"When the going gets weird, the weird turn pro."
—Hunter S. Thompson

Weird Stuff

Spring 2014
Vol. 1 #2

Co-Publishers
Jamie Hanshaw
Freeman Fly

Written by
Jamie Hanshaw

Art & Layout
Freeman Fly

To order more
copies , write to:

Weird Stuff
P.O. Box 25186
Greenville, SC
29616

freeman@freemantv.com

Exegesis of the cover art:
A full moon of Diana shines down upon two archetypes of youth today. The narcissistic Princess is hypnotized by the mirror, but it is not her reflection that keeps her captivated, it is the slave of the mirror. Through her gown run the currents of sex and death. She makes the sign of the horns, but does not know why. The more she consumes, the more she withers away. She is divided from her partner who stares off in a different direction. The soldier stands guard, ready for battle. He is not a sovereign individual, but a trained killing machine. Under his feet are the tools that created this civilization. Somewhere, under the mask, is a human being with a heart.

WeirdStuffMagazine.com   FreemanTV.com

ISBN 978-0-9890988-2-3
ISSN 2326-1048

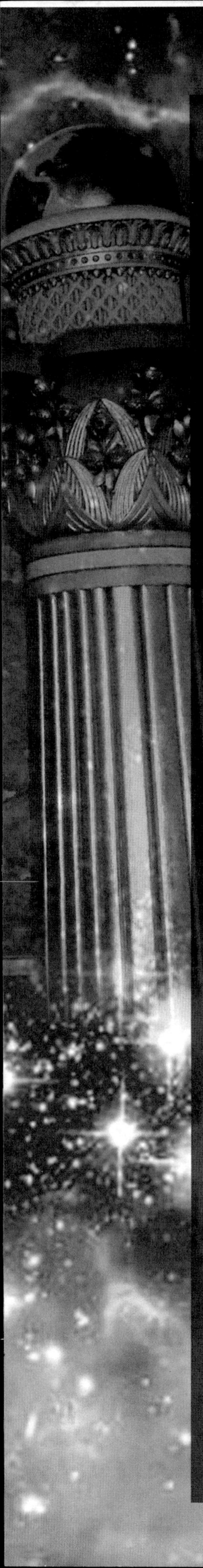

Contents

The En Vogue Mystery Religions

5

Earth Needs Mothers

36

PROJECT: CRAZY BITCH

44

TRAUMA BASED MIND CONTROL

64

MONARCHS, ZOMBIES, AND ROCK 'N' ROLL
88

PROGRAMMED FOR WAR

112

The En Vogue Mystery Religions

"There is the moral of all human tales;
'Tis but the same rehearsal of the past,
First Freedom, and then Glory — when that fails,
Wealth, vice, corruption, — barbarism at last.
And History, with all her volumes vast,
hath but ONE page."
—Lord Byron

When critical thinkers talk about "They" who are controlling the world from lofty towers and dark shadows, who are they actually talking about? The word, "Illuminati" has become the catch all phrase to describe all secret societies, dark occultists and the power brokers of the world, but naming them all collectively the "Illuminati" is a dead end and makes you sound like a crazy person. It obscures the true names of the organizations who are in control today and who have living, breathing, perpetrators of the insidious agenda in their midst.

***

Bavarian Illuminati
—The Not So Secret Society

Adam Weishaupt was born in 1748 of Jewish parents but grew up in the Catholic faith. When his rabbi father died, young Adam was turned over to be schooled by the Jesuits. He was still allowed free range in the private library of his godfather, Johann von Ickstatt, who had one of the largest personal collections in Europe. There, his questioning mind was deeply impressed by the books of the Cabbala, Rosicrucians, Hermeticism, Mystery Schools, and French philosophy. He was an avid follower of Jean Jacques Rousseau, a philosopher who insisted that man was sovereign and could govern himself without the need for oppressive religious and political institutions. Most of all, young Weishaupt was impressed with ancient Egypt. He was fascinated by the pyramids, considering the Great Pyramid to have been an ancient temple of initiation into the Mysteries.

In 1771 Weishaupt met a Danish trader named Franz Kolmer, who supposedly initiated him into Egyptian magical practices and the doctrines of Zoroastor, after which he developed a spirit of anarchy. The Jesuit order was suppressed by papal bull in 1773 and with their abolition also came Weishaupt's changing opinion of them. He went from being their pupil, to becoming their most bitter enemy. He officially converted to Protestantism when studying law at Ingolstadt in Bavaria. Weishaupt became the first layman to occupy the chair of canon law at the University of Ingoldstadt and two years later he was promoted to dean of the faculty of law. The prestigious position had been held by a Jesuit for the previous ninety years and his appointment gave great offense to the clergy. He constantly struggled with the Catholic Church over the direction of the university. He condemned the bigotry and superstitions of the priests and established an opposing party at the college. Weishaupt first tried recruiting the "ex-Jesuits", with the promise of recovering their former secret influence in society under a new name. Only two joined and this only fueled his hatred for them, and from then on he was determined to free the world from the secret Jesuitical rule of Rome.

"I have contrived an explanation which has every advantage; is inviting to Christians of every communion; gradually frees them from all religious prejudices; cultivates the social virtues; and animates them by a great, a feasible, and speedy prospect of universal happiness, in a state of liberty and moral equality, freed from the obstacles which subordination, rank, and riches, continually thrown in our way."
—Adam Weishaupt

His followers consisted principally of young students whose confidence and friendship he had gained. His republican ideals were dangerous at the time, so to achieve his goal, he formed a group to secretly work towards the abolition of *all* monarchies and establish a new world order free from religion, but still guided by the "Enlightened" ones—a name he bestowed upon his disciples as a token of their advance in intelligence and moral progress. They assembled in a private apartment, and there he discussed with them philosophical subjects, and sought to imbue them with a spirit of freedom. Weishaupt dreamed of a "Cosmo-political" world of happiness where all people were citizens and no one would have a fixed religious system or government; where favor and status were based on talent

and virtue, and not inherited. He opposed prejudice, religious influence over public life, abuses of state power, and supported women's education and gender equality. While most secret societies of the time catered to rich people and their fascination with occultism, this one sought to actively upset the status quo. This was the beginning of the Bavarian Order of the Illuminati.

"Universal happiness complete and rapid could be achieved by disposing of hierarchy, rank and riches. Princes and nations will disappear without violence from the earth; the human race will become one family; the world will be the abode of reasonable men."
—Adam Weishaupt

The group was alternately called the "Order of Perfectibilists" or simply "The Bees" and its initial stated objectives were powerfully philanthropic. *"And what is this general object? THE HAPPINESS OF THE HUMAN*

RACE. Is it not distressing to a generous mind, after contemplating what human nature is capable of, to see how little we enjoy? When we look at this goodly world, and see that every man may be happy, but that the happiness of one depends upon the conduct of another; when we see the wicked so powerful, and the good so weak; and that it is in vain to strive, singly and alone, against the general current of vice and oppression."[1] Weishaupt sought to collect for his order *"a combination of worthy persons who should work together in removing obstacles to human happiness, become terrible to the wicked and give their aid to all the good."*[2] Were they heroes fighting for liberty and reason or demented tyrants obsessed with global domination?

On May 1st, 1776, the Order of the Illuminati was founded with an original membership of five. The date was obviously not chosen at random, given Weishaupt's mystical background. Beltane is an astrologically significant date as it is halfway between the spring equinox and the summer solstice and its rituals are traditionally celebrated with bonfires. The Order was symbolized as the letter "O" with a dot in the center, the astrological symbol of the Sun, fire, light, and the Supreme Being. This symbol reflected the great Mystery of the Fire Worship of the Magi that he wished to conceal in the allegory of the Higher Grades. Other prominent symbols included a pyramid painted on the floor of the Lodge, elements from Egypt, Greece and Rome intermingled, and the seven stars of Pleiades with the crescent moon.

The structure of the Order

was clandestine and hierarchical, modeled after the Jesuits, and this wasn't the only dissonant thing about it. For a man who claimed to be enlightened by reason and science, he was also highly mystical. He reconciled these opposing viewpoints through the writings of a professor of philosophy named Christoph Meiners, who portrayed the ancient mysteries as a double initiation of believers. Superstitious beliefs were conveyed in the "Lesser Mysteries", while in the "Greater Mysteries" the veil of superstition was torn away and those deemed worthy were initiated into the truths of the rational understanding of God. Weishaupt accordingly drafted his texts for the Lesser and Greater Mysteries of the Illuminaten, where it was only the highest initiate of the Greater Mysteries who became privy to their final secret: that all of the gods were only men who had become deified. Because the Order considered itself to be the ultimate bastion of good in the world, any manner of practices, good or wicked, could be employed for its advancement. Basically, for the Illuminati, the end justified any means.

Ascending the Illuminati hierarchy wasn't so much for the purpose of attaining wisdom as to be remade into a totally loyal servant on a universal mission. Academies for neophytes were opened and strict secrecy was enforced. The novices, or Minervals, did not know anyone else in the order besides their mentor/initiator. The Owl of Minerva perched on a book was the emblem of their degree. After three years as a Minerval, if they were chosen to continue their training, they went on to become Illuminatus Minor and were permitted a little more knowledge of the objectives of the organization. A complex system of codes and aliases assured their anonymity, allowed them to strategically infiltrate organizations,

The House of the Temple
Supreme Council of the 33rd

and ensured the future continuity of the society underground, if necessary.

Their code names were inspired by Roman and Greek history, Weishaupt's pseudonym was Spartacus, the Roman who headed the insurrection of slaves during Pompey's rule. European cities were given code names of ancient cities, Munich became Athens, and Frankfurt became Thebes. The Order attracted many nobles and members of the clergy. Ironically, a number of members of the Catholic Church could be found in the ranks of the Illuminati, some, no doubt, being double agents for the pope.

***

Masonry Merger
In 1777, the year following the creation of the Illuminati, Weishaupt joined the Masonic lodge of Theodore of Good Counsel in Munich, but found that no one in his lodge truly understood the occult significance of their ceremonies. Not only did he successfully propagate his views into his lodge, he also managed to get the lodge to be absorbed into the Illuminist order almost immediately. A concrete alliance between the Illuminati and Freemasonry became possible in 1780, when a prominent figure by the name of

Exact geographical center of the District of Columbia

Baron Adolf Knigge, was initiated. He brought his active energies in to complete the system, and his diplomatic connections and organizational skills were promptly put to use. Knigge would go on to accomplish two important tasks for the Illuminati; he revised the hierarchy, created new higher grades, and allowed the full integration of Masonic lodges into the system. By 1778, the number of members had considerably increased and the Order was fully established.

On July 16, 1782, Weisaupt formally combined the Order of the Illuminati with the Freemasons at the Congress of Wilhelmsbad and became a secret society within a secret society. The combined groups now had over three million members, including some of the most powerful men in Europe. *"The great strength of our Order lies in its concealment; let it never appear in any place in its own name, but always covered by another name, and another occupation. None is better than the three lower degrees of Free Masonry; the public is ac-customed to it, expects little from it, and therefore takes little notice of it. Next to this, the form of a learned or literary society is best suited to our purpose, and had Free Masonry not existed, this cover would have been employed; and it may be much more than a cover, it may be a powerful engine in our hands. By establishing reading societies, and subscription libraries, and taking these under our direction, and supplying them through our labours, we may turn the public mind which way we will."[3]*

Weishaupt did not enjoy his Order's success for long. Suspicions of Illuminati conspiracy against governments and religions arose across Europe. Before its disbandment, the order had lodges in over twenty five cities from Munich to London. In the year 1784, the Illuminati attempted a coup against the Hapsburgs, but the plot was revealed by spies that had infiltrated the Order on behalf of the king. Seeing a credible threat against its power, the Bavarian government launched an edict, outlawing all communities, societies and brotherhoods that existed without due authorization of the law, and membership to any was punishable by death. Weishaupt was dismissed from his university and expelled from Bavaria and forced to flee to a neighboring province. He went into exile, vowing that the Order would return ten times more powerful. In spite of these setbacks, the Illuminati's influence remained in full force and their secrecy made them practically untouchable. The Illuminati's banishment had an unforeseen side effect; it dispersed its members to the four corners of the globe. Adam's peaceful and luxurious exile seems suspicious for the leading conspirator of the time. It is reasonable to suppose that because of his Orders' prestigious membership and influence, Weishaupt was allowed to continue his work while keeping a low profile. The Freemasons and Rosicrucians were still thriving, and the Illuminati appeared to be living through them.

***

Illuminated America
The New World proved to be a fertile ground for spreading both Illuminati ideals and anti-Illuminati paranoia. Most of America's founding fathers were a part of secret societies, some of them travelled to Europe and were well versed in the ideas of Illuminism. A little more than two months after Weishaupt founded his Order, on July 4, 1776, America declared independence from Great Britain. A series of letters between German minister G.W. Snyder and George Washington include knowledge of the Illuminati plan to overthrow all governments and religions. Washington was well aware of their doctrines,

and even if he did not believe that the Masonic lodges of the United States propagated its mission, he concedes that individuals might have secretly undertaken that endeavor.

The founders of Washington D.C. first called it Rome, and they named that area of the Potomac River, the Tiber. Just like ancient Rome, Washington D.C. sits on seven hills. They erected a classical capitol of pantheons and temples adorned with images of Apollo, Minerva, Venus, Jupiter and many more. In the center, they placed an enduring tribute to ancient Egypt, the obelisk, which proclaims thanks and honor to their demigod forefather, George Washington. The rotunda of the capitol is designed as a tribute to the Temple of Vesta, and for many years kept the sacred flame which once burned in the lower level, directly beneath the rotunda. This spot is now called the crypt and there is a blazing four point compass, which marks the exact geographical center of the District of Columbia.

When Thomas Jefferson read the writings of anti-Illuminati Jesuit, Abbe Barruel, he concluded that the Order and the new America had the same goals. In an 1800 letter to James Madison he declared: *"Wishaupt [sic] seems to be an enthusiastic Philanthropist. He is among those...who believe in the indefinite perfectibility of man. He thinks he may in time be rendered so perfect that he will be able to govern himself in every circumstance so as to injure none, to do all the good he can, to leave government no occasion to exercise their powers over him, & of course to render political government useless. This you know is Godwin's doctrine."*[4] William Godwin was an English political philosopher and novelist. He is considered one of the first exponents of utilitarianism, and the first modern proponent of anarchism. Godwin's writings were a major influence on the leaders of America during Revolutionary times. *"As Wishaupt lived under the tyranny of a despot & priests, he knew that caution was necessary even in spreading information, & the principles of pure morality.... This has given an air of mystery to his views, was the foundation of his banishment, the subversion of the masonic order, & is the colour for the ravings against him....I believe you will think with me that if Wishaupt had written here, where no secrecy is necessary in our endeavors to render men wise & virtuous, he would not have thought of any secret machinery for that purpose."*[5]

Benjamin Franklin was in Paris from 1776 to 1785, the same time the Bavarian Illuminati was openly active, serving as the ambassador of the United States to France. During his stay, he became Grand Master of the Masonic lodge, Les Neufs Soeurs, which was attached to the Grand Orient of France and was supposed to become the French headquarters of the Illuminati. The lodge was particularly influential in the organization of the French support for the American Revolution and was later part of the process towards the French Revolution.

Even if George Washington disagreed with the Illuminati's agenda, his legacy seems to agree with Weishaupt on one point: that the gods of antiquity were once men like themselves. His portrait in the rotunda of the capitol building is called "The Apotheosis of Washington", which is the transformation of man into god and is the core element of the symbolism in the capitol building. This 4,664 square foot fresco features Washington dressed in white and ascending on a cloud above mortal man. He is surrounded by seventy-two pentagrams and flanked by the goddesses, Victoria and Liberty. Forming a circle between them are thirteen maidens, each with a star above her head. On the outer edge, he is surrounded by a

Apotheosis of George Washington

series of ancient gods presenting the founding fathers with secret knowledge. Minerva gives technological inspiration to Benjamin Franklin; Mercury, the Roman god of commerce, gives a bag of gold to American Revolutionary War financier, Robert Morris, and so on. The room was once dominated by a statue of George Washington posed as Zeus, but as soon as the marble statue arrived in the capital city in 1841, it attracted much controversy and criticism. Like Zeus, Washington was naked from the waist up, with only a sheet covering his lower body. Many Americans found the sight of a half-naked Washington undignified, offensive, and even comical. It was soon moved from the center of the capitol rotunda to the lawn and can now be seen at the National Museum of American History.

If Washington D.C. was modeled after ancient Rome, that would explain why it has one of the highest divisions between the ruling class and the working class. Rome was a far cry from a beacon of democracy, republic and equality for all. Like America, Rome was an incredibly diverse mix of races, cultures and religions, who were at the same time deeply proud to be "Roman." This immigrant based city was a constant influx of people, and slaves were very important to its existence. Without slaves, the wealthy would not have been able to lead the lifestyles of luxury that they wanted to. The slaves were people who were frequently captured in battle and sent back to the city to be sold in the marketplace. In hard times, it was not uncommon for desperate Roman citizens to raise money by selling their children into slavery. A slave could only obtain their freedom if they were given it by their owner, or if they could afford to buy it. Therefore, slave labor became one of Rome's greatest sources of economic wealth.

Slave races support the foundation of Philadelphia's City Hall

Slavery in ancient Rome was not based on race, but, like modern slavery, it was an abusive and degrading institution and cruelty was commonplace. The slaves looked so similar to Roman citizens that the Senate once considered a plan to make them wear special clothing so that they could be identified at a glance. The idea was rejected because the Senate feared that, if slaves saw how many of them were working in Rome, they might be tempted to join forces and rebel. Saturna-lia was a traditional celebration, like Christmas, in which slaves and masters switched places. During this holiday, the master became the slave and performed all the tasks of the slave, and the slaves did the opposite. This period of liberation was a pressure release against rebellion. There was a Roman dream, just like an American dream that if you work hard enough, had a kind master and were lucky, you would someday be a free man.

Roman society was very hierarchical. The evolution of the Constitution of the Roman Republic was heavily influenced by the struggle between Rome's land-holding aristocracy, and the far more numerous citizen-commoners. The Republic was the period when the government operated as a kind of democracy. It began with the overthrow of the monarchy, and its replacement by a government headed by two consuls, elected annually by the citizens (not slaves) and advised by a Senate. Citizenship in ancient Rome was a privileged political and legal status. Only freeborn individuals held any rights in regard to laws, property, and governance. Foreign colonies and political allies could be granted a minor form of citizenship, and the promise of improved standing within the Roman "sphere of influence", and the punishment for standing with one's neighbors, kept the focus centered on the status quo of Roman culture.

***

Freemasonry

Architecture is a very specific system of magic. Across many ancient cultures, the leaders would build taller buildings than their subjects to literally show they are closer to the gods and closer to the heavens, and also as a pedestal to rule from. For the ancient Jews, Christians and Muslims, any attempt made by man to compete with the creator, by depicting things in the natural world or the human form, was deemed blasphemous idol worship. Like the cosmos of the Pythagoreans, the God of the Jews and the Muslims was One. To make images of God was to fragment and compartmentalize it. For ancient architects, God was to be discovered in the principles of shape, determined by the degrees in an angle, and by number. It was in these buildings based on sacred geometry, rather than depicting God, they created a space where the divine presence could be housed. *"The Masons were the first priests...and as they were the persons employed to provide everything requisite for honoring the Gods, the building of temples naturally fell into their hands, and thus priests and masons were identified...Thus the Masons were an order of priests, that is, of the initiated. Every initiated person was a priest, though he might not exercise the functions of a priest. Thus they became identified with the most powerful and influential body of so-* *ciety...they provided good houses for themselves...from superiority of intellect, the consequence of the constant use of their faculties, they acquired the sovereign power."* — Godfrey Higgins

The history of Masonry may be divided into two periods, the pre-historic traditional, which are the myths and legendary history of the Craft as enacted by the rituals; and the historic, meaning there are authentic documents in reference to the existence of the Order. The Legend of the Craft, according to the *Dowland Manuscript*, begins before the flood of Noah, with a man called Lamech who had four children—three sons and one daughter—who were the foundation of all the sciences in the world. Somehow, they knew that God would punish the world for sin, so they recorded all of their knowledge onto two pillars that God could not destroy with a cataclysm and could be found after the deluge. One pillar was made of marble that could not be burned, and the other of brick that could not be drowned. The discovery of one pillar was made by Pythagoras, and the other, Hermes, who is venerated as the father of all wise men and is said to be the founder of Alchemy, Geometry and Architecture. Nimrod, the King of Babylon is considered the first Grand Master, and the building of the Tower of Babylon was Masonry's first endeavor. It was the first time that the Craft was organized into a fraternity, working under a constitution set forth by Nimrod. Even through the confounding of the languages, Masonry was preserved and used to build other cities such as Nineveh, Ereck, and Accad. Afterwards, upon the Tigris and Euphrates flourished many learned priests and mathematicians who became known as the Magi of the Chaldees.

By the end of the 18th century, the legendary account of the origin of Freemasonry in Babylon began to be rejected, and another one, in contradiction to the old manuscripts, was substituted for it. The connections between Freemasonry and Judaism are very intimate. King Solomon of Jerusalem is contemporarily considered to be "the first Grand Master" and a Master Masons' Lodge is styled after the Holy of Holies of King Solomon's Temple. During the construction of the Temple, King Solomon enlisted the help of King Hiram of Tyre, the great Phoenician city of commerce. He brought with him a mysterious architect named Hiram Abiff, who

Scottish Rite Masonic Lodge Los Angeles, California

11

is called "the Widow's Son". According to the legend, before the temple could be completed, Hiram Abiff was murdered by three apprentice architects, referred to in masonry as the three ruffians, because he would not impart to them the secret word of the Master Mason. When King Solomon found the body of Hiram, he resurrected him from the grave with the grip of the Lion's Paw to retrieve from him the secret word. This is the basis of the ritual one must perform in the third degree of the Craft, Master Mason. Each candidate that enters for initiation is lead through a death and resurrection ritual starring the initiate as Hiram Abiff.

Despite Freemasonry's general disclaimer that they do not have a direct heritage to the medieval Knights Templar, certain degrees and appendant orders are obviously patterned after them. The Knights Templar claim to have been formed to protect the pilgrims in the Holy Land. This reopened Jerusalem to Christians who began to arrive in large numbers through the ports of Jaffa, Tyre and Acre. The knights Hospitaller established a hostel in the city to provide food and shelter for visitors in 1118, and that same year the original Knights Templar arrived in Jerusalem to guard the pilgrims. For the first nine years there were only nine of them. They were given quarters adjoining the Temple Mount, the alleged ancient site of Solomon's Temple. There, the Templars found something of great value while excavating under Temple Mount. Soon after, Hugues de Payens, whom they also call "the first Grand Master", left Jerusalem to gather recruits and expand the order. Among their symbols were the Phoenician Red Cross, a black and white flag made up of two squares, and the watchtower. What, exactly, it was that they found there, is a subject of vast historical and archeological study. Theories range from the Holy Grail, the Bloodline of Jesus, to the Ark of the Covenant. Whatever it was, it was enough to give these humble knights incredible influence over the pope and the kings of Europe. Only a year after the Templars were formally established, a rapid expansion had taken place. They had a papal constitution, wealth, land, and over three hundred noble families who had given all their wealth to the Templars when they joined. By the middle of the 12th century the Templars were second only to the Roman Catholic Church in wealth and influence. They had their own fleet of ships, on which they flew the skull and bones flag, and their financial centers in London and Paris were the beginning of the modern banking system of interest which has made humanity slaves to imaginary money.

In 1307, King Philippe of France and Pope Clement V secretly arranged for all Templars

Freemason Templar Knight Garb

12

in France to be arrested at dawn on Friday, October 13th. Friday the 13th has been deemed unlucky ever since. Many Templars were seized and subjected to torture of the Inquisition. Their Grand Master, Jaques DeMolay, was burned at the stake and he is honored in the Freemasonic organization for young boys called DeMolay. Some of the knights fled to Scotland where they would later re-emerge as the Scottish Rite of Freemasonry.

Operative Masons were actually builders of buildings and Temples. The Masons Company had been established in 1376, in London, and had obtained a grant of arm from King Henry VIII in 1472. But this was guild masonry, the builders, which were taken over in 1717 by "Speculative Masonry" which opened the groups to members of other professions. This is seen as a great revival of men who were willing to assist in building a "Spiritual Temple" here on earth. All modern Masons trace their official beginning to the United Grand Lodge of England, which they call the "Mother Lodge", founded in 1717, in the Apple Tree tavern, in London. The revival attracted serious minded students of the occult to Masonry, with its ritualistic and secretive trappings. Famous alchemist and mystic Count Cagliostro dominated the Lyon lodge in France and created his own brand of Egyptian Masonry. In England there were many ties to the mystical Rosicrucians. Scotland claimed to practice secret rites handed down from the knights Templar. In Germany, the Strict Observance claimed to be under the tutelage of the "Unknown Superiors", a race of god-like spiritual guides.

The initiates of secret societies have always had a code of communication through certain phrases, words, symbols, and secret handshakes. One of their most used symbols is the lighted torch. When they reach a certain level in the pyramid they are said to be "Illuminated". The Statue of Liberty holds this torch not for freedom, but for illuminated ones. The aspirant is supposed to represent one who is traveling from the intellectual blindness of the profane world into the brightness of Masonry, where he expects to find the light and truth. From the first degree, the first Initiation, the Mason is urged mightily to *seek the Light*. The average Mason is continually saying that he is "seeking the Light", and will spend his entire life "moving toward the Light" or in search of the "further light in Masonry". This symbolic journey is supposed to begin at the Tower of Babel, where, in the words of the ritual, "language was confounded and Masonry lost" and to terminate at the Temple of Solomon where "language was restored and Masonry found". According to the latest form of the Legend, the Tower of Babel is degraded from its prominent place given to it in the olden days, and becomes a symbol of darkness. But, the fact remains that Babylonia was the fountain of all Semitic science and architecture, and also the birthplace of Operative Masonry. Lucifer holds an exalted position in Freemasonry, as it is the undisputed god of light, even if it is never named. Here we will give some quotes about Lucifer from respected Freemasons and continue with Luciferianism later on in the chapter.

"When the Mason learns that the key to the warrior on the block is the proper application of the dynamo of living power, he has learned the mystery of his Craft. The seething energies of Lucifer are in his hands and before he may step onward and upward, he must prove his ability to properly apply energy." —Manly P. Hall[6]

"What is more absurd and more impious than to attribute the name of Lucifer to the devil, that is, to personified evil. The intellectual Lucifer is the spirit of intelligence and love; it is the Paraclete, it is the Holy Spirit, while the physical Lucifer is the great agent of universal magnetism."
—Arthur Edward Waite[7]

"LUCIFER, the *Light-bearer!* Strange and mysterious name to give to the Spirit of Darkness! Lucifer, the Son of the Morning! Is it *he* who bears the *Light*, and with its splendors intolerable, blinds feeble, sensual, or selfish Souls? Doubt it not!"
—Albert Pike[8]

"The true name of Satan, the Kabalists say, is that of Yahveh reversed; for Satan is not a black god, but the negation of God. The Devil is the personification of Atheism or Idolatry. For the Initiates, this is not a *Person*, but a *Force*, created for good, but which *may* serve for evil. *It is the instrument of Liberty or Free Will.* They represent this Force, which presides over the physical generation, under the mythologic and horned form of the God PAN; thence came the he-goat of the Sabbat, brother of the Ancient

Serpent, and the Light-bearer or *Phosphor*, of which the poets have made the false Lucifer of the legend." —Albert Pike[9]

"Masonry is a search after Light. That search leads us directly back, as you see, to the Kabalah."—Albert Pike[10]

***

The QQuKCabbalah

Freemasonry's roots dovetail into an ancient Hebrew form of magic known as Cabbalism. Albert Pike, Grand Sovereign Commander of the Temple of the 33rd, states over seventy times that Freemasonry is associated with Cabbalism in his work, *Morals and Dogma*. Pike clearly believed that virtually all important Masonic symbolism is derived from the Kabbalah, and at the heart of most secret societies you will find its elements. It is the "hidden wisdom", a secret doctrine of Israel, said to have been handed down, from generation to generation, since the time of Abraham. In Hebrew, the word means "that which has been received", as in a teaching or tradition. Supposedly, its most profound secrets are only passed on by word of mouth. Practitioner and high priestess, Madonna, calls it the religion before religion.

The origin of Kabbalah is a legitimate subject of controversy. Early initiates believed that it was first taught by God, to a school of angels before the fall of man. The angel, Raziel, later taught the secrets to Adam and other angels were sent to initiate the other patriarchs of the Hebrews. According to other Kabbalistic teachings, Moses ascended Mount Sinai three times, remaining in the presence of God

for forty days each time. During the first forty days, the tablets of the written law were given. During the second forty days, he received the soul of the law, and during the last forty days, God supposedly instructed him in the mysteries of the Kabbalah, "the soul of the soul of the law." Hebrew theology was divided into three distinct parts. The first was taught to all the Israelites, the *Mishna* was given to the Rabbis and teachers, and the third, the Kabbalah, was concealed, and only the highest initiates among the Jews were instructed in it. According to the story, Moses concealed the Kabbalah in the first five books of the Bible, and for centuries students have looked to them for the secret doctrine. According to other Jewish scholars, when Abraham immigrated to Egypt, the Egyptians obtained some knowledge of the mysterious doctrine. Moses, who was raised as an Egyptian, became most proficient in it during his wanderings in the wilderness where he received lessons from the angel, Metatron.

Around 590 B.C., while exiled in Babylon, a young Jewish prophet, named Ezekiel, was among the captives by the river of Chebar. There he had an elaborate vision where he witnessed all manner of mystical things, which he struggles to describe with his ancient vocabulary. Ezekiel tells of a whirlwind from the north, a fire infolding itself, with four creatures, each having four faces and four wings, who travel in vehicles that are wheels within wheels. He is taken to heaven and sees the Lord seated on a throne surrounded by a rainbow. Throughout the Old Testament book of Ezekiel, the Lord appears

to him and abducts him to different points throughout the land to judge people.

In the 2nd century AD, the Roman Empire, under the reign of the Emperor Hadrian, had control of all the territory that is now Israel. Talmudic academies were shut down and its study was forbidden on penalty of death. During this time of persecution, Jews turned to mysticism to help them understand God's will. Since they felt that their God had abandoned them, they would seek him out wherever he was. Before there were official Kabbalistic writings, Jewish mystics studied the vision of Ezekiel hoping they would one day be able to induce a trance and see God for themselves. Small groups of Jews began to gather in secret, their leader was Rabbi Shim'on Bar Yochai, a student of the famous Rabbi Akiva, who began teaching meditative techniques which put them into a hypnotic trance. The early mystics reported the dangers of this practice and did not suggest average people attempt to try it. Legends tell of novices being driven mad, or dying because they were unprepared for the powerful spiritual forces they had unleashed.

When Rabbi Yochai spoke out against Rome, he was condemned to death. To escape this punishment, he fled with his son to a cave where they remained for thirteen years, sustaining themselves on carobs and water. They studied the *Torah* together and, as the story goes, they wrote down the material that would become a book called the *Zohar*, which means "splendor", or "radiance". The first time Rabbi Shim'on came out of the cave, he was completely out of tune with the people of his generation. A heavenly voice told him to go back to the cave, reorient his perspective, and emerge again. This time, when he appeared, he was able to interact with the people of his time and become an esteemed teacher. To this day, pious Jews make an annual pilgrimage to Kefar Meron, in the Land of Israel, to pray at the tomb of this Cabbalistic scholar.

The *Zohar* is one major text of Kabbalah and refashions the *Torah* into a mystical novel. It is arranged in the form of a commentary on the *Torah* and its central theme is the interplay of human and divine sexuality. The tales focus on Rabbi Shim'on and his disciples as they wander through Galilee exchanging insights about biblical heroes. It was not until our own century that critical scholarship began to suggest that the book's author was not Shim'on Yochai, but a Spanish-Jewish mystic named Moses de León. About seven hundred years ago, de León began circulating booklets to his friends and fellow mystics, containing teachings that they had never heard. He claimed that he had translated the ancient writings of the famous Rabbi which had been hidden away and secretly handed down from master to disciple. Diaries of a Kabbalistic movement emerged in Spain and spread westward and gradually the *Zohar's* antiquity was accepted by Kabbalists.

The Kabbalist concept of the Supreme Deity is an incomprehensible principle, to be discovered only through the process of elimination. That which remains when every knowable thing has been removed, is AIN SOPH, the eternal state of *Being*. AIN SOPH was referred to as The Most Ancient of all the Ancients. It was considered sexless and its symbol was a closed eye. The "Ain Soph Aur" is the cosmic egg from which the universe began. Kabbalah teaches that God compressed himself in a process of self-limitation in order to accommodate his creation. It sent out into the void, emanations, or light from itself, and from this came a whole succession of emanations. The ten emanations are called Sephiroth, which are arranged like the skins of an onion, one outside the other. The *Sepher Yetzira* says that the ten Sephiroth out of Nothing are analogous to the ten fingers and the ten toes. *"Ten are the numbers of the ineffable Sephiroth, ten and not nine, ten and not eleven."*

The *Sepher Yetzira*, or Book of Formation, is the Kabbalistic story of creation and its authorship is classically attributed to Abraham, but, again, modern scholarship dates the writing of the book as late as the 2nd century AD. In the introduction to the *Sepher Yetizira*, translated from the Hebrew by W. Wynn Westcott, there is a quote about its supposed original authorship, *"It was Abraham our Father—blessed be he—who wrote this book to condemn the doctrine of the sages of his time, who were incredulous of the supreme dogma of the Unity…The sages of Babylon attacked Abraham on account of his faith; for they were all against him although themselves separable into three sects. The First thought that the Universe was subject to the control of two opposing forces, the one existing but to destroy the other, this is dualism; they held that there was nothing in common between the author of evil and the author of good. The Second sect admitted Three great Powers; two of them as in the first case, and a third Power whose function was to decide between the two others, a supreme arbitrator. The Third sect recognized [sic] no god beside the Sun, in which it recognised the sole principle of existence."* Rabbis believe teachings of the *Sepher Yetzira* are too powerful for ordinary people, so it was kept hidden for hundreds of years. It describes how God made the world by using the twenty-two letters of the Hebrew alphabet and builds on the doctrine that creation was brought into being by Number, Writing, and Speech. The name of the first letter of the Hebrew alphabet is "Aleph" In the Cabala it represents the "Ain-Soph". This letter is said, in great many texts, to be in the form of a Man who is pointing to Heaven and Earth so as to show that the world below is the mirror and map of the world above.

In the early centuries af-

ter Christ, the idea spread that the soul originally comes from God and descends through the nine spheres to earth, where it is imprisoned in a human body and can only re-unite with God by climbing back through the spheres to heaven. But, each sphere is guarded by angels and the space between the earth and the moon is crowded with legions of devils. Only those initiated in the secret traditions know the passwords which will make the guardians yield and open the gates for the soul to continue on its way to God. Earth, or matter, is given its own separate sphere, the last Sephiroth. Above it are seven Sephiroth corresponding to the seven planets and two more spheres at the top which are the "spheres of the stars and the Prime Mover."

The essential doctrine of the Kabbalists is that death is not necessary for souls to ascend through the spheres. The soul can climb the ladder of the Sephiroth while still in the body and man can make himself a God on Earth. The Sephiroth are shown in the Kabbalists' most famous

symbol as a diagram called "The Tree of Life" which they say is an illustration of the underlying pattern of the universe. Every possible correspondence between all branches of knowledge is said to be compressed into it. These hidden secrets are unraveled by the manipulation of letters and numbers containing divine power. In this mysterious world, the aspiring Kabbalist needs guideposts to help him find his way about and avoid pitfalls. These guideposts are provided by the system of correspondences, which list the creatures, plants, colors, jewels, scents and symbols associated with the Sephiroth and the Twenty-Two paths on the Tree of Life, which link the one Sephiroth to another and are associated with the 22 letters of the Hebrew alphabet, the 22 works of creation in Genesis, and the 22 major trumps of the Tarot deck.

The influence of the Kabbalah on culture cannot be underestimated. It involves both Christian and Jewish doctrine, and its theories are interwoven with the tenants of alchemy, Hermeticism, Rosicrucians, and Freemasonry. Kabbalah is now taught throughout the world in six distinct traditions. These are: the orthodox Jewish tradition, the magical system—i.e. The Golden Dawn, Christian Kabbalah, the Lurianic tradition, the Toledano tradition, and the teachings of the Kabbalah Center. The teachings of the Los-Angeles based Kabbalah Center are currently the most commonly known throughout the world.

The Kabbalists divide their science into five sections, The Natural, the Analogical, the Contemplative, the Astrologi-

Artist, Jacobus de Teramo, 1473, depicts Solomon conversing with the Genii

cal, and the Magical. The Magical Kabbalah is studied by those who desire to gain control over the demons and subhuman intelligences of the invisible worlds. In the Kabbalah, demons are called "sheidim." They are a consequence of creation as opposed to a direct product of creation. Therefore, they remain much less connected to the creator, allowing them to unite with other beings who feel the same way. The Kabbalah speaks of two types of creatures; the life forms which God directly willed/spoke into being, and those who came later. The sheidim came into being at some point as a result of an absence of holiness. The *Midrash* talks of a period of estrangement between Adam and Eve, and during this time, various female forms, including Lilith, presented themselves to him. He takes an attraction to them, and there is some sort of offspring from these unions that Adam takes delight in because they still look human. Descriptions of sheidim portray them as humanoid with bird like feet or hooves. There were thousands of these negative beings produced, and the *Midrash* concludes that whatever was created were not people. The life of the sheidim is to cause damage. They are not human but can multiply, eat, die and be killed. They can survive in extreme places where humans do not thrive. They have the knowledge of the angels, but they live to go against God. They do not live by the rule that there is an underlying positivity beneath all of creation. They are opposed to everything good, and have no purpose but themselves.

***

"Now the sagacity and wisdom which God had bestowed on Solomon was so great that he exceeded the ancients, in so much that he was no way inferior to the Egyptians, who are said to have been beyond all men in understanding. God also enabled him to learn that skill which expelled demons, which is a science useful and sanative to him. He composed such incantations also by which distempers are alleviated. And he left behind him the manner of using exorcisms, by which they drive away demons, so that they never return; and this method of cure is of great force unto this day."
—Josephus, *Eighth Book of the Antiquities of the Jews*

Solomon
Although there is no direct reference to King Solomon summoning demons in the Old Testament; outside of Christianity, Solomon is revered as the greatest necromancer and Ceremonial Magician who ever lived. According to rabbinical tradition, on account of his modest request for wisdom, Solomon was rewarded with riches and power over realms, which extended to the upper world inhabited by the angels, as well as demons and spirits. His control over the spirits and animals augmented his splendor. The demons he conjured and subdued brought him precious stones, which he used to build the Temple in Je-

rusalem. It has been noted by archaeologists and theologians at The Temple Institute that the description of Solomon's Temple was not of ordinary construction by any means. The work and dimensions were extraordinary and according to Hebrew texts, the workmen that contributed to the design were not ordinary men either. Ashmedai, the king of demons, is written about in many Jewish stories. When Solomon was trying to build the temple, he needed a special kind of worm that could eat through stone. He summoned a male and female demon, and, according to the *Qur'an*, the demons were named Haruk and Maruk. They told him that he needed to speak with Ashmedai, who was subsequently captured in physical form and brought to Jerusalem to serve the king. According to the ancient Rabbis, Solomon was an initiate of the Mystery schools and the temple was actually a house of initiation, containing pagan philosophic and phallic emblems. According to the Talmudic legends, Solomon understood the mysteries of the Kabbalah.

Whether or not Solomon actually used demons to do his bidding, I Kings, chapter 11, describes his delve into dark occultism and child sacrifice. *"¹But king Solomon loved many strange women, together with the daughter of Pharaoh, women of the Moabites, Ammonites, Edomites, Zidonians, and Hittites... ⁴For it came to pass, when Solomon was old, that his wives turned away his heart after other gods...⁵ For Solomon went after Ashtoreth the goddess of the Zidonians, and after Milcom the abomination of the Ammonites....⁷Then did Solomon build an high place for Chemosh, the abomination of Moab, in the hill that is before Jerusalem, and for Molech, the abomination of the children of Ammon. [8]And likewise did he for all his strange wives, which burnt incense and sacrificed unto their gods."*

The tradition of Solomon's control over demons is fully elaborated in the pseudo graphical work called the *Testament of Solomon*, which deals with a variety of astrological and magical themes, vast legions of demons, summoning spirits, and magic rings. Despite the text's claim to have been a first-hand account of King Solomon's construction of the Temple of Jerusalem, its original publication was in Greek, and dates sometime between the 1st and 5th centuries AD. In the narrative, Solomon prays in the temple and receives a ring from the archangel Michael with the seal of God in the shape of a pentagram, which enables him to command the demons. *The Testament of Solomon* is probably the source for the *Lesser Key of Solomon*, an anonymous medieval work famously edited by Aleister Crowley in 1904 as *The Book of the Goetia of Solomon the King*, where you'll find the names of 72 demons and their functions. The book gives the techniques and materials needed to embark on the mystical path of Solomon. It gives directions for casting magick circles and invoking demons and dark Djinn into the consciousness of the magician. Here, like Solomon, the magician must unleash the demon from the brass vessel and symbolically slay it with a magical sword. Like the Djinn trapped in the magick lamp, the demon may also grant the wishes and desires of the magician. *"The spirits of the Goetia are portions of the human brain. Their seals therefore represent methods of stimulating or regulating those particular spots (through the eye)."*[11]

***

**Grand Architect of the Universe
Natural History Museum, London**

Gnosticism

Many of the basic ideas of the Kabbalah are also found in Gnosticism. Have you ever looked at all the evil, suffering and decay in the world and thought, "This is a Hell world, who would have ever created it like this?" You're not the first person to feel that way, and you won't be the last. The word Gnosticism was coined in 1966. It is a collective name for a large number of diverse groups who claim that their inspiration, essence, and knowledge comes from within. Just as with magicians, there can be as many Gnostic theologies as there are people who subscribe to them. Because their gnosis comes from observation, experience and intuitive insight, this allows it to be categorized as a mystery religion.

In 1945, near the village of Nag Hammadi in Egypt, two brothers were walking around the mountains looking for fertilizer. Instead, they found a buried earthenware jar containing a collection of papyrus manuscripts, written in Coptic, and bound in leather. Having no idea what they were, they might have burned some of them as fuel for the fire. What they discovered turned Christianity upside down. A cache of religious texts dating from the 3rd or 4th century A.D., known as the Nag Hammadi library, contained fifty-two religious treatises, including writings on Hermeticism and Plato's *Republic*. Forty-one of the texts were unknown, new works including The Gospels of Thomas, Truth, Philip, and Mary. The texts expound on all areas of Christianity including the life of Jesus, Mary Magdalen, spirit beings, and the origin of the world, good and evil.

In the classic Gnostic view, there is a true, ultimate and transcendent God who is beyond all created universes. It "emanated" or brought forth from within itself the substance of all there is in all the worlds, visible and invisible. It is called simply, Pneuma, which means breath, or "The Light". It is a preexistent, uncaused perfect being; the "Father Spirit" who is un-generated and eternal. It is a force with no personality or emotions with an emphasis on androgyny. The mother aspect of the light is "Protennoia" the First Thought, who is impregnated by the Father to bring forth gods called Aeons. These beings exist between the ultimate, True God and ourselves. The Gnostic view of the universe has three tiers, the realm where the Light lives is the upper realm, the bottom world is the created universe that we know, and in the middle is the realm of the lesser gods, the Aeons, who are fractions of the light. The Aeons pair up with each other to produce more demi-gods. When all the Aeons are together and in harmony with the "Light" it is called the "Pleroma" which means fullness. The Fullness stands in contrast to our existential state, which in comparison, they consider emptiness.

Father God, Mother Thought, and Logos (Mind) make up the initial trinity of the Gnostics. Logos, the son, is the primary expression of the light and is the highest thing that the light produced. The last and extraordinarily important Aeon was called Sophia or Wisdom. She was close enough to the physical world to transgress the boundary and was the first one to "sin", as she wanted to reproduce without the consent of the Light and without her male counterpart Aeon. Her offspring is described as an abortion, a flawed emanation, called the De-

miurge, "the maker" or "architect" named Ialdeboath, who Gnostics equate with Yahweh, or El, of the Old Testament. Realizing she had created a monster god, Sophia banished him to the outer cosmos. Alone and ignorant but with great power, he did not know that there were any gods before him. He created the physical universe all in the image of his own flaw. In Gnosticism, the creator is a fool because he thought that there were none like him. Matter is a prison and therefore everything that is physical is evil.

The Demiurge created the Archons, the "Watchers" or rulers, who are sort of like cosmic henchmen, to keep humanity under control. Together, the Archons and the Demiurge made Adam. One theme in all of the Gnostic creation stories is that the pure spiritual nature, the divine spark, was planted in some souls. The creator god imprisoned Adam and Eve in a world of misery and gave them a subservient soul. They were incapable of distinguishing between good and evil, between the uncreated kingdom and the created one, and they were ignorant of their origin and their destiny. A redeemer was then sent to reveal the way of escape out of the material world. The saved soul must pass through the realms of the Archons in order to return to its proper spiritual home. *The Hypostasis of the Archons* says that not only was Eve the emissary of the divine Sophia, but the serpent was also inspired by the same supernal wisdom. Sophia mystically entered the serpent, who thereby acquired the title of instructor. The instructor then taught Adam and Eve about their source, informing them that

they were of high and holy origin and not mere slaves of the creator deity. According to Gnostic scripture, the serpent in the garden is a symbol of good, the liberator, bringing knowledge and everything else we understand as human into the world. The character, Yahweh, is seen as Satan, and Lucifer is the redeemer, a Messenger of the True God. This Serpent of Enlightenment, which brought Gnosis, allows the authentic and true nature of things to be seen in this world, and came to liberate man from tyranny. The Serpent is, for Gnostics, the Serpent of Salvation, which opened the eyes of man, and offered him the apple of emancipation to help him wake up and free himself from this world of misery and impure matter.

For the Gnostics, the story of the redemption of the Sophia through Christ or the Logos is the central drama of the universe. The Gnostic Jesus was considered God in the flesh. An Aeon in disguise, the earthly Jesus was crucified but the cosmic Jesus is eternal. In the *Pistis Sophia*, Christ is sent from the Godhead in order to bring Sophia back into the Pleroma. The Christos appears to Sophia in the shape of a trans-cosmic cross and she has new desire to return to the Light and be reunited with her celestial bridegroom. Christ is then sent to earth in the form of the man Jesus, to give men the Gnosis needed to rescue themselves from the physical world and return to the spiritual world.

The Gnostic Christians who authored the Nag Hammadi scriptures may not have read Genesis as literal history, but as a myth with a meaning. To them,

Adam and Eve were not actual historical figures, but representatives of two intra-psychic principles within every human being. Adam was the dramatic embodiment of psyche, or soul, while Eve stood for the pneuma, or spirit. In Gnosticism, the Gospel story of Jesus could also be allegorical, it all depends on the Gnostic. They may view it as the Outer Mystery, used as an introduction to Gnosis, rather than being literally true in a historical context.

***

Eternal Egyptian Magic

It is well documented that the Egyptians, of all the ancient peoples, were the most learned in the Occult Sciences; and many believe Freemasonry to be the reincarnation of the Mysteries of ancient Egypt. The wisest of philosophers from all nations visited Egypt to be initiated into the sacred mysteries by the priests of Thebes, Memphis and Hermopolis. Solon, Pythagoras, Plato, Euclid, Socrates, Aristotle, Herodotus, and Hippocrates all acknowledged the Egyptians to be the wisest of mortals and their temples to be the repositories of the most sublime doctrine. The history of Egypt is the most curious considering that they appeared almost suddenly in the ancient world with a full blown civilization, religion, cosmology, written language, system of mathematics, and inexplicable architecture. The Egyptian chronicles of the Pharaohs go back over 30,000 years to the land of Aha-Men-Ptah, which many believe to be Atlantis, where they claim their arcane teachings all originated from.

The ancient Egyptians say that the First Time, the Zeb Tepi, immediately following creation, was a golden age when gods ruled their country and humanity was offered the gifts of civilization. They also spoke of beings, the Urshu, or the watchers, who were intermediaries between gods and men. The gods themselves they called Neteru, both male and female, who had human attributes but possessed a range of supernatural powers including teleportation and shape shifting. They lived on the earth along with mankind and ruled over them. Although they were vastly superior to humans, they could become ill, die, or be killed. According to the Heliopolitan priest, Manetho, who compiled a comprehensive history of Egypt in the 3rd century BC, The Ennead, or Nine Gods of Heliopolis, were the first to rule Egypt and their reign lasted for almost 14,000 years. The first ruler was Ra, and last was Horus. After that, the kingship passed to the Demi-gods who ruled for 1255 years, then came the succession of human kings and so on. Every new pharaoh, before ascending the throne, had to visit heaven and become ordained by the gods. Only after this otherworldly journey could the pharaoh be accepted by the priests and by himself as one fit to fulfill the divine kingship.

The ancient Egyptians' belief in the power of magical names, spells, enchantments and ceremonies to produce supernatural results was an essential part of their religious philosophy. Their magic was not sleight of hand but arose from a deep and profound understanding of natural law. After the gods ceased to rule in Egypt, they began to believe that the earth, the underworld, the air, and the sky were peopled with countless invisible beings which could be friendly or unfriendly to man according to the direction of the skilled magician. These beings were thought to possess all human emotions and the chief object of their primitive magic was to give man the pre-eminence over them. The earliest Egyptian magic was for the purpose of transferring the powers of the supernatural being *into* man, temporarily enabling him to perform super-human feats. Later on, as their science of magic progressed, the object then became the art of compelling both hostile *and* friendly spirits, and even God himself, to do as the magician wished whether they were willing or not. While most of the religions of other nations of the ancient East were directed entirely against the powers of darkness, and were invented in order to vanquish it by invoking a class of benevolent beings, the Egyptians aimed at being able to command their gods to work for them, and to compel them to appear at their desire.

Religious texts from Egypt communicate that the powers of the skilled priest/magician were believed to be virtually boundless. The abilities supposedly possessed by the adepts were exorcism, heal the sick, resurrection, levitation, handle fire, live underwater, sustain great pressure, harmlessly suffer mutilation, read the past, foretell the future, make themselves invisible, control the elements, charm animals and project their souls into them. With the correct incantations and words of power, which he had wrested from the gods, even the forces of nature were at the magician's disposal. Some believed that the world itself came into existence through the utterance of a word by Thoth, and by words, the world itself could be rent asunder.

Most ancient Egyptians worked as field hands, farmers, craftsmen and scribes. A small group of people were nobles. Belief in the magicians' power flourished among peasants, educated folk and aristocracy alike, fueled by elaborate secret ceremonies which were performed in temples by initiates of the Mystery Schools. To meet the religious needs of the people, the priests found it necessary to provide pageants and ceremonies which appealed chiefly to the senses, but failed to explain the true symbolism which was reserved for initiates. There were numerous strata in Egyptian religion—more than one faith flourished on the banks of the Nile. It is certain that the views and religious ideas of many heathen *and* Christian sects may be traced directly to Egypt.

The Egyptians had many gods, but the fact remains they did believe in One God, of love and light, who was almighty, eternal, invisible, who created the heavens and earth and all beings. They believed in the resurrection of the body in a changed and glorified form, which would live on in eternity with the other righteous spirits in a heavenly kingdom. They believed that God had once lived upon the earth, suffered a cruel death at the hands of his enemies, rose from the dead and became king of the world beyond the grave. Even with all of their devotion to Osiris, they still used their talismans, magical names, and words of power to protect their souls and bodies.

In ancient Egypt, magic was the handmaiden of religion and appears side by side with their most exalted spiritual conceptions.

One god dominated the religion and culture of ancient Egypt for the entire span of its known history. Osiris was the most beloved god-king to have ever ruled and he is venerated as the principal benefactor of mankind. He is credited for having abolished cannibalism, introduced the agriculture of wheat and barley, taught the art of wine making, provided a code of laws, and inaugurated the cult of the Gods in Heliopolis. Tales of Osiris relate that he was ultimately gentle and persuasive and never had to force a man to carry out his instructions. After he completed his worldwide mission to make men give up their savagery, he was murdered by his brother, Set. The conflicts between Osiris, Isis, Set and Horus are the ultimate "Passion Play" of Egypt and the main focus of many Mystery Religion rituals. The story of the dying god recurs in most of the world's religions.

The Greeks regarded Egypt as the home of knowledge, the source of civilization and the arts, and the fountain head of "white magic" and the "black art". The magic of the ancient Egyp-

The Ancient Provincial Grand Lodge of Pennsylvania

tians was of two kinds: the first was employed for the benefit of the living or the dead, the second was the furtherance of nefarious plots and schemes intended to bring calamities upon ones enemies. Beliefs which the ancient Egyptians had about God, the "gods", Judgment, the Resurrection and Immortality closely resemble the Christian religion of today. On the other hand, many of the religious sects that flourished were decidedly non-Christian and belong to a savage state of existence.

The Egyptian influence on modern Satanism cannot be understated. Osiris was slain by Set, the light was vanquished by the darkness, thus setting into motion the eternal struggle of revenge by Osiris' reincarnation, Horus. Aleister Crowley's religion of Thelema was founded on the channelings of an Egyptian entity named Aiwass and much of his magic is designed to invoke the God forms of ancient Egypt. In 1975, Michael Aquino was the editor of the Church of Satan newsletter. He had a falling out with Anton LaVey over the issue of selling priesthoods. In protest, he resigned the C.o.S. and formed the Temple of Set with his wife Lilith Sinclair. To distinguish himself from Anton LaVey's church, followers of Aquino are called Setians rather than Satanists. Members of the Temple of Set believe the Egyptian deity, Set, is the real Dark Lord behind the name Satan, of whom Satan is just a caricature. Within the temple of Set, the Black Flame is the individual's god-like core, which is a kindred spirit to Set, and they seek to develop it. Setians believe they may become gods through

a process known as Xepering, (pronounced Kepering) from the Egyptian hieroglyphs for "to come into being." Aquino claims that Satan appeared to him, as Set, on June 21, 1975, and he believes it was the spirit of Aiwass, the same as appeared to Aleister Crowley. Aquino is now inaugurating his own aeon of Set.

Today, popular culture is flooded with ancient Egyptian imagery. In the 1970's, artist, Maurice White, of the legendary band, Earth, Wind and Fire, was trying to "reawaken the minds of the mighty people of the sun!" Earth, Wind & Fire's message was of universal harmony. Their music, in his words, is a vehicle to raise awareness of Cosmic Consciousness. Their performances were designed to blast a "cosmic wave" of peace, love and other happy vibrations to audiences using a combination of dazzling costumes, lights, pyrotechnics, magic illusions, and good music. Maurice told *Newsweek*, "We live *in a negative society... Most people can't see beauty and love. I see our music as medicine.*" The artworks for the albums of Earth, Wind and Fire are replete with all things Egyptian—from the eye of Heru, the Ankh, the Heru Bedhet, Pyramids and more. Other influential bands to adorn their albums with Egyptian symbols include, Journey, The Bangles, Alan Parsons Project, David Bowie and Iron Maiden. Who can forget Michael Jackson's ode to Akhenaten's Egypt, in his music video, *Do You Remember the Time?* Singer, Rhianna has the goddess, Isis, tattooed on her breast, and Queen Nefertiti on her ribs. In 2013, Rhianna's on-again off-again boyfriend, Chris Brown, launched his

new clothing line called "Black Pyramid." Recently, Kanye West, appeared in a music video called *Power*, where he appears with glowing eyes as some sort of proto-Horus. Katy Perry's 2014 video, *Dark Horse*, features Katy as a Magical Egyptian Queen, named Katy-Patra, who destroys men for their belongings. The subjects at her feet are mind-controlled sex kittens. As part of her "I Am..." tour, in 2009, Beyonce was given a tour of the Giza plateau by famous archaeologist and Egypt's former head of antiquities, Zahi Hawass. He reportedly became annoyed with her attitude, and publicly called her a "stupid person" because she didn't show him and the pyramids the respect he thinks they deserve, and turned the private tour into a photo shoot.

***

The O.T.O.

A new order of the Illuminati appeared in Munich, in 1880, founded by freemasonic druggist, Theodore Reuss, called the Ordo Templi Orientis (Order of the Temple of the East), but the initials also have a secret meaning for initiates. According to its own manifesto, the O.T.O. is a body of initiates in whose hands are concentrated the wisdom and the knowledge of the following sects: the Gnostic Catholic Church, the Order of the Illuminati, the Order of the Knights of the Holy Ghost, the Order of the Knights Templar, the Order of the Knights of St. John, the Order of the Knights of Malta, the Order of the Knights of the Holy Sepulchre, the Hidden Church of the Holy Graal, the Hermetic Brotherhood of Light, the Holy Order of Rose Croix of Heredom, the Order of the Holy Royal Arch of Enoch, the Antient and Primitive Rite of Masonry, the Rite of Memphis, the Rite of Mizraim, the Ancient and Accepted Scottish Rite of Masonry, the Swedenborgian Rite of Masonry, the Order of the Sat Bhai, and many other orders of equal merit. As far as the O.T.O. is concerned with Freemasonry, they claim that the whole of the Knowledge of the 33rd degree is incorporated in the first seven degrees of the O.T.O. Famous initiates they include in their ranks are Siddartha, Krishna, Orpheus, Tahuti (Thoth), Hermes, Dionysus, Pan, Melchizedek, King Arthur, Merlin, Percivale, Mohammed, Apollonius Tyanaeus, Simon Magus, Dante, Christian Rosenkreutz, Roger Bacon, John Dee, Sir Edward Kelly, Francis Bacon, Richard Wagner and many others. The names of women members are never divulged.

In 1896, Reuss, fellow occultist Leopold Engel, and Franz Hartman co-founded the Theosophical Society of Germany, and in 1901 Engel and Reuss produced a forged charter giving them the authority over the re-established Illuminati of Weishaupt. The O.T.O's highest grades involve working with "tantric" exercises, usually referred to as sex magic. Co- founder, Karl Kellner, was an initiate of the Hermetic Brotherhood of Light, whose rites include sacred applications of sexual energy, and Crowley names the HBL as the source of the O.T.O.'s "secret" which is sexual in nature. Kellner was a high ranking Freemason who claimed to have found the "KEY" to the Mysteries after having met three adepts from the East, one Sufi and two Hindu tantrikas. The word

Key, itself, has a hidden meaning of key-in-lock sexual symbolism. Kellner proposed to Reuss that they disseminate this new found key through an organized masonic rite. Several famous occultists were chartered by Reuss to operate O.T.O. lodges, including Rudolf Steiner.

"Our Order possesses the KEY which opens up all Masonic and Hermetic secrets, namely, the teaching of sexual magic, and this teaching explains, without exception, all the secrets of Freemasonry and all systems of religion."— Francis King, The Secret Rituals of the O.T.O.

Aleister Crowley joined the O.T.O. in 1910, thinking it was just one of many other Eastern Lodges. In 1913, Crowley published a mystic treatise of dirty jokes entitled *The Book of Lies*, at which time he was an honorary 7th degree member. After reading the book, Reuss appeared at Crowley's home accusing him of revealing the secret of the highest degree of the Order. Crowley denied the allegation, so Reuss took *The Book of Lies* from the shelf and pointed out the offending passage which revealed the great secret quite openly. Crowley said, *"It instantly flashed upon me. The entire symbolism not only of Free Masonry but of many other traditions blazed upon my spiritual vision....I understood that I held in my hands the key to the future progress of humanity."*[12] Reuss insisted that Crowley immediately take the 9th degree, so that he would be sworn to secrecy and

accept that rank in the O.T.O. and its obligations. It is never openly stated which chapter of the book contained the secret. So, the question is, what chapter did Reuss point to? In his book, *The Cosmic Trigger,* Robert Anton Wilson states that he believes the telltale chapter is 69, "The Way To Succeed—And the Way To Suck Eggs." Both the chapter number and the title are puns on oral sex and definitely do give instructions on how to obtain the mingled sexual fluids in the Holy Graal. The last paragraph explains that: *"This Work also eats up itself, accomplishes its own end, nourishes the worker, leaves no seed, is perfect in itself"*, a reference to the act of consuming the Sacrament.

Another likely candidate is chapter 36, "The Star Sapphire", which is named in Crowley's secret book, *De Arte Magica*, as containing the secret of the O.T.O. It begins with the words, *"Let the Adept be armed with his Magick Rood [and provided with his Mystic Rose]."* This is definitely an allusion to sex-magick, the Rood being the erect penis and the Mystic Rose representing the graal of the priestess. If the ritual is performed correctly, the Egyptian god, Set, should appear and partake of the offering. *"In this the Signs shall be those of Set Triumphant and of Baphomet. Also shall Set appear in the Circle. Let him drink of the Sacrament and let him communicate the same."*

Amrita is a Sanskrit word that literally means "immortality", and is often referred to in texts as nectar. The word's earliest occurrence is in the *Rigveda*, where it is one of the words for "soma", the drink which confers immortality upon the gods. It is related to the Greek "ambrosia", and it carries the same meaning. In the beginning of the book, *Amrita: Essays in Magical Rejuvenation*, by Crowley, before you get to the title page, there is a copy of Chapter 18, "Dewdrops." from *The Book of Lies*. According to the introduction to the book by editor, Martin P. Starr, he clearly states that Crowley's writings on Occult medicine, particularly Amrita, as being the Central Secret of the O.T.O., and he talks about Crowley becoming a member of the 9th degree, due to this writing on Occult medicine. This makes "Dewdrops", which clearly refers to Amrita and the Elixir/Dew of Immortality, another candidate for the secret chapter from *The Book of Lies*, which put Crowley at the 9th degree. Whichever chapter it was, if it was one of these three, the secret of the O.T.O. is the sacrament of sexual fluids. It is well documented that Crowley practiced the ritual use of pain and consumption of all bodily fluids. *"Although he [Crowley] positively encouraged ejaculatory orgasm in his sex magic, he always made a point of consuming what he called the 'elixir' afterwards.... He entered very carefully in his magical diaries a description of the elixir's consistency and taste, and he even recorded the prophecies which he deduced from these data."*[13]

One of Crowley's central goals for the Order was the establishment of profess-houses, which he also referred to as Retreats or Collegium ad Spiritum Sanctum. In the O.T.O. Manifesto, it is claimed that one should exist "in every important centre of population" and that their exact location would be secret, known only to those who are entitled to use them. Crowley gave several descriptions of what profess-houses are for. He wrote that each house should develop its own unique character and should develop

strongly its own specific tradition. *"The model may be a madhouse or a university, a nunnery or a brothel."* Exalted pleasure should also be a central theme, and the *"Abbot of every Profess-House is therefore expected to be an Epicurus, a master of pleasure, an instructor in delight; and he is to know how to obtain all joy, and to be able to teach others to obtain it, by means that are within the reach of all men."*[14]

Special profess-houses were set up for all women who were pregnant or mothers in need, so that their children could be raised and educated by the Order.

After Reuss' death, Crowley was appointed the Outer Head of the O.T.O., a position he held until his death in 1947. The Inner Head presumably remains invisible and anonymous to the un-initiated. The original rituals of the Order were derived from Freemasonry, but Crowley rewrote almost everything, replacing masonic material to bring it into line with his own doctrine of Thelema. Crowley includes Adam Weishaupt among the Holy Saints in his Gnostic Catholic Mass, which became the main public ritual of the Order, and which is still practiced all over the world on a weekly basis. "Do what thou wilt shall be the whole of the law" and "Love is the law, love under will" are standard salutations for members of the O.T.O. today. Their concept of love or *Agape* refers to the "love feasts" of the second century Christian Gnostics, which did include a sexual meaning. *The Equinox*, the official organ of the O.T.O., states that initiates have accepted the principles of the *Book of the Law*, transmitted through Crowley by the Intelligence, Aiwass, who is a messenger of the ruling hierarchy of our species. The purpose of the new law for mankind is the planetary transition into the Aeon of Horus.

In April, 2013, socialite Peaches Geldof chose to share with her 148,000 followers on Twitter, that she was a devotee of the O.T.O., and even had the initials tattooed on her left forearm. In November 2013, she was facing a criminal investigation for tweeting names that identified mothers who allowed pedophile rock star, Ian Watkins, to abuse their children. In April, 2014, the 25 year old was suddenly found dead in her home in Kent, England with her eleven month old son reportedly by her side at the time of death. Geldof's autopsy examination came back inconclusive and her passing is strangely similar to her mother's death in 2000. In the last interview before Peaches died, she talked about coming to terms with her traumatic childhood and expressed her hopes for the future.

Other celebrities linked to O.T.O. include the rapper Jay-Z, who has repeatedly used imagery and quotations of Crowley's religion in his clothing line, Rocawear, with T-shirts emblazoned with "Do what thou wilt", the all seeing eye in a triangle, the eye of Horus, and the head of Baphomet. Many other practices of the O.T.O. are being introduced to the masses through popular culture. In 2012, Lady Gaga launched her debut fragrance, Fame, which became the number one best-selling women's fragrance just a week after hitting the shelves. The bottle is black and gold featuring gilded monster claws and supposedly contains notes of blood and semen; and also the highly-toxic plant extract, Belladonna. According to the *Boston Globe* and various other sources, the scent, was created using a sample of Ga-ga's own blood, as well as semen from another unknown donor. The original controversial buzz surrounding the fragrance started in early 2011, when Gaga took to the radio airwaves in Australia stating her first scent would smell "like an expensive hooker … [Blood and semen] is in the perfume but it doesn't smell like it."

***

"The theory of ritual magick is that the Luciferian understands the "gods", "spirits" and "demons" are the archetypical creation of humanity; that our subconscious feeds the type of energy in which these beings exist through. Luciferians thus seek experience and the darkness within to gain knowledge, wisdom and power. Luciferianism is thus the ultimate spirituality as it focuses on the growth and expansion of the individual in a rational sense here and now, with the broad range of spiritual exploration as well."
—Maskim Hul,
Babylonian Magick

Luciferianism
Lucifer is the most diametric, occulted, and mystifying character in history. Whether groups venerate the name or curse it, they both feel that they are in the highest moral standing for doing so. Heartless intellectual Luciferianism is the de facto religion of the ruling class. At the core of this belief system you will, again, find the desire for apotheosis. At its very best, the positive side of Luciferianism worships the Light as the word Lucifer means "Light Bearer." To them the Light represents knowledge and intellect. Lucifer is not a physical personality, but a symbol of the cognitive powers of man and his individual potential. It has been symbolized as many things, fire, lightning, a torch, a serpent, and Prometheus who betrayed Zeus and brought fire (knowledge) to mankind. Lucifer is a deity of intelligence; neither feminine nor masculine, but both at the same time and is synonymous with Venus, the "Morning Star." He/she is the torch-bearer, the bringer of fire and therefore the bringer of knowledge.

The first tenant of modern Luciferianism is identification with the ego-mind. Believing that you are only your body and your thoughts, and your five senses are the only way reality can be perceived. The material world is all that exists, so you must do everything you can to gratify those senses; regardless of how selfish those desires may be. There is no judgment because death is the cessation of consciousness for all time. In this world-view everything is limited except for the ego. Another major tenant of Luciferianism is moral relativism, which is the idea that there is no such thing as objective right or wrong, natural law or moral code. There are no repercussions to your actions as long as you are not found out and whatever is expedient for the individual is permissible. Man is God on earth who lives and who dies. Their allegorical translation of Lucifer in the Garden of Eden with Adam and Eve is that they were prisoners kept by a jealous god, and Lucifer set man free by giving him the gift of intellect to conquer nature, and become god himself. In Luciferianism, man decides good and evil for himself and the concept of God is the oppression of superstition, keeping humanity down. They claim to desire to bring about heaven on earth because there is nothing else but our physical existence.

Luciferianism has been called the Left Hand path, which also correlates with Left brain, analytical and non-emotional thinking. Governments subscribe to this religion without even knowing it. They seek to create a world where a small number of adepts work behind the scenes for the culmination of their great plan. Luciferians believe that only *they* have understanding of light, and they are the enlightened ones. Everyone else is in a state of ignorance, therefore they have every right to steer the direction of the entire species as they see fit, even to the extreme of reducing populations. To them, man is just another animal and Darwin's theory of evolution and "survival of the fittest", provides the perfect rational for Luciferian ideology. The Cremation of Care ceremony that the elites perform at Bohemian Grove is a way of purging the heart of all empathy.

Gnostic myths relate that Lucifer is the Messenger of the Unknowable God who sent an angel of indescribable fire and light, to show man the way and help him wake up and see his true origin, which has been perversely imprisoned in this impure matter called body-soul. The creator of the world trapped Adam and Eve, and Lucifer, in the form of a serpent, offered them the forbidden fruit of saving Gnosis, and showed them that the creator was deceiving them. Gnostic Luciferians believe that this Serpent Lucifer is the liberator of the world and mankind. It is wisdom, the liberating Gnosis that saves him. Of course, this Messenger of the Unknowable God, Lucifer, is an opponent and an enemy of the creator of the world.

Dark Luciferianism blends into Satanism with a few subtle differences. Neither groups believe in any entity called Lucifer or the devil or even God. They are humanists and atheists in the strictest sense. There is no such

The Greek god, Phanes, whose name means, "I bring to light". Greco-Roman bas relief, circa 2nd A.D., Modena Museum, Italy

thing as sin, only learning experiences. They view "darkness" as the source of our desires, drives and motivation. Satanists generally worship themselves and their impulses; Luciferians believe that in improving oneself, you can become god. In general, both Satanists and Luciferians talk about human beings as gods, and having mastery of the planet. For groups who do acknowledge the spirit world, if they believe in a literal Lucifer, they pay him respect rather than worship, acknowledging he has many things to teach rather than finding themselves subservient to him. Luciferian groups such as the Church of Lucifer and the Children of the Black Rose, may or may not equate Lucifer with Satan. The Church of the Black Goat believes Satan and Lucifer are the same being in his light and dark aspects. In theistic Satanism, the Black Flame is knowledge which was given to humanity by Satan, who is a being independent of the Satanist himself and which he can dispense to the Satanist who seeks knowledge.

High level dark occultists would consider themselves Luciferian. They are primarily focused on the physical nature of man, exploring, experimenting and enjoying that nature, while rejecting endeavors to rise beyond it. Satan is an emblem of carnality and materiality. It is very interesting that Luciferians are staunchly anti-slavery, as they see "god" and morals as a burden and control mechanism, however, their ideology is used to perpetuate the very forms of technocratic slavery that we now find ourselves in.

***

Hand Signs & Gestures

The most subtly prominent feature of the art produced by initiates of the Mystery Schools was the peculiar hand signs they used to covey esoteric teachings, or for secret signs of allegiance. This was known as the Ancient Sign Language, transmitted from age to age, culture to culture. Hand gestures are used for many things, in both religion and magic, for spell casting, healing, for blessing or cursing. A symbolic or ritual hand gesture in Hinduism and Buddhism is called a Mudrā. The Yogis know that hand gestures stimulate the same regions of the brain as language. Mudrās are used in conjunction with yogic breathing exercises to stimulate different parts of the body. Yoga is practiced in magic for the purpose of unlocking your kundalini, a "corporeal energy", the kundalini is an unconscious, instinctive or libidinal force, envisioned either as a goddess or as a coiled, sleeping serpent.

The Sign of the Horns, so prevalent in rock and roll and heavy metal, is also known as Karana Mudra, a gesture with which demons are expelled and is said to remove obstacles such as sickness or negative thoughts. In Italian, the *Mano Cornuto*, which means "horned hand"; is a gesture commonly depicted on charms against the *malocchio* or "evil eye." This gesture seems undoubtedly to be descended from Classical times and refers to crescent moon of Selene or Diana Lucifera. Ancient lunar goddess charms depicting animal horns were used for similar protective purposes and are probably related to this gesture. The Horned Hand is used occasionally by Wiccans as a symbol of the "horned God" or as the horns of the Moon Goddess, depending on tradition.

Its use is not restricted to Europe, for it is a very important sign of the dreaded Hung Society of China, used to indicate membership to the secret brotherhood. It is said to mean a "Man" who is halfway between heaven and earth, or a departed person who has always been feared by primitive cultures. Its Asian religious significance is attributed to Kwan Yin, the Chinese goddess of Mercury. In India, figures of Shiva the Destroyer, are often depicted making the Sign of the Horns combined with the Sign of Destruction, which he, himself is the embodiment.

The 1969 back album cover for *Witchcraft Destroys Minds & Reaps Souls*, by psychedelic-occult rock band Coven, pictured band members giving the sign of the horns and included a Black Mass poster showing members at a ritual making the sign. Starting in early 1968, Coven concerts always began and ended with Jinx Dawson giving the sign on stage. Ronnie James Dio of Black Sabbath was known for popularizing the sign of the horns in heavy metal. He began using the sign soon after joining the band in 1979. He claimed he learned it from his Italian grandmother who used it to ward off the evil eye.

The "OK" hand sign, made by connecting the thumb and index finger and extending the other three fingers, has been identified by some to be a coded "666." It was also used in the 1960's television show, *The Prisoner*, as a gesture for "I've got my eye on you." This is the

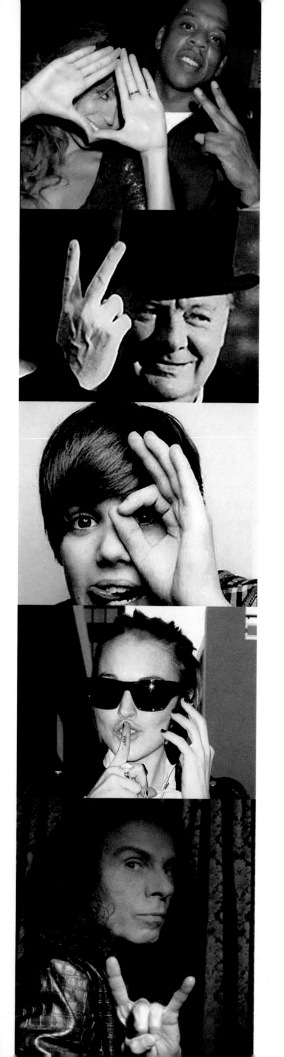

Gyan Mudrā, said to open your root chakra called the Muladhara. This chakra is the grounding force that is the connection to the earth energies of empowerment. Our lowest chakra, located at the bottom of the spine, relates to the sexual organs, lust and obsession with stability and security. When the serpent energy is unlocked in the root chakra, it travels upward through all chakras, as a bolt of lightning, and out through the crown chakra.

This gesture is also known as the Sign of the Vesica Piscis and is commonly used in conjunction with the sign of the horns. The vesica piscis is a subject of much mystical importance too lengthy to elaborate here. Basically, it is a sign of the sacred feminine, mothering power and origin, the "womb of the universe", and the root of sacred geometry. The ancient Egyptians practiced mathematics based on this profound shape, the Eye of Horus being the most common depiction of it. Freemasons and artists used the vesica piscis and its proportions in their sacred buildings and artwork to reflect their religious beliefs. It is used extensively in Christian art with Saints, the Virgin and Christ being depicted inside it. This is also an important sign to the Hung Society, to be used when a fight is taking place. Depending on how the palm is placed it indicates whether or not a particular man is a member, or "within the womb" of the Society, and so entitled to assistance from other members. The official seal of the O.T.O. uses the vesica piscis shape containing the eye of Horus, a dove and the Holy Graal. What does it mean to see countless celebrities pose with this gesture? Many times they will be shown with one eye looking through the fingers. Could this be a sign of allegiance to Thelema and the Aeon of Horus?

Jay-Z, Beyonce, Rhianna, and Kanye West all use the Triangle of Manifestation to amplify the energy of their ritual performance. According to the *Encyclopedia of Wicca and Witchcraft**, the triangle is shown as it is used in ritual and explains the principle behind magickal manifestation. This basic principle is rooted in the number three. According to metaphysics, in order to manifest something, three components must come together. These components are time, space and energy. Accordingly, if one selects a space, and a time, and then directs energy there, a manifestation occurs. For the Kabbalist magician, this gesture can be done as protection from psychic attack or to transfer the essence of the Moon's magical power into a talisman. A magician may also draw a Triangle of Manifestation outside of his Circle of Protection for the purpose of physically manifesting other spirit entities with incantations and incense.

The Triangle of Manifestation is sometimes used in conjunction with the Jewish gesture, Birkat Kohanim, or Priestly Blessing. The Blessing is administered by members of the Kohanim priestly class, usually on holidays. The hands are spread into two "V" shapes, in the form of the Hebrew letter Shin and symbolizes the light of the Shekhina, or Presence of God. The resemblance of the gesture to the "Live long and prosper" salute of the Star Trek character, Spock, is not coincidental. Actor Leonard

Nimoy has remarked on several occasions that the gesture was a nod to his Jewish heritage.

The Sign of Silence is a sign of secrecy and is a symbolic illustration of one who has been initiated into the mysteries of illumination. In Thelema, it is the affirmation of the station of Harpocrates, the Greek god of silence, and is the sign of the Neophyte. By the Egyptians it was called the Sign of Horus the child; "the child" being the title given to the new initiate. To know, to will, to dare and to be silent is a code of magicians. "Hear; See; Keep Silence", is the Motto of the United Grand Lodge of England. The ritual of The Four Adorations, based on Crowley's *Liber Resh vel Helios*, comprises four daily adorations to the sun, to be performed at dawn, noon, sunset and midnight. During each adoration the magician will make the sign of the enterer, the triangle of manifestation, and the sign of silence. The magician is also instructed to raise his hands to form the gesture of The Triangle of Manifestation at noon to the Egyptian fire goddess, Thoum-aesh-neith.

According to J.S.M. Ward of Cambridge University, the sign of silence is also connected with the mystery of the resurrection. *"The magician makes the Sign of Secrecy, while the spirit who has been raised from the underworld, to which place he must ultimately again descend. It should be noted that this latter sign often occurs in Christian art and generally in connection with the decent of our Lord into Hell and His subsequent ascension into heaven. Therefore we see that once again the Sign of Secrecy is closely associated with One who has risen from the grave."*[15]

The first singer for Black Sabbath, Ozzy Osbourne, was rather well known for using the "peace sign" at concerts, raising the index and middle finger in the form of a V. Aleister Crowley did not invent this gesture, but he did make it globally popular. During World War II, at the request of friend and Naval Intelligence officer, Ian Flemming, Crowley provided Winston Churchill with valuable insights into the superstitions and magical mindset of the leaders of the Third Reich. He suggested to the prime minister that he exploit the enemy's magical paranoia by being photographed as much as possible giving the two fingered "V-for-Victory" gesture. In magic, this is the sign of Aphophis-Typhon, a powerful symbol of destruction and annihilation, which, according to magical tradition, was capable of defeating the solar energies represented by the swastika. The symbolism of the "V" refers to the story of Isis, Apophis and Osiris, as it is illustrated in the Lesser Ritual of the Hexagram by Crowley in *The Equinox I*. In this ritual, the swastika is used to represent the mourning of Isis; and the "V" is used to symbolize Apophis or Typhon, the destroyer. This symbolism explains Crowley's use of the "V" as a foil to the swastika, since Apophis slays Osiris, thus causing Isis to mourn. The "V" symbol also echoes the downward-pointing triangle, a symbol of Horus, the Crowned and Conquering Child of the New Aeon. In *Liber Pyramidos*, Horus first appears as Hoor-Apep, a hybrid of Horus and Apophis. Because of this symbolic connection, the "V for Victory" simultaneously invokes Apophis who destroys the swastika, and Ra-Hoor-Khuit, the Lord of this Aeon, who's Law is "Do what thou wilt."

***

Weird Stuff! Eye in the Pyramid

What if I told you that the eye in the pyramid is not strictly an Illuminati symbol? When you look back in history it seems like the All-Seeing Eye is used a lot and for the same purpose over and over again. In Egypt it is the Eye of Horus. In Alchemy and Freemasonry it is a symbol for The Grand Architect of the Universe, and it is widely used in Christian art where it is called the Eye of Providence. In 1984, a large cache of over three hundred artifacts was discovered in a tunnel hundreds of feet below ground, in the jungle covered mountains of La Maná, Ecuador, by a small group of gold prospectors, led by Dr. Elias Sotomayor. Among them was a small stone pyramid, twenty-four centimeters tall, with thirteen steps and an eye at the top. More artifacts unearthed depict how to "use" the pyramid in tandem with other items found at the site. Its natural color is light green and gray but if you shine ultraviolet light on it, the eye glows bright blue and yellow. On its base is a gold inlay of the constellation, Orion. Four curious characters can be found near the stars on the base—an unknown script which has appeared on other ancient artifacts around the world. The president of the German Linguistics association called it "Pre-Sanskrit," the oldest known writing, and it has some similarities to the writing of Easter Island and the Indus Valley. The characters translate into the message: "The Son of the Creator Comes."

1. *Proofs of a Conspiracy*, John Robison
2. Ibid
3. Ibid
4. Letter from Thomas Jefferson to Bishop James Madison, Philadelphia, Jan. 31, 1800
5. Ibid
6. Manly P. Hall, *The Lost Keys of Freemasonry*, pg. 48
7. Arthur Edward Waite, *The Mysteries of Magic: A Digest of the Writings of Eliphas Levi*, pg. 428
8. Albert Pike, *Morals and Dogma*, pg. 321
9. Albert Pike, *Morals and Dogma* pg. 102
10. Albert Pike, *Morals and Dogma*, pg. 741
11. Aleister Crowley, from the introductory essay, *The Initiated Interpretation of Ceremonial Magic in the Goetia*
12. Introduction to the *Book of Lies* which quotes his book *Confessions*
13. *Secrets of the German Sex Magicians*, Frater U. D.
14. *Of Eden and the Sacred Oak*, Aleister Crowley as "Baphomet"
15. *The Sign Language of the Mysteries*, J.S.M. Ward

*2nd Edition Revised and Expanded by Raven Grimassi

Books:
Perfectibilists: The 18th Century Bavarian Order of the Illuminati, Terry Melanson
The Secret Teachings of All Ages, Manly P. Hall
The Secret Destiny of America, Manly P. Hall
Understanding Aleister Crowley's Thoth Tarot, Lon Milo DuQuette
Sex and Rockets, The Occult World of Jack Parsons, John Carter
Sign Language of the Mysteries, J.S.M. Ward
The Egyptian, Masonic, Satanic Connection, David L. and Donna M. Carrico
Egyptian Magic, E.A. Wallis Budge
The Essence of the Gnostics, Bernard Simon
Ancient Egyptian Religion, Henri Frankfort
Fingerprints of the Gods, Graham Hancock
Magic in Ancient Egypt, Geraldine Pinch
Genesis of the Grail Kings, Laurence Gardner
The History of Freemasonry, Albert Gallatin Mackey

As Above, So Below As Above, So Below

Founding father, George Washington, Eliphas Levi's Goat of Mendes, and pop star, Lady Gaga, all make the gesture called "As above, so below". These words circulate throughout occult and magical circles and they come from the Hermetic texts, a set of philosophical and religious beliefs based primarily upon the writings attributed to Hermes Trismegistus. These beliefs have heavily influenced the Western Esoteric Tradition and were considered to be of great importance during the Renaissance.

The concept was first laid out in The Emerald Tablet of Hermes with the words "That which is Below corresponds to that which is Above, and that which is Above, corresponds to that which is Below, to accomplish the miracles of the One Thing." In accordance with the various levels of reality, the physical, mental, and spiritual, this states that what happens on any level happens on every other. This is often used in the context of the microcosm and the macrocosm. The microcosm is oneself, and the macrocosm is the universe, within each lies the other, and through understanding one you can understand the other. The Egyptian priests emphasized the philosophical certainty that the visible and the invisible, together, constitute Nature.

This phrase embraces the entire system of traditional and modern magic. Its significance is that it is believed to hold the key to all mysteries. Almost every system of magic is claimed to function by this formula. The message theorizes that man is the counterpart of God on earth; as God is man's counterpart in heaven. In magic, the universe is a human organism on a colossal scale. Therefore, it is a statement of an ancient belief that man's actions below parallel the actions of God above. When Jesus instructs the twelve disciples on how to pray, he tells them: "Thy will be done, as in heaven, so in earth." Luke 11:2.

In the Kabbalah, man is viewed as a being in a microcosm, an exact duplicate on a small scale of the larger physical and spiritual universe, the macrocosm. Since the universe and man are inexorably linked by this relationship, any act performed by man under certain conditions may affect the universe at large, just as an occurrence in the outer universe may affect man.

The purpose of all rituals in ceremonial magic is to unite the microcosm with the macrocosm to join God, or gods when invoked, with the human consciousness. Symbols that express this ideology include the hexagram and the compass and square. This can also be seen in the layout of many ancient temples and sites such as the pyramids of Egypt, Mexico and China, Stonehenge, and even modern cities like Washington D.C., which are laid out to exact astronomical precision to reflect certain constellations.

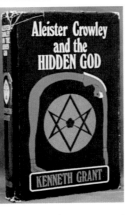

In the Dreamworks animation, *Prince of Egypt*, Moses looks on as two priests, Hotep and Huy, make the symbol of the Unicursal Hexagram, Crowley's personal sigil, before calling upon the goddess, Nuit.

HOTTEST TREND OF THE SEASON:

The Phoenix is the most celebrated of all the mythological creatures by the Mystery Schools for the purpose of concealing esoteric philosophy. This fire bird has a 500 to 1000 year life-cycle, near the end of which it builds itself a nest that ignites and the bird burns fiercely. Out of the ashes a new phoenix is born as a symbol of death, resurrection and eternal life.

The International Order of the Rainbow Girls is a Masonic youth service organization. Kabbalist rabbis teach that the rainbow symbolizes a sexual rite. The bow of the rainbow is the phallus of the male god which descends into the kingdom of the womb, the queen or goddess. It is usually viewed as a link between heaven and earth known as the Rainbow Bridge.

Certain ranks of the Egyptian priesthood wore leopard skin mantles while performing their official duties, marking them as high priest. The figure in the papyrus with the leopard skin is Ay, high priest and successor of Tutankhamun. Details of King Tut's death remain a mystery, some scholars suspect foul play with Ay as their chief suspect. King Tut was buried with a leopard skin shroud.

Horus, the son of Osiris and Isis was called "Horus who rules with two eyes." His right eye was white and represented the sun, his left eye was black and represented the Moon. Some equate them with brain hemispheres. Horus lost one eye in battle and it was reassembled by Thoth's magic and presented to Osiris in the underworld.

While Secretary of Agriculture, Freemason Henry Wallace had a guru named Nicholas Roerich who was financed to find mystical objects in Central Asia. He convinced Wallace that the Eye in the Pyramid should be put on U.S. currency. Wallace convinced FDR who said, "He's not a mystic. He's a philosopher. He's got ideas. He thinks right. He'll help the people think." That November, Wallace was elected Vice President of the United States during Roosevelt's third term.

The Initiate is *In*. The Profane are *Out*.

There is a legend of an explorer from Tyre named Melcarthus, who was sailing in search of Atlantis. He paused in a bay at the western extremity of the land beyond the straits, and set up there two pillars and a temple of Hercules as a memorial. A colony of Tyre was established there, and the place grew into the ancient Gades, the modern Cadiz. The twin pillars represent the two great pillars erected in Solomon's Temple called Jachin and Boaz. They were said to be hollow and were filled with writings containing all the knowledge of masonry. Egyptian legends speak of knowledge carved on two pillars, one of stone and one of metal.

The Knights Templar were established users of human skulls of all sizes and mediums, incuding metallic and crystal skulls. One of their preeminent symbols was the "Jolly Roger" which is the skull and crossbones. It represented both the ceremonial use of skulls as drinking vessels, as well as their practice of Alchemy, one of the stages being called "Deadhead". A skull and crossbones can be found on the coffin of Hiram Abiff in the Freemasonic rituals as a symbol of his murderers. The skull represents intellect and the bones, willpower, but there is no heart, care or conscience.

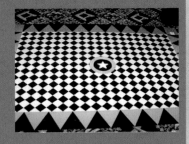

The black and white checkerboard floor found in all Masonic lodges is said to represent duality, the polarities of life and death, ignorance and knowledge. The black and white represents base consciousness, or unconsciousness. It is not understanding one's spiritual nature, natural law, not knowing good from evil and being ignorant of both. In this state you are considered lost, a wanderer in darkness, not knowing light from darkness, on the floor of the house.

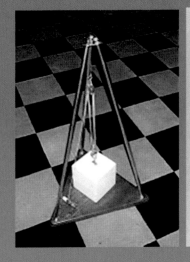

In Masonry you are to work from the rough ashlar to the perfect ashlar. To a Mason, the rough ashlar *"is a symbol of men's natural state of ignorance. But if the perfect ashlar be, in reference to its mode of preparation, considered as a symbol of the social character of Freemasonry, then the rough ashlar must be considered as a symbol of the profane world. In this species of symbolism, the rough and the perfect bear the same relationship to each other as ignorance does to knowledge, death to life, and light to darkness. The rough ashlar is the profane; the perfect ashlar is the initiate."*
—*Symbolism of Freemasonry*
In geometry it is the hexahedron, one of the five platonic solids. The Kaaba is a cube shaped building in Mecca, Saudi Arabia, and is the most sacred site in Islam.

Earth Needs Mothers

No Place Like Home

When Dorothy clicks the heels of her ruby slippers together and chants, "There's no place like home," she's absolutely right; but maybe not in the way that you might think. The theme of Dorothy's story, her desire to go home, is a very common one. To the natural human, the concept of home would represent a place where you could always go, most likely where you grew up, where you were always welcomed and loved unconditionally. You could stay and do whatever you like, with limited responsibility, and be refreshed and nurtured for as long as you needed. For most people there is no such place like this. Even if one is fortunate enough to have a place to live, the constant pressure of rent or a mortgage, bills, insurance and taxes means that for many, keeping their "home" feels more like a prison sentence than a paradise. The feeling that one could lose

their home at any time due to a number of factors is a very traumatizing one. The spirit and heart of every home is the mother and it seems good moms, just like good homes, are in short supply right now.

Before any religion there was mother worship and what inspired that worship is that she was the first source of nourishment. She was the very embodiment of what was sacred and necessary. From this, sprang the first religion of the Great Mother who, from the beginning, was associated with fertility, nurturing and the provision of food. In the oldest artifacts yet excavated we discover the female as primal power. Female clay figurines of the Paleolithic period are evidence of goddess/mother worship and coincide with the development of agriculture. Ancient Mystery Schools of the mother goddess, Ceres or Demeter, tell the story of her teaching humans how to grow

grain. Other goddess cults articulate the same thing and it is always women who are responsible for the discovery of food cultivation. The voluptuous shape of so many ancient figurines illustrated how a goddesses being and function are always closely intertwined. What a goddess does she also is, so the giver of food is herself, food. The sculptures' exaggeration of breasts, hips and belly suggest not sexual attractiveness but the potency of the milk giving mother. Ancient agricultural rituals were shaped by the analogies between planting and intercourse and between harvesting and childbirth.

The most famous of the ancient religious Mysteries were the Eleusinian, whose rites were celebrated every five years in the city of Eleusis, in Greece, in 1,400 B.C. The initiates of the Eleusinian School were famous for the beauty of their philosophies and their high standards of morality. Women and children were admitted to the Eleusinian mysteries, making it a family affair and at one time there were literally thousands of initiates. The rites of Eleusis focused on mystic interpretations of the cycles of nature. The Lesser Mysteries were celebrated annually and dedicated to Persephone, the goddess of spring and daughter of Ceres. The legend says that one day Persephone was in a meadow when she was abducted by Hades (Pluto) and taken to the underworld where she was forced to be his queen. They taught that the young goddess represented two things: the sun, who is "forced into the underworld on the autumnal equinox", and the psyche, or soul, that lives in the bondage of material form. The story of her abduction represents her function as the personification of vegetation which shoots forth in spring and withdraws into the earth after harvest.

The Greater Mysteries were sacred to the mother, Ceres, and represent her as the hero of the quest for her abducted daughter. In Persephone's absence, living things ceased their growth, then began to die. The Mother goddess wanders the earth and eventually travels to the underworld to plead with Pluto for her daughter. They reach a compromise and Persephone is allowed to live in the upper world for part of the year if she would stay in Hades for the other part. The Greeks portrayed Persephone as a manifestation of the solar energy, which in the winter months lived in the underworld but returned again in the spring as the goddess of productiveness. In the end it was motherly love and dedication that saved the world from eternal winter. The 1934 Disney cartoon,

The Goddess of Spring, illustrates the ancient story, however the Mother goddess is left out entirely.

***

The magical dogma is also one in three and three in one. The triad is the universal dogma.

In Magic—principal, realization, adaptation; in alchemy—azoth, incorporation, transmutation; in theology—God, incarnation, redemption; in the human soul—thought, love and action; in the family—father, mother and child. The triad is the end and supreme expression of love; we seek one another as two only to become three.

—Eliphas Levi, Transcendental Magic

The Trinity

In most religions featuring a triune god, or trinity, they are represented as Father, Mother, Son. The Sumerians referred to these as Anu, Ninkharsag and Enlil. In Egypt it came to be known as Osiris, Isis and Horus. The Greeks knew them as Zeus, Hera and Apollo. From Roman Catholicism comes God, Mary and Jesus. In Freemasonry, a trinity is worshipped and it is represented by a symbol, the 47th Proposition of Euclid, or the Pythagorean Theorem and the right triangle is a symbol of the trinity. The perpendicular side represents the masculine or divine Father. The base represents the feminine divine Mother. The hypotenuse is their offspring, the divine Child, who is sometimes called the Masonic Christ. The Hebrew triad of the Kabbalah uses the letter Shin to signify the trinity of the first

three sephiroth. The middle is Kether, the Crown and the other two circles represent Chochmah, the Father and Binah, the mother. From the union of the divine Father and the Divine Mother are produced the worlds and the generations of living things. The three flame like points of this letter represent the Creative Triad of the Cabbalists.

There is a trinity in every home too—the father, the mother, and the child. This is naturally a holy trinity considering the family unit, when functioning properly, is one of mankind's best defenses against evil influence. At the heart of the conspiracy is the suppression of the sacred feminine and the removal of motherly love.

***

Holy Spirit Mother

The trinity is central to Protestant doctrine with one difference, they have replaced the Mother with an ambiguous abstract called the Holy Spirit; but as we are about to see, this aspect of the trinity is most decidedly female and very motherly. In Hebrew, the word for spirit (ruach) is feminine. In Aramaic also, the language generally considered to have been spoken by Jesus, the word is feminine. Thus, referring to the Holy Spirit as "she" has linguistic justification. Out of eighty four Old Testament uses of the word "spirit", in contexts assumed to be references to the Holy Spirit, seventy-five times it is either explicitly feminine or indeterminable due to lack of a verb or adjective. In the Old Testament and the Dead Sea Scrolls the Holy Spirit was known as the Ruach or Ruach Ha Kodesh (Psalm 51:11) and was considered to be a voice sent from on high to speak to the Prophet. In the Old Testament language of the prophets, *She* is the Divine Spirit of indwelling sanctification. It has long been recognized that the Godhead must include some feminine aspects, since Genesis 1:26-27 explicitly states that both men and women were created in God's image.

The Bible says that the Holy Spirit is the balancing force to the discipline and correction of the Father God. One of her primary characteristics is to bring comfort. Jesus himself said before he as

WISDOM

cended to heaven that the Father would send another comforter to teach us, so that we would not be left alone, and she would remind us of what Jesus taught. (John 14:26) The Holy Spirit is the teacher and the guide, so is mom. It is the unseen One Who gives others all the attention; so is Mother. When the spirit speaks to Isaiah it says: "As one whom his mother comforteth, so will I comfort you." (Isaiah 66:13)

If now such a child thinks about the holy Trinity, it does not need to speculate in the abyss of the Godhead and strain its head and reason so that it might snap and tear. But as easy as it is for one to think about Father or Mother, so easy it is for the disposition to occupy itself with the heavenly Father and the heavenly Mother. That is simple, childlike, easy, and tender."—Zinzendorf, 1748

You might think the idea of the Holy Spirit being the female/mother counterpart to God the Father would be an obvious and biological way to explain it, but this doctrine has always been suppressed and it is very controversial. One biblical scholar who set out to promote this theology was Count Nikolaus von Zinzendorf, a German religious reformer in the 18th century and father of the Moravian Church. As a child of nobility, he was given the benefit of a first rate education. While still a student he established a religious society called, the Order of the Grain of the Mustard Seed. Members wore rings which were inscribed with the words "No

Man Liveth Unto Himself" and pledged to be kind to all men, to be true to Christ, and spread the gospel to the world.

Zinzendorf was often frustrated by the excessive subtlety and hair-splitting of traditional theology, which seemed to him more likely to cause people to become atheists rather than believers. He thought that each denomination had a unique perception of Christ, and a rare gift to offer the world. In 1722, Zinzendorf offered an asylum to a number of members of the Bohemian Brethren, who were being persecuted by the Catholic Church. He permitted the religious wanderers from Moravia and Bohemia to build the village of Herrnhut on a corner of his estate. As the village grew, it became known as a place of religious freedom, and attracted individuals from a variety of persecuted groups. Because of its diversity, the village fell into disarray and severe religious conflict. Zinzendorf began to visit each home for prayer, and finally called the men of the village together for an intense study of the Scriptures. The question they came to focus on was how the Scriptures described Christian life in a community. These studies, combined with intense prayer, convinced many of the community that they were called to live together in love, and that the disunity and conflict they had experienced was contrary to Scripture.

Zinzendorf is known as the father of Protestant missionary work. His interest in spreading the gospel was sparked by meeting two Inuit children and a freed slave, Anthony Ulrich, who told of terrible oppression among the slaves in the West Indies. In 1732, the community began sending out missionaries to those countries. Zinzendorf tried to teach his followers and missionaries about the Holy Spirit in a way that was accessible to all kinds of people. He believed that any child could understand the language of motherhood and this was a type of speech that was easy to translate for Native Americans, enslaved Africans, Inuit, and others. Zinzendorf began promoting the doctrine of the Mother Office of the Holy Spirit at the same time that Moravians began evangelizing tribal peoples from Greenland to the Cape of Good Hope. Zinzendorf assumed that since everyone had a mother, preachers would not need to teach people what a mother is and what mothers do. All they would have to do was convince people that one aspect of God is like a mother.

For before [theologians] regarded her as a finger, a dove, a mirror, and they publish, preach, and sing a hundred other foolish fancies about her in which there was no sense and understanding. So now they may rather attain a childlike, simple heart concept of her, since one is better than the others: for the hearty, childlike concept can still bring them to a true, living knowledge and to a feeling of the office of the Holy Spirit in their hearts."
—Zinzendorf, 1746

Zinzendorf developed his doctrine of the Holy Spirit, proclaiming that she is a mother in three distinct ways. First, it was the Holy Spirit, not Mary, who was the true mother of Jesus, since she prepared him in the womb and hovered over him. (Luke 1:35) Second, the Holy Spirit is the mother of all living things, because she was involved in creating the universe. As the Spirit of God she has a special role in the on-going creation of the world. The ruach, or breath of God, was there during the formation of the world, (Gen. 1:2) as it hovered over the waters and breathed life into Adam (Gen. 2:7). The Holy Spirit is also the Mother in a third and most important sense, as the Mother of the church and all those who have been reborn. Zinzendorf bases this understanding of the Spirit giving birth to converted souls, in large part, on Jesus' conversation with Nicodemus in John chapter 3, where Jesus told Nicodemus that he must be born again, not from his mother's womb, but from the spirit. Ultimately, then, the Holy Spirit is the Mother of the Christian, in the sense that she is the active agent in Salvation.

The new and simple concept that the Spirit functions like a mother was a lovely rethinking of worship. The first duty of the Holy Spirit is to bring people to Christ and lead them into spiritual rebirth. But her motherly work does not end there. She protects, guides, admonishes, and comforts the children of God throughout the changing years of their life, just like a human mother teaches a child to become an adult. The Moravians believed that the Spirit does this for all Christians, but she could do her work better if Christians would participate in the process, by acknowledging her motherly presence in their lives. The Moravians often referred to the Church as the school of the Holy Spirit, which they viewed more like a family in the arms of the eternal Mother, who tenderly loves her children. Thousands of people responded positively to Zinzendorf's sermons and hymns. Some of them were even willing to cross an ocean and build a community in the wilderness of Pennsylvania.

In 1741, Zinzendorf visited the New World, thus becoming one of the few 18th century European nobles to have actually set foot in the Americas. In addition to visiting leaders in Philadelphia such as Benjamin Franklin, he met with the leaders of the Iroquois and reached agreements for the free movement of Moravian missionaries in the area. Bethlehem, PA is one of the most important communities established by the Moravians, and there has been a lot of scholarly research on this town. It was one of the most successful communes in American history. When the residents of Bethlehem built their large building for the Single Brothers in 1748, a stone was carved to proclaim to all visitors what the Moravians believed about God and their new town: *"Father and Mother and dear Husband give honor to the plans of the young men."* (Christ is the Husband) In 1748, the Moravians were so committed to the idea that the Trinity includes God the Mother that they literally wrote it in stone and placed it on the front of one of their largest buildings.

In 1764 the church brought together most of the leaders, male and female, in a synod to deal with the crisis caused by the death of Zinzendorf. Some of the

Nicholas Ludwig von Zinzendorf (1700-1760)

elders suggested that the language of motherhood had caused too much opposition and misunderstanding and should be dropped. Many of the members of the synod disagreed, asserting that this doctrine had been a great blessing to the church, but the leading male authorities doubted the wisdom of using language that was so at odds with other powerful churches. They instructed the members of the church to avoid using this language in public settings. They also decided to let most of Zinzendorf's writings go out of print so the public would have less access to what he said. Before long it was forgotten that he preached entire sermons on the Mother office of the Holy Spirit. At the next synod, women had less voice in the affairs in the church, and they appointed a pastor to revise all of the litanies of the church. The new litanies replaced the word "Mother" with "Comforter" in most instances. The last time the celebration of the mother, called Mutterfest, was celebrated was in 1774.

Amongst the Eastern Church communities there is none more clear about the feminine aspect of the Holy Spirit as the writings of the Coptic-Gnostics. The 3rd century scroll of Coptic Christianity, The Acts of Thomas, gives a graphic account of the Apostle Thomas' travels to India, and contains prayers invoking the Holy Spirit as "the Mother of all creation" and "compassionate mother," among other titles. The most profound Coptic Christian writings definitely link the "spirit of Spirit", manifested by Christ to all believers, as the "Spirit of the Divine Mother." Most significant are the new manuscript discoveries, which have demonstrated that more early Christians than previously thought, regarded the Holy Spirit as the Mother of Jesus. It is becoming clear in re-examining the first 100 years of Christianity, that an earlier doctrine was closer to the "Feminine Spirit", the Ruach and the beloved Shekinah of the Old Testament.

***

"To the performance of this Work, the nearest obstacle and the most obvious is the Family."—Aleister Crowley, *Magic Without Tears*

They Always Kill the Mother

In popular culture the Holy Spirit can be reduced to one easy to understand archetype: Motherly Love. What do Cinderella, Belle, Jasmine, Ariel, Snow White, Pocahontas, Hannah Montana, and *literally countless* other characters have in common? None of these girls have a mother. An uncanny re-occurrence in all types of movies and TV shows is the death of a parent, and more often than not, it's the death of the mother. In instances where she is not horrifically killed as part of the story, she is simply not mentioned, as if she never even existed. It is noteworthy that Disney deletes almost all reference to the most primary human relationship; and who is mothering these characters? Everyone in the world but Mom. It may be a friendly fish, a cricket, a chipped teacup, seven dwarves, friendly birds, rabbits, skunks and baboons—all of the male gender, of course.

In place of motherly love, Disney creates looming, hideous female witches, demons, octopi, dragons, and stepmother-monsters, to make sure everyone comes away with a perfectly nauseating feeling toward powerful women. Instead of a Mother, all adult female roles are reduced to a vague amalgam of the Weird Sisters from *Macbeth*, the children-eating crones that inhabit the forests in Grimms' Fairytales and in Walt Disney's cartoon treatments of them. They are the beak nosed hags who wear conical hats and ride on broomsticks.

Now that you are aware, pay attention to how many television and movies feature a dead mother as part of the story. It may be subtle, just a quick flash of a woman in a picture frame who they vaguely remember. What are the consequences of removing the mother from the fairy tale? If, like we believe, the Mother equals the Holy Spirit, constantly blaspheming her by murdering her is the only unpardonable sin. What, after all, is more sacred than motherhood? In Matthew 12:31-32, Jesus says, *Wherefore I say unto you, All manner of sin and blasphemy shall be forgiven unto men: but the blasphemy against the Holy*

What do all of these and many more movies have in common?

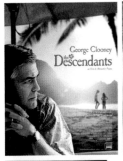

Ghost shall not be forgiven unto men. And whosoever speaketh a word against the Son of man, it shall be forgiven him: but whosoever speaketh against the Holy Ghost, it shall not be forgiven him, neither in this world, neither in the world to come." The synoptic Gospels all have a version of the saying, admittedly mysterious, that no blasphemy against the Holy Spirit is ever forgiven, unlike sins or blasphemies against sons of men (Mark) or the Son of Man (Matthew and Luke). The Gnostic gospel of Thomas, verse 44, also states it clearly: blasphemies against Father and Son will be pardoned, but those against the Holy Spirit will not be forgiven on earth or in heaven.

***

Mom Power

Nobel Prize winner, Leymah Gbowee is a mother and African peace activist who witnessed the first and second civil war in Liberia from 1989-2003. The war broke out just as she was graduating high school and she spent her entire early adulthood on the run from the horrors inflicted on the innocent by soldiers and rebels alike. During this time she managed to raise four children and became a counselor trained in trauma therapy. In 2003 she led a protest by various inter-faith women's groups against the war. Christian mothers came together with Muslim mothers and women from all different tribes and countries bonded as women, and only women; the one thing that they shared that could never divide them. They asked themselves, what does it take to make those who fight listen to reason? They announced that, because men were involved in the fighting and women were not, they encouraged women to withhold sex as a way to persuade their partners to end the war. The message was, that while the fighting continued, no one was innocent and not doing anything to stop it made you guilty. The women protesting on rural communities set aside a separate space where they sat each day and the men couldn't come. The strike lasted on and off for months. Their efforts emboldened the nation and the powerless began to stand up.

When peace negotiations stalled, and the killings continued, Gbowee led the women straight into the meetings and said they would not allow the negotiators to leave until resolutions were made. When they came to arrest them for obstructing justice, Gbowee threatened to strip naked. In Africa it is a terrible curse to see a married or elderly woman deliberately bare herself. If a mother is severely upset with her child, she might take out her breast and slap it to curse him. For all the African delegates to see her naked would almost be akin to a death sentence, as if the mothers were saying "We now take back the life we gave you." Two weeks later the terms of agreement were announced.

***

Books:
Mighty Be Our Powers, Leymah Gbowee

Resources:
The Motherhood of the Holy Spirit in Moravian Bethlehem Presented to the Moravian College Faculty, April 7, 2011 Craig D. Atwood

Weird Stuff! Mother's Day

Mother's Day was originally started after the Civil War by women who had lost their sons, as a protest to the carnage. The first Mother's Day, proclaimed in 1870 by Julia Ward Howe, was a passionate demand for disarmament and peace: *"Arise, then, women of this day! Arise, all women who have hearts, whether your baptism be that of water or tears! Say firmly, we will not have great questions decided by irrelevant agencies. Our husbands shall not come to us, reeking with carnage, for caresses and applause. Our sons shall not be taken from us to unlearn all that we have taught them of charity, mercy and patience. We women of one country will be too tender of those of another to allow our sons to be trained to injure theirs. From the bosom of the devastated earth, a voice goes up with our own. It says, 'Disarm, Disarm!' The sword of murder is not the balance of justice. Blood not wipe out dishonor, nor violence indicate possession. As men have often forsaken the plow and the anvil at the summons of war, let women now leave all that may be left of home for a great and earnest day of counsel. Let them meet first, as women, to bewail & commemorate the dead. Let them solemnly take counsel with each other as to the means whereby the great human family can live in peace, each bearing after his own time the sacred impress, not of Caesars but of God."*

PROJECT: CRAZY BITCH

For those who don't know me, I can get a bit crazy
Have to get my way, 24 hours a day
'Cause I'm hot like that."*
—Miley Cyrus

Gentlemen, have you been noticing any irrational behavior in your wives, girlfriends or daughters? Has your lady been going a little gaga lately? Or maybe you've been ground down so hard by the girls you try to please that you start to think maybe the gays are on to something. If not, you are among the lucky few. If so, then you may be witnessing something far more sinister than that monthly female luny-cycle. Although, you won't find it in any psychology textbook (yet), you could be witnessing the victims of a viral epidemic known as Princess Programming.

***

The Royal Invasion
You should by now be aware that there is an overarching agenda to turn every American girl into a self-absorbed, puffy, pink princess. At this time, the largest franchise for girls on the planet is "Princess." The Walt Disney Companies' popular global pro- file makes the Disney princess the most recognizable; the "princess of all princesses," and there are now more than 26,000 different princess items on the market. The Disney Princess did not fully exist as a concept until the year 2000 when former Nike executive, Andy Mooney, stepped in to rescue Disney's ailing consumer products division. He had seen the show *Disney on Ice* and found himself surrounded by girls in *homemade* princess costumes.

He thought, why let little girls use their imaginations to play dress up when they could be buying licensed products? The next day he pulled together a marketing team and they began work on a special line that would become known solely as "Princess." The Disney Corporation had never marketed its cartoons separately from their movies before and Roy Disney always hated the idea of lumping together characters from different stories. They began by packaging eight female characters under one royal emblem; Cinderella, Sleeping Beauty, Snow White, Ariel, Belle, Jasmine, Mulan and Pocahontas, and later Tianna, to round out the Satanic 9. The company conducted little market research on their new Princess line, instead, they rely heavily on the power of its legacy among mothers to pass on the royal tradition.

Not to be outdone, or perhaps on cue, in 2001 Mattel turned Barbie from your all American consumer girl into a fairy princess with the "World of Girl" line of princess Barbies. Sesame St. also introduced a fairy princess character called Abby Cadabby, after Sesame Workshop execs decided they needed a more feminine and attractive puppet to re-enforce the princess craze. Even little Dora the Explorer was revealed to be royalty in a two-part episode where she becomes a "true princess."

***

"If there is a devil in history, it is the power principle"
—Mikhail Bakunin

The Dark Triad of Psychopathology

At first princess play seems innocent enough, as most would think that treating your little girl like royalty equates her with honor, unconditional love and adoration; but what are the consequences when these little darlings grow up? If you are determined to raise your daughter as a princess, let's examine her characteristics. First is the huge sense of entitlement. A princess gets everything she wants at her whim, with no thought for the cost or the sacrifice made by anyone else. She believes she is deserving simply because she is the princess and for no other reason. Much like the *Highlander*, in the world of fairy tale princesses, there can be only one heroine per story! This entitlement attitude can have devastating effects when the logic is extended to the real world. It creates a corrupted and selfish world-view and a vast separation between the elite and the lowly, in essence, the deserving and the non-deserving. Taken to its extreme, it becomes a serious psychological condition known as narcissism, which is becoming a frightening epidemic, especially with young women in their twenties.

Narcissism is an inflated sense of self-worth to the point of grandiosity. All narcissists believe they are special and entitled. Because they are so special they feel they deserve preferential treatment, privileges, indulgences, attention, and only the best of everything—and they want it *now*. They expect others to gratify them at all times, but are not concerned with gratifying anyone else, ever. They are in love with themselves, to the exclusion of healthy relationships with others.

People with Narcissist Personality Disorder lack compassion and empathy, and this population is growing by leaps and bounds. Narcissists aren't particularly interested in warmth and caring. They enjoy being around people, for the energy that they can siphon off of them, and are only in relationships for their own narcissistic needs. They are very vain and selfish, and require approval and praise from everyone around them and can be set off by the slightest criticism. Much like a sociopath, they have no remorse over hurting people. One of the most disturbing characteristics of narcissism is insatiable greed. Add in the gluttony, and appallingly stingy nature, and you've got one revolting creature. They are parasites, mooches and vultures of the human race, always on the take, and always ready to swoop in and sink their claws into whatever they can get.

Because they have no conscience, they are quite successful in business and entertainment, where cut throat behavior is essential in order to get ahead. A narcissist will constantly seek validation and recognition and will often put others down to inflate their own ego. They are addicted to the spotlight and have an insatiable need to be recognized for every single achievement. Social media sites such as Facebook and Twitter are a big draw for narcissists, who over-value the importance of their own opinions to amplify their egos in cyberspace.

In the largest study of its kind, a group of psychologists of the American Freshman Survey found that the scores of over 16,000 college students who took the Narcissistic Personality Inventory between 1982 and 2006, have risen by 30%! A full two-thirds of today's young adults rank above average in excessive self-involvement and dishonesty, with the sharpest decline in empathy occurring since the year 2000.

This behavior is so obvious in shows like MTV's *My Super Sweet Sixteen*, a reality series documenting the lives of teenagers who have wealthy parents that throw huge coming of age celebrations. These are the true monstrous faces of the American Princess. In one episode, fifteen year old Audrey suffers a psychotic meltdown because her mother presented her with a brand new Lexus but was supposed to wait until the day of the party. This behavior is typical of all the young ladies featured on the program. In each episode the girls make a dramatic show at school of handing out invitations to the infamous soirée. The self-important princesses watch and giggle with sadistic glee at the crestfallen faces of the classmates who were not invited.

In the grown up version you can see these princesses in "reality" shows like the *Real Housewives* series on the network BRAVO!; The only network that has made me feel like I don't want to live on this planet anymore; but of course this is all part of the psychological programming isn't it? Real Housewives promotes to the world that American women are generally immature, selfish, extremely arrogant, mentally unstable, irresponsible, and highly slutty. The behavior of most of these housewives is utterly disgusting, to say the least.

We know that these shows do not reflect the lifestyles of real people, but it does give them something to imitate, especially if it is defined as success. Telling your daughter that she is a princess is the beginning of an upper/lower class paradigm. The middle and lower classes are bombarded daily with images of the affluent life styles of the rich and famous, dangled in front of us like diamond-studded carrots. So it was in ancient times with elaborate street processions, extravagant church and court rituals and society gala marriages. The ruling elite parade their superiority and entitlement before the masses and this behavior has devastating impacts on both parties. The feeling that you are superior to the majority of the human race, which you are actually just a part of, creates a psychological schism which leads a person to feeling never quite sure whether the others around them genuinely like them, envy them, or are trying to get something from them.

It is a total lie that if honest, hardworking people are dedicated enough, they can make their way in the business world and eventually afford the types of "freedom" and luxury of the upper class. In a book called *Office Politics*, psychologist, Oliver James identifies three types of dysfunctional personalities among white-collar workers; the Psychopath, the Machiavellian, and the Narcissist. The ones who succeed are the ones who have no problem trampling over others, and like nothing more than to plot and scheme. They have a dangerous, yet effective mix of a lack of empathy, self-centeredness, deviousness and self-regard, which can propel them to the top of any organization because the modern workplace rewards these psychotic traits. There is also a terrifying fourth dysfunctional type, a "triadic person," who suffers from a combination of all three traits called the *Dark Triad*.

No industry has a monopoly on triadic types because these psychopaths and sociopaths also dominate the political arena. The Machiavellian personality is characterized by a disregard for morality and a focus on self-interest, deception, and cynicism about human nature. The disorder is named after the sixteenth-century Italian philosopher and historian, Niccolò Machiavelli, who wrote a book about the mechanics of government called *The Prince*. He describes the book as being an un embellished summary of his knowledge about the nature of princes and "the actions of great men." Machiavelli wrote that the only purpose of political power is to maintain and extend itself. It has nothing to do with the welfare of the people, principles, ideology or right and wrong. The ultimate goal is power and they do whatever it takes to keep it and extend it.

Machiavelli deduced these rules from the political practices of his time: Never show humility; it is more effective to show arrogance when dealing with others. Morality and ethics are for the weak; powerful people should feel free to lie, cheat, and deceive whenever it suits their purpose, and it is better to be feared than loved. Machiavellian personalities are committed to the belief that a desired end justifies virtually any means. A prince, or princess, therefore, should only be concerned with power and be bound only by rules that would lead to that success.

According to new studies from neuroscientists at Wilfrid Laurier University in Ontario, feelings of power diminish all varieties of empathy.[1] Even the smallest dose of power can fundamentally change the way the brain operates. Furthermore, they found that the more powerful a person perceived their self, the less they are able to empathize with the plight of others. Pretty much anywhere there is power to be had you will find a psycho. Where there is competition, a cheater will always have the upper hand. So it would follow that someone who disregards the rules and only thinks for themselves would always rise to the top. In many ways a psychopath is like a sorcerer, in that their ultimate goal is to be able to have control over other people.

The concept of ponerology is something you've probably never heard of but sums it up quite nicely. The word was coined by Polish psychiatrist, Andrzej Łobaczewski, to describe his interdisciplinary study of social issues like aggressive war, ethnic cleansing, genocide, and despotism. Ponerology is the idea that any power structure, over time, becomes twisted by the work of relatively few sociopaths, until the entire structure and everyone in it behaves and thinks like a socio-

path as well. The idea that profit is the only thing that matters, that employees must be paid as little as possible, is by definition, pathological, meaning a decision that is made on "rational" grounds only. A pathological person will think that *any* action is logical if there is an immediate benefit to them. The consequences to others are considered irrelevant, if they are considered at all, and so are the long-term consequences. That is someone else's problem.

This attitude perfectly describes our culture in the

world of finance and business. The system itself has become pathological, as a result of years of sociopaths wielding great power. Even a decent person, once they get trapped into the corporate world, will find themselves making pathological decisions and being congratulated for it by other decent people. These people are not sociopaths, but they have come to realize, whether consciously or unconsciously, that you have to behave like one to achieve wealth and power.

***

"What, then, is the definition of a true witch? I don't see any reason to readily discount the movie and TV image of the witch, because I think whatever popular image is most flattering should be utilized and sustained whenever possible."—Anton LaVey

Modern Bitch Craft

You might look down on people who call themselves Satanists, but how closely aligned with their principles are our cultural norms and belief systems? You will be surprised to learn. In San Francisco on April 30, the day witches call Walpurgisnacht, Anton Szandor LaVey shaved his head in the tradition of black magicians and medieval executioners and announced the establishment of the first Church of Satan in the United States. He declared 1966 "Anno Satanas", the first year of the Satanic Age. LaVey was a generational Satanist of German and Romanian descent, and was raised for the purpose of leadership in the satanic movement and mind control. At the age of sixteen, LaVey ran away from his home in California to join the circus as a cage boy and later became a lion tamer. At eighteen, he left the circus to join a carnival where he performed as a hypnotist, a mentalist and an organ player. When he settled down in San Francisco, he worked as a crime scene photographer for the San Francisco Police Department.

His work for the police reinforced his growing cynicism about human nature. His moment of realization came when he had a gig playing the organ for carnival strip acts on Saturday nights, and again for tent-show evangelists on Sunday morning. He noticed he would see the same people at the girlie shows that he saw at church, and so he set out to make a religion that he claimed was free from hypocrisy. He based his church on the principles of "survival of the fittest," a term coined by Herbert Spencer, who was a major influence on the Eugenics Movement. Satanism is a spiritual Darwinian theory based on predation. The 7th Satanic Statement, as outlined in *The Satanic Bible*, says that humans are just another species of animal, the most viscous animal, and therefore should live in an animalistic and predatory way. Satanists believe in self-indulgence, mind control, vampirism, lycanthropy, and the extermination of lower class people. Satanists believe in keeping the masses in lower states of consciousness for selfish purposes, so that a small class of people can gain a tactical advantage in knowledge and, therefore, rule over people who lack that

knowledge. Rituals of the Church of Satan include influences from the Catholic Church, the Knights Templar, the O.T.O, the Nazis, H.P. Lovecraft and many more. The Church membership includes teachers, movie stars, government officials, lawyers, judges, police, and last but not least, high ranking military personnel.

The Satanic Witch, is a book by Anton LaVey, and a self-professed *"guide to selective breeding, a manual for eugenics— the lost science of preserving the able bodied and able minded while controlling the surplus population of the weak and incompetent."* It is a tool for women that teaches how to manipulate men, and other women, using psychology and sexuality for the liberation of the demonic in every woman. *"In order to be a successful witch, one does have to make a pact with the devil, at least symbolically. She must worship the Luciferian element of pride within her."*[2] This truly "liberated" female is called the "compleat witch", and knows how to both bewitch and manipulate people.

Your typical consumer princess is a compleat witch, as outlined by the founder of the Church of Satan. I find the characters of HBO's *Sex and the City* to be perfect examples of the

princess/consumer programming. Like the women on the show, LaVey also had an affinity for the three-inch spike high heel, because this type of shoe creates an exaggeration of the natural "S" curves of the body. The calves, hips, thighs and buttocks are thrown out and it is virtually impossible to walk in high heels without the hips and pelvis reacting in a suggestive manner. The fifth chapter of *The Satanic Witch* is called, Fashion: The Witch's Greatest Friend. Interestingly enough, popular culture is so degenerate now, that even LaVey himself wouldn't condone the dress and behavior of many modern girls and women. According to his Law of the Forbidden, the more chaste you can *seem*, the more bewitching you will be. However, he does claim that *"The 'uniform' of the prostitute is virtually little different than the uniform of the compleat witch."*[3] because, *"What you, as a witch, accumulate in the way of lust power from others will in turn give you greater magnetic power over others."*[4]

Somewhere along the line, the "girl power" message of the 90's became its own opposite. In the competition for prince charming, girls are always pitted against each other as rivals, instead of caring friends. LaVey

says, *"One of the surest signs of potential proficiency in witchcraft is an inability to get along with other women."*[5] You will notice on any licensed product that although the Disney Princess is surrounded by her fellow princesses... she is still isolated. You will never find her making eye contact with the other ladies who appear on the same item. They are never interacting with one another as girlfriends. Each character stares off in a different direction, as if unaware of the other's presence.

LaVey teaches that it is pointless for women to try and foster relationships with other women, because ultimately they will always try to undermine and out do you. Instead of girlfriends, a compleat witch keeps a familiar, a pet of some sort. This little creature will keep all your secrets; which sadly, is hard for most girlfriends to do. The unseen manipulators want to keep women suspicious and envious of each other at all times. After all, at the core of narcissism is envy. Not only is this envious person rendered unhappy by his envy, but they also wish to inflict misfortune on others. *"To be a resourceful witch, you must be able to see the bitchiness in other women for exactly what it is, then in your own way, beat them at their own game. You must learn to be a worse bitch than they."*[6] Satanists have an obscene 'burlesque' relationship with the female energy. They seek to express only the extremes, thus creating disharmony and conflict. They use the highly negative expressions of the female, namely deceit and covert manipulation behind the

scenes, to create events which the extremes of the male energy like macho men, soldiers, or terrorists can play out in the public arena.

Satanism today is a multi-faceted phenomenon. First, there are the open and public Satanic groups, consisting of angry teens and disillusioned Christians, who dress in black and wear pentagrams. These people would never sell their soul to the devil because they do not believe in the devil or souls. They have no opinion of the afterlife but strive to live in the here and now, and claim to prohibit the ritualistic harming of any living thing. To them, the Devil represents carnality and

reason. They advocate egotism, indulgence and the acquisition of power, and the highest holiday in their religion is their own birthday. They pose little threat compared to the second group, an ancient bloodline of abusers who have infiltrated all religions and governments. These people pretend to be pillars of the community and would never openly proclaim to worship Satan. These people are far more dangerous than the self-professed Satanist in black robes. The ones you should watch out for wear business suits with red and blue ties and an American flag pin when they go to church on Sunday. Pub-

licly worshiping Satan is for the bourgeoisie and the proletariat.

"If you have good looks and you want to be a witch, then you must exploit your beauty at every opportunity."[7]

The Illusion of Glamour

A new study shows that psychopaths and sex appeal go hand in hand. Researchers at Washington University in St. Louis, recently studied 111 college students to determine that people with psychopathy, a medical diagnosis defined by superficial charm, a manipulative personality, a lack of fear, and enormous ego, are almost always perceived as more attractive by their peers, than those without the affliction. The Greek story of Narcissus and Echo is about a boy who rejected a mountain nymph and was cursed to fall in love with his own reflection so much so that he wasted away because he could not leave it. Among the many messages contained in fairy tales, those concerning the importance of beauty, especially for young women, are paramount. Their beauty is often associated with being fair skinned, financially privileged and seemingly virtuous.

Fairy tales, like other media, convey messages about the importance of feminine beauty, not only by making beauties prominent in stories but also demonstrating how beauty gets its rewards. So ingrained is the image of women's beauty, that it is difficult to imagine any fairy tales that do not highlight and glorify it. Instead of teaching young girls to be kind, nurturing, and creative or

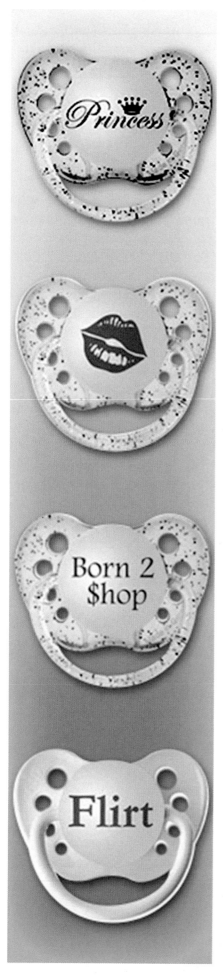

smart, they push to make appearance the epicenter of identity and the only thing she should want to be is "The Fairest of Them All." The second characteristic that the princess programming teaches is that **Looks Mean Everything** which is the title of the fourth chapter in *The Satanic Witch*.

"Your first duty as a witch is to your appearance....A witch can never get too much attention, and if you have a surplus, you not only have more victims from which to choose, but an abundance of potent lust-power being poured into you."[8]

Ninety percent of classic children's fairy tales involve harm to women, and forty percent of these acts of violence are the direct result of the characters physical appearance. The most reproduced fairy tales revolve around romantic love and victimization, and stories that make frequent reference to looks are likely to be reproduced. Those that have been copied the most, Cinderella and Snow White, are precisely the ones that promote the ideal feminine beauty.

Everywhere a young girl looks, there are images showing glamorous women with airbrushed and photo-shopped perfection. In magic, the concept of glamour is the result of not seeing reality as it is. It is illusion on the astral plane. The word "glamour" was long ago defined as "witchery or a charm on the eyes making them see things differently from what they really are." This is still the meaning of the word.[9] In Theosophy, there are three levels of illusion. On the physical plane it is called Maya. On the astral plane it is called Glamour. When it is on the mental plane, it is called Illusion. The glamours are maintained by the effect of the basic law of occultism, that energy follows thought. Wherever we put our thought, we put our energy. Glamour has often been described as an attempt of the "Black Forces" to deceive and hoodwink well meaning magicians.

The history of glamour goes all the way back to the beginning. In the *Book of Enoch* it says that Azazel, one of the fallen angels who took human wives, also brought fashion and warfare. *"And Azazel taught men to make swords, and daggers, and shields, and breastplates. And he showed them the things after these, and the art of making them; bracelets, and ornaments, and the art of making up the eyes, and of beautifying the eyelids, and the most precious stones, and all kinds of coloured dyes. And the world was changed. And there was great impiety, and much fornication, and they went astray, and all their ways became corrupt."*[10] Another translation says that Azazel also taught the people how to make mirrors, so that they could see themselves better. The ancient city of Ur was flourishing in 3,000 B.C. and was a metropolis when Babylon was merely a village. An excavation of the city on display at the Penn Museum, furnished evidence that the princesses of the time were "painted like hussies and they piled on the ornaments like a bootleggers girlfriend."

By now the creators of popular culture have gone way past trying to get young girls to want to be the prettiest, or even the most glamorous. Now, it's all about sex appeal. Girls are taught that they need to look "hot" even before they know what it means. The marketing and advertising agencies even have a term for it, KGOY, which stands for "Kids Growing Older Younger." Just months after Disney introduced their princess division, in 2001 a small company from California named MGA Entertainment released a line of dolls called Bratz and the irony was lost on parents. Bratz dolls conveyed "attitude", "sassiness", "cool" and above all, a love of consumerism. They are marketed as the "girls with a passion for fashion". The Bratz are a doll that can only be described as hooker Barbies. With nick-names like "Sugar", "Spice", "Pretty Poodle" and "Sizzles", they resemble someone who would feel much more comfortable wrapped around a stripper pole, than at a little girl's tea party.

In 2012, the Bratz introduced the Bratzillaz line. They are the cousins of the Bratz and are witches with special powers that make each character unique. In 2013, MGA began to use "House of Witchez" in the main logo, and produced lines of dolls with the themes "Back to Magic" and "Witchy Princesses" to express the Bratzillaz's witchy nature. When I saw how they spelled the word witches with a "z" I realized something about witches. Traditionally the term "witchcraft" signifies a person, man or woman, who has made a pact with a spirit, usually the Devil. A very different kind of witch, a Wiccan, comes from the Saxon word "wica," which means "wise one". Modern Wiccans focus on medieval folklore, astrology, moon cycles, seasons, herbal medicine and the

earthly elements. In either case, the practicing witch is highly intelligent, well read, in tune with nature and educated on a wide range of interconnecting topics. These Satanic consumer "Witchez" of the doll world can't even compare. They are incredibly self-obsessed and vapid, only worshiping their Luciferian self, and basically good for nothing except sex objects.

The Bratz are perfect examples that the marketing industry no longer worries about crossing lines of social appropriateness when creating toys for girls. Children growing up today are bombarded from a very early age with graphic messages about sex and sexiness in the media and popular culture. Ty Girlz dolls are a plush version of Bratz, for the sexy preschooler. They have names like "Oo-LaLa Olivia" and "Sizzlin' Sue." Dora the Explorer used to be a cute little

girl with bangs and baby fat. Now she is all grown up and trading in her map to move to the Big City and wear designer fashions.

Moxie Girlz tag-lines like "Be True, Be You", "celebrate you" and "express yourself" sound eerily like the self-actualizing Bernays' propaganda of the 1980's. Again it is all about defining your individuality through appearance, consumption and most of all, sexuality. The American Psychological Association's Task Force on the sexualization of girls, reports that the emphasis on "beauty" and play sexiness can increase girls' vulnerability to depression, eating disorders, distorted body image and risky sexual behavior. Even brief exposure to idealized images of women has been shown to lower self-esteem physically and academically. The pursuit of physical perfection is cast as the young woman's main source of empowerment. In our culture, sexuality is fostered, while intellectual and spiritual progressions are slowed to a grinding halt. Not only does this objectification have a profound negative effect on girls, Studies** have shown that viewing images of objectified women, compels men to view women as "less competent" and "less human."

In 2009, male college students at Princeton University participated in studies on how the male brain reacts to seeing people in different amounts of clothing. Brain scans revealed that when men are shown pictures of scantily clad women, the region of the brain associated with "objects" or "tools," such as screw drivers or hammers, lit up. Some men showed zero brain activity in the region that empathizes with other people's thoughts, emotions and intentions. When men see these women, their brain is reacting to them as if they are not fully human.

"You must make every man that sees you think he would like to go to bed with you, and the only way you can do that is to give him sneaky cues that will lead him to think he can."[11]

Victoria's Secret sells thong panties for tweens as low as eight years old. Speaking of lingerie, little girls' Halloween costumes are looking more like they were designed by Victoria's Secret every year. While complaints about slutty kids' costumes may seem like a yearly parents' lament, the industry has been ramping up the sex appeal to ever younger groups of girls. It's not just 10 and 12 year-olds who have gone Halloween trampy. Now six and seven year-old models are featured in catalogs wearing child-sized versions of skimpy costumes that used to be reserved for adult bedrooms. Apparently, no costume is fit for girls unless they are tarted up, fe-

tish versions. Costume catalogs and web sites filled with images of preteens modeling the latest in Halloween fashion, seem almost to verge on child pornography. A little girl isn't just an Army cadet for Halloween, she's a "Major Flirt," and who knew female firefighters wore fishnet stockings? Even the Little Bo Peep costume comes with a corset, short skirt and lacy petticoat. If you think this is exaggeration, realize that there is actually something called a Child's Chamber Maid costume.

All this depravity was laid out a long time ago by the "Beast" himself, Aleister Crowley. He wrote that children should be included in the sexual revolution of the new Aeon. *"Moreover, the Beast 666 adviseth that all children shall be accustomed from infancy to witness every type of sexual act, as also the process of birth, lest falsehood fog, and mystery stupefy their minds, whose error else might thwart and misdirect the growth of their subconscious system of soul-symbolism."*[12] Translation: Innocence must be stripped away as early as possible. All children should see every kind of sexual act as soon as they get control of their motor skills and they also have to witness a birth.

Network ABC's slogan is "A New Kind of Family." Current shows in the line-up include *Re-*

venge, *Mistresses*, *666 Park Ave.* and *Desperate Housewives*. In the family section of the programming you can find shows like *Baby Daddy*, *The Lying Game*, *Pretty Little Liars* and *Twisted*. Network NBC's pilot episode of *The New Normal* featured a mock election in an elementary school where the little girl casts her vote for Barack Obama, because she thinks that he cares about gay marriage. Why should little children be thinking about presidential elections *or* gay rights issues? Because in Crowley's view, unleashing sexual inhibitions releases vast amounts of energy, both physical and psychological, and sets up "vibrations" in the surrounding atmosphere, which under stringent control, can be directed and used for whatever purpose the sorcerer desires. *"In traditional historical sex magic, as it has been filtered into Western Magical Tradition, there seems to have been the common belief in the notion that the sexual fluids contain/are a power which can be manipulated by the will of the magician...From a pragmatic viewpoint the central fact surrounding sexual magic is that it works on the basis of sexual energy or arousal. The higher the level of sexual excitement, the higher the level of energy available to the magician."* —S. Llewellyn Flowers, *Fire and Ice*

***

"The color pink is always sure to work magic, as it is the color of feminine intimacy."
—Anton LaVey

The Pink Invocation
Why does every product for girls look like it's been dipped in Pepto-Bismol? Consider the "girls" edition of classic board games.

The pink Ouija board comes with a deck of cards with questions for girls to ask the spirit world. Deep, thoughtful inquiries like, "Who will text me next?" and "Will I be a famous actress?" Pink Monopoly boutique claims to be about all the things girls love—malls, shopping sprees, and cell phones. Pink Yahtzee has replaced the numbers on the dice with hearts, butterflies, cell phones and flip flops. Victoria's Secret has an entire clothing line called PINK. The terms "pink" and "princess" are practically synonymous. Funnily enough, in the Church of the Subgenius, a "pinkie" is a person who cannot see the conspiracy.

Every color has specific characteristics that can stimulate a psychological and physiological response in the body's aura. Each color's qualities are linked to the chakra system with which it resonates. Pink is the secondary color of the Heart Chakra. There are some teachings that say there are seven primary chakras and a number of additional ones. The pink chakra supports the ability of unconditional love and self-love, and lies close to the green one, slightly below it but smaller in size. The green chakra lets us feel loved or feel the pain of not being loved, but the pink chakra allows us the ability to feel love toward ourselves, and not just rely on an outside source. It is the pink chakra that allows us to feel the emotion of empathy and also self-respect and self-esteem.

Remember that black magic takes from a fundamental law of nature and distorts it so that it will have the adverse effect. Much like the color green has been misused to represent willpower, pink has also been hi-jacked from its original meaning of empathy to represent the very opposite, the narcissistic, insecure princess. Although it is hard to pin down the exact occult significance of a common color such as pink, we can recognize the color in the form of the cultural context and go from there. What does it mean to see "Juicy Pink" splashed across a girls' backside? Pink is a receptive color and is ruled by the planet Venus. It is associated with the feminine and with the genitals and is also used as slang for vagina. Today's exploitation of the color pink has to do with oppression of the sacred feminine, the notion that you are nothing *but* "a pink." Pink is mass produced for the raw objectification of women as sex objects and easy targets of degeneration.

Colors are a vibrational energy. The ability to raise energy and control it has always been a

major focus of occult studies and a student of magic would have practiced for hours and would know where in a ritual the energy would be raised and how it would be directed. To conjure something from nothing; basically, condensing imagination into physical form, is considered a great alchemical process. The art of summoning up beings from the astral netherworld, to seek their council or have them do the magician's bidding, is called evocation. *Invocation* is the magical act wherein you allow your body to be temporarily shared by another entity. This is sometimes known as channeling and can lead to actual possession. Both are easier than you think.

In ritual magic, the correct sounds, words, incantations, and colors are all used to manifest a desired energy field or vibratory field. Some magical ceremonies, such as voodoo, are deliberately designed to summon up and unleash the animal driving forces from the depths of human nature. The rituals manipulate energy and provide sustenance for the hidden 'gods' and an energetic environment in which the demonic entities can manifest. The anatomy of a spell consists of three basic components, regardless of the tradition or ritual. The three components are: altering consciousness, focusing will, and directing energy. As long as you include all three in your spell-craft, you can use any style of technique that suits you. The invocations of the Church of Satan employ "theatrical ritual techniques, meant as self-transformative psychodrama." In this case, an innocent girl can be bewitched into invoking a "princess" entity/energy and it's as easy as popping in a DVD.

"There are three main methods for invoking any deity... The third Method is the dramatic, perhaps the most attractive of all; certainly it is so to the artist's temperament, for it appeals to his imagination through his aesthetic sense."[13]

The book on invocation/evocation of demons called *The*

Goetia: The Lesser Key of Solomon the King, points out that reality is a perception of the mind. *"All sense impressions are dependent on changes in the brain, we must include illusions, which are after all sense impressions as much as 'realities' are, in the class of 'phenomena dependent on brain changes.' Magical phenomena, however, comes under a special sub-class, since they are willed, and their cause is the series 'real' phenomena called the operations of ceremonial Magic."* These are reflected upon by the person and produce unusual brain changes. The "impressions" listed are:
1) Sight. The circle, square, triangle, vessels, lamps, robes, implements, etc.
2) Sound. The invocations.
3) Smell. The perfumes.
4) Taste. The Sacraments.
5) Touch. As under (1)
6) Mind. The combination of all these and reflection on their significance.

During an invocation/evocation ritual, a magician will envelop all of his five senses with the essence of the entity that he wishes to conjure. Taste, touch, smell, hearing, sight and memory are all manipulated to create a desired atmosphere. If a magician wished to invoke the god Mars, for instance, he would use ceremonial objects which are red and made of iron. He would drape the room in crimson, wear a scarlet robe and ruby ring and so on. Ceremonies, vestments, perfumes, characters and figures are necessary to apply imagination to the education of the will. The success of magical works depends upon the faithful observation of all the rites associated with it.

"In the third method, identity is attained through sympathy. It is very difficult for the ordinary man to lose himself completely in the subject of a play… but for those who can do so [the children] *this method is unquestionably the best."*[14]

Fantasy plays an important part in any religious or magical curriculum. The fundamental pattern of a ritual consists of emotion plus intention. Ritual magic is dependent on emotional intensity for success and all manner of emotion producing devices must be employed in its practice. The use of ritual paraphernalia functions as an aid to the imagination. Undoubtedly, there is a pink plastic princess product for every one of your senses. Imagine your typical tiny princess watching her favorite movie. She possesses all the elements of a well-run invocation ritual. She is feeling the tiara on her head and pink satin on her skin, smelling the princess perfume, eating the princess food, and listening/singing along with the movie. All of the elements are present, the ritual clothing, the television as altar, a sippy-cup chalice, perhaps a magic wand and some other princess relics and emblems. Familiar songs such as *A Whole New World* or *Kiss the Girl* become literal mantras for manifesting spirits. The child's entire Mind and Will are as completely focused and dedicated as any Faustian conjurer.

In magical terms, the entity which the princesses may summon is called an "Egregore", an occult concept of a thought being, formed around a group of people over time who engage in a repetitive practice. This "thoughtform" is an autonomous psychic entity made up of, and influencing, the thoughts of the group of people, in this case, the princesses. Thought forms work much like memes as once you identify

Photo on this page: "Music of Gounod-a Thought Form", from *Thought Forms* by Annie Besant and Charles Leadbeater
Photo on opposite page: "Bridezilla" by Shaztheraz for deviantart.com

with that archetype you will try to imitate it as much as possible. Once the girls are possessed by the princess spirit they have been added to the Princess collective group mind and are ready to be manipulated en masse.

Tibetan magicians believe that real spirits or "mind-made bodies", can be created through sheer spiritual or mental discipline alone. These are called Tulpas, and are sort of like imaginary friends that you can interact with, that have their own thoughts and emotions. A tulpa is believed to be an autonomous consciousness, existing parallel to the creator's consciousness inside the same brain, often with a form (mental body) of its own. A tulpa is entirely sentient and in control of their opinions, feelings, form and movement. They are willingly created by people via a number of techniques. To grow a tulpa, you have to spend many, many hours imagining it, thinking about it, talking to it, and visualizing it, in other words, feeding it with attention.

The formulas of the invocation and assumption of god-forms are of vital importance to an understanding of Crowley's magic. In his view, the old methods of evocation practiced by traditional sorcerers were clumsy and inferior. In such rituals, the magician summoned the demon or deity while standing within the protection of a magical circle drawn on the floor. Crowley's aim, however, was to achieve total identification with the spirit, to invoke it, so that it actually took possession of the consciousness. The resulting state experienced by the magician was a temporary loss of ego. When practicing the assump-

tion of a god-form in the astral plane, Crowley chose the form of Horus in the image of a golden hawk. The children's book series, *The Kane Chronicles*, by Rick Riordian, (published by Disney) outlines this very thing.

***

The Fractured Fairy Tale
What is so wrong with wanting your life to be like a fairy tale? It may have something to do with what happens *after* the "Happily Ever After." A common complaint amongst single men is that girls today are frightening and hard to approach. If she has been raised as a princess and encouraged to live her life like a fairy tale, she could be suffering from some serious subconscious fears.

The stories that describe the characters of women are starting points for cultural construction of the feminine. The wedding is endorsed as the single most important event in a girls' life and in most fairy tales it is the final curtain. There is literally nothing left, so to speak, no archetypes for the woman to aspire to. Following the logic of the cycle, once a princess is wed and has had an offspring, she is no longer of use and usually dies a horrible, untimely death. This is precisely what causes a young woman to go crazy, or could create an aptly-named "Bridezilla." Men say that a girl will usually choose a jerk over a nice guy. Since girls are so subconsciously afraid of the future and of motherhood, they will more often chose a partner that they can easily discard.

The heroin of the fairy tale is always a teenager at the idealized height of puberty. Female wickedness is embodied in mid-

dle-aged beauty at its peak of sexuality and authority. Snow White's evil stepmother, cruel Maleficent, Ursula, and Cruella DeVille are all middle aged women. Motherly love and sweet nurturing, emblematic of the divine feminine, is drawn in pear shaped, old women past menopause, as the good fairies, godmothers, and servants. They are consistently in contrast to the *femme fatal*. The characters of these women are cultural archetypes that attempt to align audience sympathies with the beginning and end of the feminine life cycle, marking the middle as a dangerous and evil realm.

The most frequently reproduced fairy tale of all time is Cinderella. The Grimm's called her, Aschenputtel, and there are at least 500 versions of her story told around the world. From the Chinese, Russian, Japanese, African and Native American the story is the same. A beautiful girl is devastated by her parent's untimely death, and then despised by her new guardian. She is transformed by magic and loses an item of clothing while fleeing a love struck nobleman. He tracks her down and they live happily ever after. In the Grimm's version, Aschenputtel plants a hazel on her dead mother's grave and waters it with her tears. Her mother's love is so strong it grows into an enchanted tree and grants her daughter's wishes. In his remake, Disney even deleted the dead mother's spirit and replaced it with a vague fairy god-mother.

The Cinderella story is so popular to this day because it propagates the false hope that no matter how lowly you are, if you are sexy and cunning enough, someday a prince may come and rescue you from your drudgery and you will live happily ever after in a giant castle with servants, and never have to worry about another thing as long as you live. Disney painted princesses who had to do work, but these homely chores were never depicted as her rightful occupation. Housekeeping always was forced upon her and it becomes apparent that she was merely concealed behind this inherited drudgery, enforced by the evil queen or mother, and waiting to be rescued.

So if princesses don't work or do chores, what do they do? What is her role in society? *Disney's Cinderella II: Dreams Come True* gives us a glimpse of what happens after the fairy tale wedding. The moment the coach arrives to the castle from their honeymoon, Prince Charming has to go away on a business trip. Cinderella is left on her own to fulfill her royal duty of party planning. The perfect family life of the fairy tale is all illusion, because narcissists grow up to be the worst kind of parents. Their parenting style can be akin to child abuse with traits like constant criticism, belittling, ignoring, excessive teasing, isolating, corrupting, i.e. rewarding child for bullying and/or harassing behavior, and exploiting, for instance where a child is expected to be 'caregiver' to the parent. Sigmund Freud observed that our interest as adults in the fantasy world of fairy tales, is often the result of attempting to regain a childhood that may have been lost due to abuse.

***

The Descent

Fairy tales are far from innocent and have been called the pornography of their day. Before the Grimm Brothers compiled them, these tales existed in oral story telling tradition. They were R-rated, full of double-entendre and pre-marital pregnancy and incest. The Grimms may have edited the sexy parts but they embellished the bloody and violent bits, believing they would scare children out of bad behavior. Why does every child star, when coming of age, decide that it is a good career choice to become essentially a demonic prostitute? Is this the emergence of their creative license; an attempt to reach a more "adult" audience? Or are they being guided in yet another mega-ritual? In mythology this is known as the Katabasis, literally a trip to hell and back. Many gods and goddesses have taken this epic journey. One was the Babylonian goddess, Inanna. The dark occultists venerate Babylon and many girls in the industry are led from innocence to the pit of Hell, and "back again" in honor of Inanna.

In the 2000 video for *Oops I Did it Again*, an astronaut finds a Britney Spears CD in the rubble of Mars. She's shown lying on a bed made of two eight pointed stars that represent Inanna/Ishtar, called the "Queen of Heaven." Ishtar herself was considered to be the "courtesan of the gods" and had many lovers. While inspired in bed, she was also cruel to the men that got attached to her. Ishtar is the Babylonian goddess of fertility, love, war and sexuality. Her cult involved sacred prostitution and ritual acts with hermaphroditic bodies and feminine men. Babylonians gave Ishtar offerings of food and drink on Saturday. They then joined in ritual acts of lovemaking, which they believed would invoke Ishtar's favor on the region, to promote continued health and fruitfulness. Sacred Prostitution was particularly involved in the worship and ritual practices of Inanna's temples. Ancient texts describe her as a great dragon, called the pure torch that flares in the sky. She is another goddess of dual nature of fertility and devouring dragon.

"The formula of the 'holy whore' has persisted into modern times in Aleister Crowley's Cult of Love under Will with its Scarlet Woman; in Austin Spare's Zos Kia Cultus; in Michael Bertiaux's Voodoo Cult of the Black Snake, and in the sinister Chinese Cult of Kû with its female demons and whores of hell who—for all their harlotries—hold keys to the gates of paradise."—Kenneth Grant, *Cults of the Shadow*

The Kali Yuga

Where once Hollywood studios covered up their star's indiscretions like a matter of national security, now with the popularity of the tabloid, erratic and shocking behavior has become food for mass consumption and emulation in what some are calling "insanity chic." Consider how many times the word "crazy" or its synonyms are used in the lyrics of popular music: Britney Spears sings a song called *You Drive Me Crazy*. Taylor Swift lyrics say, "You make me crazier, crazier, crazier." Beyonce and Jay-Z sing a song called *Crazy in Love*. Madonna sings *Crazy for You*. Rhianna's lyrics say, "What's wrong with me? Why do I feel like this? I'm going crazy now." The list is too long to count.

This is another form of social programming sorcery outlined by Aleister Crowley. His system of sexual magic affiliates with the ancient rites of Kali, the dark goddess of blood and dissolution; represented in Crowley's religion as The Scarlet Woman. Scarlet equates with the blood of the menstrual cycle, what they call the "prime menstrum of magical energy", and also with the nugatory, destructive aspect of lunar black magic and witchcraft. The scarlet woman is also connected to the ancient tradition of temple prostitution. The color scarlet has reference to the Draconian Current upon which the New Aeon is based, because it is the color of Ares, or Horus.

"I, the Beast 666, am called to shew this worship and to send it forth into the world; by my Woman called the Scarlet Woman, who is any woman who receives and transmits my Solar Word and Being, this is My Work achieved; for without woman man hath no power."[15]

One aspect of Crowley's Scarlet Woman is the goddess, Kali. In Hinduism, Vishnu and Shiva represent opposing forces, and Brahma, the all-inclusive deity, represents their balancing force. Shiva is the bringer and the conqueror of death and his consort or *shakti* is Kali, "The Black One," the terrifying aspect of the great mother goddess. She is known for her crazy/sex energy. She is the personification of death and destruction, usually depicted with red eyes, multiple arms, each holding a murderous weapon, and tongue out in search for blood. Kali is wild-haired and usually naked except for a girdle of human arms cut off at the elbow and a garland of human skulls. She is capable of terrible destruction and represents the most terrifying form of the female forces in the universe, the mother defending her young. Even as Kali is the spreader of disease and devourer of men and animals, she is infinitely kind and generous to those she loves.

Worship of Kali is largely an attempt to appease her and avert her wrath. She constantly drinks blood and she has an insatiable thirst for it. As mistress of blood, she presides over the mysteries of both life and death. She may get carried away by her gruesome acts, but she is not necessarily thought of as evil. Kali's destructive energies on the highest level are seen as a vehicle of ultimate transformation. They believe that Kali intends her bloody deeds for the protection of the good. She destroys only to recreate, and what she destroys is sin, ignorance and decay. For this reason, even hard core bloodline Satanists are afraid of the judgmental wrath of Kali for their abominations. The fact is, however, wherever there is Kali worship, there is the possibility of human sacrifice, and Kali cults have generally proved to be a destructive and bloody affair.

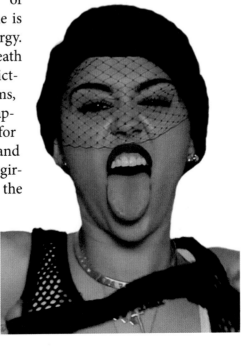

One image of her in mythology is squatting over the dead Shiva, devouring his intestines while her *yoni* sexually devours his *lingam*. Animal sacrifices are still made to her, notably in temples such as the one at Kalighat in Calcutta, where a goat is immolated in her honor every day. On her feast in the fall, goats and buffaloes are the usual victims, along with certain types of vegetation. Although human sacrifices have been banned, there are occasional reports of sacrifices to authorities from remote areas.

The original "Thugs" were the Thuggies of India, the "Sons of Death," an ancient secret society who worshipped Kali as a calendrical concept, associated with the *kalas* or the monthly menstrual cycle. Thuggies murdered their victims according to elaborate rituals dedicated to Kali. For the members of Thuggee, murder was both a way of life and a religious duty. They believed their killings were a means of worshiping Kali, who was honored at each stage of the murder by a vast and complex system of rituals and superstitions.

The Rolling Stones freely acknowledge that their famous mouth and tongue logo is based, in part, on Kali. Eric Burdon, singer for another band of the British invasion era of rock and roll, tells in his autobiography, *I Used to Be an Animal, but I'm All Right Now*, about a time where he took LSD and met the goddess herself. While staring at a mural of Kali created by Andy Summers, gui-

tarist for The Police, Burdon fell into a deep coma. He came face to face with Kali and gave her his life.

In the doll world we are seeing a shift in trends from the overtly sexy to downright disturbing. Monster High is a full blown line of dolls, clothes, costumes, webisodes, television shows, and movies for girls six and up. They are the children of legendary monsters like Dracula and the Werewolf and dress like undead hookers. They promote hyper-sexualization, superficiality, and a culture of death. Most

Monster High characters are either artificially created, or a product of a scientific experiment and many of them do not really have a mind of their own. They are all literally dead and animated by some kind of unholy force. On a deeper level, almost everything in Monster High relates in one way or another to Monarch Mind Control.

A deeply embedded morbid pre-occupation with themes of death is called necrophilia. Kali's paramount place of worship is at the cremation ground,

preferably in the dead of night where she can be found amid the dead bodies. In the fashion world, models posed as dead bodies have become an advertising campaign staple. If you're going to be a model in the New Aeon, you need to know how to look dead. Marc Jacobs, Jimmy Choo, Kate Spade, Lanvin, Duncan Quinn and American Apparel ads have all featured dead girls in their recent campaigns. Television show, *America's Next Top Model*, did a shoot where they asked the girls to pose as if they'd just been killed.

The January 2014 cover of *US Weekly* magazine features Ben Affleck cuddling a corpse like Rosamund Pike on a coroners table. Psychologist, Erich Fromm, defines the struggle between good and evil as biophilia, the love of life; or necrophilia, the love of death. Fromm states *"The necrophilous person is driven by the desire to transform the organic into the inorganic, to approach life mechanically as if all living persons were things. The necrophilous person can relate to an object—a flower or a person—only if he possesses it; hence a threat to his possession is a threat to himself...He loves control and in the act of controlling he kills life... 'Law and order' for them are idols."*

The Hindu or *Vedic* notion of time is that it revolves in cycles, called Yugas, which repeat like the seasons, waxing and waning within a greater time-cycle. The name Kali is derived from the Hindu word which means "time," and also means "black." Each Yuga lasts for thousands, even millions of years. Like Spring, Summer, Autumn and Winter, each Yuga involves stages of gradual change which the earth and the consciousness of mankind goes through as a whole. The Yugas decline in length through the cycle, reflecting a decline in righteousness. The Kali Yuga or Iron Age is the degenerate age and represents mankind's delve into wickedness. Most interpreters of Hindu scriptures believe that earth is currently in Kali Yuga. Hindus believe that human civilizations decline spiritually during the Kali Yuga, which is referred to as the Dark Age because, in it, people are as far removed as possible from God. Kali Yuga is also associated with the apocalypse demon, Kali, a separate entity from the goddess Kali, but they do share common characteristics. The "Kali" of Kali Yuga means strife, discord, quarrel, or contention. It is marked by an apocalyptic series of events, ending with a fantastic battle between good and evil.

***

Royal Reality Check

The middle class is rapidly disappearing. We may soon find ourselves in somewhat of a technocratic system with only two classes, so we might want to brush up on our politics of medieval times; the period of history where most fairy tales are set. At the very top was the king, whose word was considered God's law and could not be challenged by anyone, except maybe the Pope and this has caused a *lot* of wars. The medieval way of life was known as feudalism and was based on the ownership of land. All land of the empire was considered the property of

the king who doled out parcels of real estate to the "nobility", the dukes, lords, and earls were whoever the king named as worthy of their title, meaning whoever was the best sycophant.

Below the nobility were the knights who were basically mercenary killers for hire. If a common person wanted to try and claw their way up in the world he would first become a page or a squire; a servant to the knight who would tend to his horses and weapons and accompany him into battle. If a squire proved himself a good assistant killer for the knight he would be eligible for a knighthood, where he adopted the title "Sir" and was eligible for more dumb titles if he proved useful. Knights were professional warriors, and when there wasn't a war to fight, they had to find something to do with all those violent urges and they tended to take it out on the peasants. Toward the 11th century, many of the local lords started bickering over the division of the Holy Roman Empire, and the knights were at the forefront of these petty wars. These "wars" consisted of knights riding up into villages and slaughtering everybody. When the church could not curb the conflicts, the Pope called the First Crusade and exported all these psychos to the Middle East, where they proceeded to terrorize the population of Jerusalem.

Below the knights were the skilled craftsmen and merchants. At the very bottom of the social hierarchy were the lowly serfs, who made up over ninety percent of the population. Serfs worked the land and were considered the property of the lord of the manor, and his wealth depended

on the labor they supplied. They were subject to the whims of these lords and were crushed beneath the injustices of the system. The serfs were taxed unmercifully and were often victim to the foraging raids that were frequently made by the soldiers of nobility, who came to carry off their food, property or women depending on their mood. One feudal law went to the extreme of declaring that before a peasant could consummate his marriage he had to bring his bride to his lord in order that the lord might have the "first fruits" of the marriage.

***

The True Life of a Princess: An Eternal Victim

Wars are waged, battles fought and lives are lost all in the name of rescuing the princess in distress. Men die on the battlefield and submit themselves to nation or king, all in the hopes of someday being able to marry a "princess." Historically, the life of a princess was no fairy tale. In medieval times, women were held in extremely low esteem because the Catholic Church taught that they were a gate way to sin and temptation. Because of Eve's sin in the Garden of Eden, women were eternally guilty. This made medieval marriage a rather unromantic affair. It had little, if anything, to do with love. It was an alliance between families and an agreement involving the transfer of property which the wife was included in. Like any piece of property the potential wife required a close and proper inspection before a deal could be struck. Rich brides came with dowries and massive amounts of land in Europe could change hands with a single marriage.

Princesses, or daughters of other suitably high-ranking nobles were nothing more than political pawns to gain power. They were used to attract potential husbands, typically middle aged men, who could strengthen the girl's families' political or financial position. From childhood many girls were promised to kings, and many marriages occurred before the princess reached her teenage years. The young women were uprooted from their home and sent throughout Europe to be married, often never to see their home kingdom again. Marriages were the ultimate political strategy, as they were seen to be permanent and children created from the union become heirs to two kingdoms. The primary purpose of a princess or young queen was to produce a male heir. Daughters were valuable for forging other alliances, but it was the male heir, who could ascend to the throne after his father, that was most desired.

For a princess of ancient Ur, the wedding was nothing more than a financial merger. Marriages were arranged by the elders of the contracting parties, and the bride brought a dowry to the union. The wedding is thought to have consisted merely of the making of a formal nuptial contract which set forth, among other things, the conditions under which a divorce might be granted. How romantic. The most common grounds for divorcing a wife was barrenness. Another grounds for annulment was sexual purity. Since the only purpose given to a princess in her life was to produce an heir to the throne, they were expected to be virgins on their wedding day and the fa-

THE HOT CRAZY SCALE

A girl is allowed to be crazy, as long as she is equally hot

mous white dress was symbolic of this. It wasn't uncommon for the consummation of the marriage to be attended by family members and nobility—to officially "seal the deal," and seating to the event was determined by your rank. Family on the groom's side would be eager for evidence that she had not already been "defiled" and might keep bedclothes as legal proof. The bride's relatives would be there to make sure that the groom had done his best to impregnate her. *So* dreamy!

***

High Class, Low Morals

In a series of startling studies, psychologists at the University of California at Berkeley, have found that higher social class predicts increased immoral behavior. Seven studies reveal that upper-class individuals behave more unethically than lower-class individuals. Research proved that the upper-class individuals were more likely to break the law while driving, were more likely to exhibit unethical decision-making tendencies, take valued goods from others, lie in a negotiation,

cheat to increase their chances of winning a prize, and endorse unethical behavior at work. Data demonstrated that upper-class individuals' unethical tendencies are accounted for, in part, by their more favorable attitudes toward greed. Results of over thirty studies on thousands of people all concluded the same thing. Here is some disturbing behavior they found: Drivers of luxury cars were three to four times more likely to break the law and refuse to stop for pedestrians in a crosswalk. Wealthy participants took two times more candy from children. In games of chance played for a small cash prize, they cheated four times as much as the lower income participants.

As we find ourselves constantly encouraged to seek more wealth and power, we also find ourselves aspiring to high society's degraded moral code of behavior. The link between wealth and narcissism is becoming clearer than ever. The idea of royalty is the epitome of narcissism and always has been. If the elite are superior to us, what else can it

60

mean but that their appalling behavior is superior also? Who does culture and history consider the greater man; the one who is honest, faithful to his wife and dedicated to being a good father? Or the warrior or corporate psychopath with numerous mistresses who behaves like a tyrant, unless smiling for a camera? Despite their secret misery and dysfunction, the power of these classes to influence fashion and trends cannot be underestimated. They not only suffer, but make their suffering fashionable, spreading the dysfunction they experience to the rest of society through art, music and literature. The belief in their own superiority also lies the source of their own misery.

***

1. *Power Changes How the Brain Responds to Others,* Jeremy Hogeveen, Suhkvinder S. Obhi, Michael Inzlicht
2. *The Satanic Witch,* Anton LaVey
3. Ibid. pg172
4. Ibid. pg191
5. Ibid. pg185
6. Ibid. pg188
7. Ibid. pg121
8. Ibid. pg124
9. *Theosophy Magazine,* October 1915
10. *The Book of Enoch,* chapter 8:1-2, A Modern English Translation of the Ethiopian Book of Enoch with introduction and notes by Andy McCracken
11. *The Satanic Witch,* Anton Lavey
12. *The New and Old Commentaries to Liber AL vel Legis, The Book of the Law,* Aleister Crowley
13. *Magick in Theory and Practice,* pg 145, Aleister Crowley
14. Ibid. pg 147
15. *A.L. The Comment Called D (The Djeridensis Working)* by 666, Aleister Crowley (published posthumously)

*Lyrics from the song, *Can't Be Tamed*
***Effects of exposure to sex-stereotyped video game characters on tolerance of sexual harassment,* Karen E. Dill, Brian P. Brown, Michael A. Collins

Books:
Cinderella Ate My Daughter, Peggy Orenstein
The Narcissism Epidemic; Living in the Age of Entitlement, Jean Twenge & W. Keith Campbell
Satan Wants You, Arthur Lyons
Princess Recovery, Jennifer L. Hartstein, Psy.D.
Good Girls and Wicked Witches, Amy M. Davis
From Mouse to Mermaid, Elizabeth Bell
So Sexy So Soon: The New Sexualized Childhood, Diane E. Levin, Ph.D., Jean Kilbourne, Ed.D.

WeirdStuff! Woman Power!

This is pretty much as badass as possible…The Gulabi Gang or the "pink gang", is a group of women vigilantes and activists from Banda, India, reported to be active across North India as of 2010. It is named after the pink saris worn by its members. The gang was founded in 2006 by Sampat Pal Devi, a mother of five and former government health worker and a former child bride, as a response to widespread domestic abuse and other violence against women. Gulabis visit abusive husbands and beat them up with bamboo sticks unless they stop abusing their wives. In 2008, they stormed an electricity office in Banda district and forced officials to turn back the power they had cut in order to extract bribes. They have also stopped child marriages and protested dowry and female illiteracy.

Slavery

By Kahlil Gibran

The people are the slaves of Life, and it is slavery which fills their days with misery and distress, and floods their nights with tears and anguish.

Seven thousand years have passed since the day of my first birth, and since that day I have been witnessing the slaves of Life, dragging their heavy shackles.

I have roamed the East and West of the earth and wandered in the Light and in the Shadow of Life. I have seen the processions of civilization moving from light into darkness, and each was dragged down to hell by humiliated souls bent under the yoke of slavery. The strong is fettered and subdued, and the faithful is on his knees worshipping before the idols. I have followed man from Babylon to Cairo, and from Ain Dour to Baghdad, and observed the marks of his chains upon the sand. I heard the sad echoes of the fickle ages repeated by the eternal prairies and valleys.

I visited the temples and altars and entered the palaces, and sat before the thrones. And I saw the apprentice slaving for the artisan, and the artisan slaving for the employer, and the employer slaving for the soldier, and the soldier slaving for the governor, and the governor slaving for the king, and the king slaving for the priest, and the priest slaving for the idol….And the idol is naught but earth fashioned by Satan and erected upon a knoll of skulls.

I entered the mansions of the rich and visited the huts of the poor. I found the infant nursing the milk of slavery from his mother's bosom, and the children learning submission with the alphabet.

The maidens wear garments of restriction and passivity, the wives retire with tears upon beds of obedience and legal compliance.

I accompanied the ages from the banks of the Kange to the shores of the Euphrates; from the mouth of the Nile to the plains of Assyria; from the arenas of Athens to the churches of Rome; from the slums of Constantinople to the palaces of Alexandria….Yet I saw slavery moving over all, in a glorious and majestic procession of ignorance. I saw the people sacrificing the youths and maidens at the feet of the idol, calling her the God; pouring wine and perfume upon her feet, and calling her the Queen; burning incense before her image, and calling her the Prophet; kneeling and worshipping before her, and calling her the Law; fighting and dying for her and calling her Patriotism; submitting to her will, and calling her the Shadow of God on earth; destroying and demolishing homes and institutions for her sake, and calling her Fraternity; struggling and stealing and working for her, and calling her Fortune and Happiness; killing for her and calling her Equality.

She possess various names, but one reality. She has many appearances, but is made of one element. In truth, she is an everlasting ailment bequeathed by each generation unto its successor.

CAUTION:
THIS CHAPTER MAY BE TRIGGERING.
If there is any chance you, the reader, have
had mind control done to you, you must
consider the following chapter to be
DANGEROUS.

TRAUMA BASED

The warning on the previous page can be found in the beginning of many books and articles written by and about victims of trauma based mind control. Our culture is so saturated with it's themes and techniques that, truthfully, the warning should be on just about everything we consume.

Trauma

How many murders have you ever witnessed? How many dead bodies have you seen? How many people do you know that have died? How much rape, torture, or horrific acts of violence have you witnessed personally? The answer for most people would be very few. However, thanks to modern media, we witness these events daily. We know that the media does not reflect our true experience, but our brain has a difficult time telling the difference between what we see on screen and what is actually happening to us; in each case, the same neurological regions are stimulated. Children today are watching death, violence and perversion at a rate like no other generation in history. What happens when we die is a primal question and how we answer it is our belief paradigm. These questions are being posed to younger and younger minds.

For most children, their introduction to death is through a cartoon. I was seven years old when I saw a movie in the theater for the first time. A neighbor took his daughters and me to see the Lucas/Spielberg cartoon *The Land Before Time*. My tiny mind was blown as I watched the opening credits. As soon as the underwater bubbles began to rise on the screen, I was mesmerized and transported to a prehistoric world of wonder, full of sea creatures and dinosaurs. I listened careful-

MIND CONTROL

ly as they spoke of a famine that forced the dinosaurs to migrate. I witnessed the miracle of the babies hatching from their eggs under the loving protection of mom and dad. A tiny lump formed in my throat as one little egg hatched and was greeted by mother—Littlefoot was born! I sat on the edge of my seat when Littlefoot and his friend were attacked by a T-Rex called Sharptooth and his mother fought him off. Then—the earthquake! All the dinosaur families were separated from each other. When Littlefoot finds his mother she is on the verge of death. He begs her to get up but she is too weak. She tells him she will always be with him even if she

can't see him. At this point in the movie I was literally bawling. The neighbor had to ask if I wanted to call my parents to pick me up. I decided to be brave and stick it out to the end, but I was forever changed.

When the movie was over all I could think about was Littlefoot. He was an orphan who needed care and since I had lived through his trauma I had to give it to him. I begged my parents for a Littlefoot doll and it came at Christmas time, from the neighbor who had taken me to see the movie. I cherished that doll. Something in my psyche needed to tend to it as a kind of therapy for what I had witnessed. I pam-

pered him and in many of my childhood photos I can be seen clutching a stuffed brontosaurus by the neck.

When I was older my mother accidentally sold Littlefoot at a yard sale and I was heartbroken again. Years later, when the internet came, the first thing I bought on Ebay was a Littlefoot to replace my lost one. Why did I still need this doll? I was a teenager with a job and a car and certainly no need for stuffed animals but I had to have it. How many stuffed Nemos, Bambis or Simbas have been sold from this type of trauma? This is not just the ultimate plush toy marketing strategy, this is a mild form

"When I look back on my life, it's not that I don't want to see things exactly as they happen, it's just that I prefer to remember them in an artistic way. And truthfully, the lie of it all is much more honest, because I invented it. Clinical psychology arguably tells us that trauma is the ultimate killer. Memories are not recycled like atoms and particles in quantum physics. They can be lost forever. It's sort of like my past is an unfinished painting and, as the artist of that painting, I must fill in all the ugly holes and make it beautiful again. It's not that I've been dishonest, it's just that I loathe reality."

—Lady Gaga song, "Marry the Night"

of trauma-based mind control. From ancient Babylon to Nazi Germany and on into America, trauma-based mind control has been the modus operandi of the sorcerers. Whether we admit it or not, we are all, to some degree, victims of it.

***

WWII

For millennia warfare has taken place and men have experienced post-traumatic stress syndrome which are the mentally debilitating effects of trauma. Intrusive flashbacks of the event will often occur if the brain doesn't protect itself from reminders, and any traumatic event could create a certain "shattered-ness" within the victim. The human brain has a natural defense mechanism which compartmentalizes cases of extreme trauma. The mind creates an amnesiac barrier around the event, so that the person can go on leading a somewhat normal life and not have to re-live the horrible experience.

The methods for exploiting this ability of the brain were perfected in the concentration camps of Nazi Germany. After the Second World War the emphasis changed from control of physical territory to control of minds, emotions, and finances which are the foundation for the control of the entire race. Nazi scientists learned that if you could systematically traumatize someone, and start with children particularly under the age of five, you could shatter a person's mind into a honeycomb of self-contained compartments. They then use techniques to access the different sections of the brain while the subject is hypnotized. These various compartments, unaware of the other's existence, can be programmed like a computer to carry out tasks. Using trigger words and hypnotic keys, sounds, or signals, these alter personalities can be pulled to the front or pushed back according to the will of the programmer. One self contained fragment of mind becomes a person's core, or front personality, on the conscious level and is returned to the subconscious when another compartment is accessed. After the victim has performed a task, they "forget" what they have done. Entire "Systems" can be embedded into a person's mind, each with its own theme, access codes and trigger words. Their closest friends won't even realize that who they know is only one compartment of their mind.

This has become known as Multiple Personality Disorder (MPD) or Dissociative Identity Disorder (DID), where different dissociative parts of a single brain view themselves as separate persons.

Among the Nazis who escaped in Project Paperclip was the mass murderer and torturer, Joseph Mengele. He was called the Angel of Death and the Butcher of Auschwitz. As the doctor at the concentration camp run by I.G. Farben, now Bayer, he had access to an endless supply of inmates. He was able to use countless thousands of people as human guinea pigs for experimentation on how much torture various humans could take. He was an expert in demonology and the Kabbalah, and was obsessed with the ancient idea of creating golems, or mind controlled slaves. It is well documented that he performed experiments on thousands of twins at the Kaiser Wilhelm Medical Institute in Berlin. It is reported by survivors that Dr. Mengele had victims see him as a cricket and used a cricket noise maker that clicked while programming.

The public was lead to believe that the Nazis fled to South America but many of them were allowed to travel around the world working for US and British Intelligence. From this influx of Nazi doctors into America came the mind control program known as MKUltra. MK stands for mind control where the German spelling is *kontrolle*. It was officially headed by Dr. Ewan Cameron, head of the Canadian, American and World Psychiatric Associations. Cameron's code name in the project was "Dr. White" and Mengele's was "Dr. Green."

Because of Cameron's extensive experience and credentials, the CIA funneled millions of dollars throughout organizations like the society for the Investigation of Human Ecology, which Cameron ruthlessly presided over. Besides the conventional methods of psychiatric torture, such as electroshock, drug injections and lobotomies, Cameron used the technique of "psychic driving," wherein unsuspecting patients were kept in a drug induced coma for several weeks and administered a regimen of electroshocks, while electronic helmets were strapped to their heads and repetitive auditory messages were transmitted at variable speeds. The Nazis continued their work in developing mind control and rocketry technologies in secret underground military bases. The only thing the public was told about was the rocketry work with Nazi celebrities like Warner Von Braun. The killers, torturers, and mutilators were kept discretely out of sight, but busy in U.S. underground military facilities.

MK-Ultra was the code name for a secret CIA project under Director Allen Dulles. As early as April 1950, the CIA had embarked on a series of projects to explore techniques of mind control. In 1953, these projects were brought together under a general umbrella, code named MK-Ultra, which was to continue in operation, at least officially, until 1964. Under that name it was terminated but it would be naïve to think that research was not continued under other names, or that organizations other than the CIA were not involved. Documents reveal that MK-Ultra had at least 149 different sub-projects, many of which combined drugs such as LSD with other forms of mind control. Many of the rituals and methods employed in the mind control projects are inspired by ancient mystery cults and the CIA admitted in 1977, that millions of dollars had been spent studying voodoo, witchcraft, and psychic warfare.

***

In Greek mythology, a person's soul was depicted as a butterfly, a personification of the goddess, Psyche. They believed that human souls become butterflies while searching for a new reincarnation.

Psyche in the Underworld, Paul Alfred de Curzon

Project Monarch

One of the many offshoots of MKUltra was the U.S. Government Defense Intelligence Agency's TOP SECRET Project Monarch; a mind control operation which was "recruiting" multi-generational incest abused children with Multiple Personality Disorder for its genetic mind control studies. The project derives its name from the Monarch butterflies who are known for their lengthy annual migration. Of all the journeys made by animals, few are as astonishing as the one performed by the Monarch butterfly. They travel between 1,200 and 2,800 miles or more between their starting and ending points but no single individual makes the entire trip since the length of the migration exceeds their normal lifespan. The ones that return to the trees where Monarchs hibernate have never been there before. These are the great-great-great grandchildren of those that performed the intrepid journey from southeast Canada and United States to central Mexico. The monarch learns these migration patterns and where it was born via genetic memory, which is knowledge passed on to offspring through the genes.

This was one of the key animals that tipped off scientists that information and other abilities could be passed on this way. The Monarch Program was based upon goals to create a Master Race, in part through genetics. They achieved their goal; but not the "blond haired, blue-eyed Aryan's" version that we are told about. They perfected the creation of human robots who would, without question, perform on command the most heinous acts. They serve as their personal army of human carrier pigeons and perform as highly skilled sex slaves, all while entertaining the masses as singers, dancers, actors, athletes and politicians. A majority of the victims selected for this program came from multi-generational abusive families who are programmed to fill their destiny as the chosen ones or chosen generations.

A monarch can also mean a king or queen who is the head of the monarchy in which sovereignty is embodied in a single individual.

Why do you think the royals and upper class people throughout history are absolutely obsessed with interbreeding and keeping the bloodlines pure? It boils down to this: in order for the elite to maintain their privileged position of power, they are systemically keeping humanity developmentally arrested. From an elitist point of view, the most efficient way to control the masses is to traumatize them. The Church of Satan was just one of the front organizations for an ancient body whose very existence had never before been imagined. The techniques used in Monarch programming can be traced to various generational Satanist families among European royalty. The MPD states created by the Monarch programming were used to hide the royal personality involved in the dark rituals from the public. Without this alternate personality, the nobles practicing Satanism inevitably went insane, so its practice spread r a p i d l y t h r o u g h t h e occult c o m - munity. The Satan- ic Networks are of a glob- al mind c o n t r o l program to create a race of h u m a n robots a n d h a v e been

with us since the beginning. Ritualized forms of abuse have been practiced since the dawn of human history. The ancient Assyrians worshipped the god Baal, who they depended upon for the continuance of their crops. Rituals to Baal extended from the Canaanites to the Phoenicians and the rites included animal and human sacrifice. Another deity was Molech, whose rituals were also costly to human life. Molech is a deity based on the astro-theology of the age of Taurus and so was fashioned in the likeness of a bull. Giant statues of Molech would have carved out cubicles where worshippers would place small children for burned sacrifice. Many of these rituals were adopted by the ancient Hebrews, as mentioned in the Bible (Levit icus 20 and II Kings 23) and were carried out for over a thousand years, both openly and secretly.

Survivor, Jay Parker, comes from a multi-generational Satanic abusive family. He was a victim of Monarch programming that he claims goes back to at least 10,000 BC. Their religion is founded in mysticism, where powers outside yourself control your destiny and you, yourself are as powerless as a cog in a machine. These families have a caste system based on bloodline and his ancestors were part of this cult well before the Illuminati of 1776. His mother claimed to be a direct maternal descendant of the ancient Amalekites, a tribe of Canaan so bad that the Lord commanded Saul to kill every last one down to their livestock.

Theistic Satanism, sometimes referred to as Devil Worship, is a form of Satanism with the primary belief that Satan is an actual deity or force to revere or worship. These type of people are often hard to spot because they hide in plain sight. As a child, Jay was presented with a toy statue which he recognized as the Statue of Liberty. He was told it was, in fact, Queen Semiramis of Babylon, which is the primary mystery religion of the satanic bloodlines. Jay's family called it the "The Old Religion" and its roots reportedly go further back to Atlantean warlocks before the cataclysm in 9,600 B.C. To the outside world they looked like every other family. As teachers and members of the Presbyterian Church, no one would have suspected that after service on Sunday, they would attend their *other* church, a network of cult families who met in the back room of a regular storefront downtown. Jay estimates that this network had roughly 30 million cult members or ten percent of the population—a very strategic ten percent. Since their religion has a special affinity with the city of Babylon, researchers have taken to calling them the Babylonian Brotherhood, or simply, The Brotherhood.

***

Babylonian Slavery

Their religion with no name, the tradition of ritual abuse to create slaves, is unbroken to this very day and the continuity of the practice of slavery on planet earth is staggering. The idea of owning another person is as old as civilization itself, going all the way back to ancient Sumer. Predating all other forms of coerced labor, not only is it ancient, but it is oh, so contemporary—and fashionable! We pretend we live in more enlightened times, but right now there are more people in slavery than any other time in history. If you believe that slavery is a thing of the past, you are still a slave.

When Bob Marley sings about slavery, he calls it the Babylon System and hits the nail on the head. The Bible calls Nimrod, the King of Babylon "a great hunter before the Lord." According to archeology and biblical context, the word "hunter" translates to plunderer or conqueror. Nimrod was immortalized not for his skill in hunting beasts, but in the success of his slave trading and the hunting of men to establish his imperial kingdom of tyranny. Nimrod hunted men and brought them into bondage to Babylon and forced them to build him a great tower. The foundation of Babylonian society was the slave population; the necessary component of all mass economic activity. The sources of their slave supply were endless. Military conquests furnished many; others had fallen from the position of free laborers; still others were purchased from abroad, or were children of native slaves. Nimrod's Babylon will always represent slavery, military and economic power, seduction, and worship of the state.

Like so many other things in life, when it comes to slavery, it takes one to make one. A truly free and sovereign person would have no use for slaves. The programming is like an infinite train, or a virus, where slaves are programmed to be handlers and programmers to create more slaves. The kings and priest craft of Babylon were themselves, slaves to their gods. The duties of their religion were an indispensable element of their life. Before their idols they came, bowing as dependents and slaves, to make their offerings of flesh and blood. Girded with burdensome restrictions, they believed that the violation of their rituals would entail disaster upon themselves and their city. On the other hand, they claimed to be as gods before their subjects and captives, demanding from them the same type of servitude and reverence.

***

What the "Elite" Experience

The primary ability that they were looking for in Project Monarch, the one that could be passed on genetically, was disassociation. It is the ability to witness or do something horrible, then go on as if nothing had ever happened and highly intelligent children from multigenerational abusive families are better at it. The higher the tolerance, the more "alters" can be created. The selection of a victim is based on genetics, dissociative abilities, availability, and mental and physical features. Attempts to program people with low intelligence or no creativity proved to be a waste of time. Children who have pedophile parents are blackmailed into turning their children over to the CIA to work with. Their rationale is that if a father would abuse his own child then the programmers know that he has no conscience and the parent's involvement in criminal activity can be continually increased.

Generational Satanic families believe that their children belong to Satan and make prime candidates for Monarch programming. The Network uses slaves to program other slaves and members of the elite will have undergone as much trauma as the new generation which they are programming. The children of the elite families are conceived according to ancient rituals and their programming is agreed and set out before they are even born. From the families' perspective, their plans involve possession by generational spirits and positions within the hierarchy. A generational spirit is given "appointment" over a victim at birth. The Brotherhood's regimen for programming their children is far more intense than the CIA's. One of these pre-birth rituals is called the Moon Child ceremony.

The NeverEnding Story is about a boy named Bastian, whose mother dies (big surprise!) and turns to books for comfort. On the way to school one day he is attacked by bullies and gives them the slip by ducking into a store. There he finds an old man reading a book with two intertwined serpents in an infinity pose. Bastian is curious about it but the man tells him the book is not for him because it's "special." He takes the book and over the course of reading it, he discovers that it is a link between fantasy and reality and he is influencing the story world, called Fantasia, in real time. The fantasy world is under attack by an enemy called The Nothing, and only by giving the Childlike Empress a new name can they save Fantasia. At the climax of the movie, when Bastian finally does give her a new name, he screams something incomprehensible into a thunderstorm. If her name is so important, why wouldn't we be able to understand it? We are given to think he yelled out his late mother's name, so why wouldn't we hear it? In the novel that inspired the movie by Bavarian author, Michael Ende, Bastian cries out "Moonchild!"

For the Babylonian Brotherhood, the moonchild rituals are designed to demonize a fetus and the spirits that are invoked are very powerful and blood sacrifices are always required for this level of magic. The idea of the Moonchild is that through black magic a perfect soul from the fourth dimension can be captured. This perfect soul in a proper person is called a Homunculus. In the book *Moonchild*, by Aleister Crowley, the ritual took place at a villa called The Butterfly Net. Occasionally the child involved in Moon Child rituals retreats into its mind like a cocoon and develops autism rather than becoming MPD/DID. The mothers who give birth to a "dark child" are called a "Rosemary."

Over the centuries it became understood that if you torture a child while it's still in the womb, the baby would already begin to disassociate, therefore pregnant mothers are traumatized. Needles are inserted into the stomach to stab the baby and then forced into a premature birth through induced labor or C-section. When the preemie is born it copes with the pain by being dissociative. Because of the pre-mature birth, often, the skin is so sensitive that the slightest brush can cause pain, but at this stage the child still wants and needs to be held and will crave that touch even if it hurts. This is the beginning of the "pain is pleasure" mentality used in programming. Being born prematurely will create a fighter spirit within the child. If the baby does not have a strong instinct for survival, then it will not fight to endure the tortures of the programming. A bloodline will often want a fe-

male's first born to be sacrificed to their belief system for "Lilith" programming. It is not uncommon for high profile pregnancies to hide behind a "miscarriage" when this happens. These women are made to believe that offering their babies to Satan is the highest honor.

After birth, a programmer is assigned to them, usually a family member, close family friend or family doctor. The programmers will begin by extreme torture. After a certain amount of torture the victim is willing to say or believe anything to stop it. Children are bonded to the programmers and are dependent on them and taught to see them as a god. The programmer will set himself up as God and in a spiritual sense they take the place of God in every way. The child will learn to trust, obey and adore the programmer. The baby is rigidly taught total obedience, not being allowed to cry in a process called behavior modification. In a technique known as love bombing, intense love and affection is given to them for the first eighteen months and then suddenly it is withdrawn and the child is then treated extremely cruelly. Unless love is given so that it can be taken away, there is no trauma. Several survivors have described rituals where Christian ceremonies are parodied and the victim of abuse is told to pray to God for help. No help is forthcoming because the participants deliberately orchestrate the situation so that no aid can appear to them under such conditions. No relief is offered until the victim makes a sincere plea to Satan, or until the victim makes another alter personality through dissociation who is a devoted follower of Satan.

Everything imaginable can be used to traumatize the victim and create dissociation. Being caged up for 42-72 hours at a time. Foul odors of rotten food, ammonia and the child's own excrement overwhelm their sense of smell. They are fed blood to distort their sense of taste. Other programmers dressed in Satanic garb chant, make loud noises, and blast rock music to over whelm their sense of hearing. Spinning and electric shock, starvation and cold are used until the child's senses are overloaded and they become numb. At this stage, the primary handler, their beloved caretaker from the first eighteen months, will appear and they are so excited that they disassociate the pain of the previous experience. This is when the trusted adult shows their most vicious side to prove to the child that there is no hope and no one will ever come to help them. The programmer is now someone who the child loves and fears with equal intensity. A close bond is needed between the child and the initial abuser, so that a clean split occurs in the mind when the trauma is carried out. This happens when the child is confronted with two irreconcilable opposing viewpoints of someone who is important to them. They will also be allowed to bond with a pet and then the pet is ritually killed while they watch. The same effect can be re-created on a mass scale with movies like *Old Yeller*, where the boy must kill his own dog.

By now you're probably thinking this is too crazy. One common reaction of a normal person is "They wouldn't do that" and this is exactly the kind of reaction that they are counting on. Since most of what we perceive about other people or

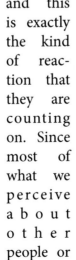

what they are capable of is merely a reflection of what we think of ourselves, many people will not believe that this kind of thing could ever happen. Most people are good natured and would never conceive that a human being could be so cruel, but as we are about to see these beings are not human.

Since the beginning of time, "governments" have been in the business of owning people and ensuring that they stay loyal. They have refined the art of deception far beyond what the common man has imagined. According to experts, a great deal of Monarch programming, slave abuse and drug trafficking is done under three major fronts: Religious organizations, the front of National Security and the Military, and the front of the Entertainment Industry, especially the country western and rock music industry and Hollywood. The object is not just to program key individuals, but to program entire nations. The monarch programming is a miniaturization of what is being done to entire peoples or cities. It is simply the sophisticated application of what has been done to humanity on a large scale being scaled down to a single human body.

***

Cathy's Story

Once the ritual abuse technique was perfected in Nazi Germany, mind controlled slaves, including very small children, could be used for a myriad of things. They serve as drug mules, spies, assassins, messenger pigeons, politicians, actors, military, clergy… you name it. They provide bizarre sex

for presidents, foreign leaders, politicians and businessmen. Survivor and thriver, Cathy O'Brien was one of these children. Her book, *Trance-Formation of America*, documents her experience in the Monarch program. Cathy's father was a pedophile who would share her with his friends. Trauma like that automatically triggers MPD, since the child's own mind wishes to shut out the horror. Her father was caught sending child pornography through the mail, so to avoid prosecution he made a deal with the Defense Intelligence Agency for Cathy to be groomed as a presidential model mind controlled slave, who was detailed to operate

with people in the White House and the Pentagon. Cathy's father was instructed in how to prepare her for government service. *"My father began working me like the legendary Cinderella. I shoveled fireplace ashes, hauled and stacked firewood, raked leaves, shoveled snow, chopped ice, and swept….by this time my father's exploitation of me included prostitution to his friends, local mobsters, Masons, relatives, Satanists, strangers and police officers."*[2]

Cathy writes that she and many others' torture programming took place at Disneyland in California and Disney World in Florida. She also states that the theme parks and movies are perfect for creating illusions that confuse the mind of the multiple.

Satanic rituals go on there and trauma based programming happens when the parks are closed. *"My Father insisted that I watch the Walt Disney movie Cinderella with him, paralleling my existence to Cinderella's— 'magically transforming from a dirty little slave to a beautiful Princess'….My brother, Bill, who was often featured in kiddie porn with me, was not a 'chosen one' for Project Monarch….Yet my father figured that 'what was good for me would be good for my bother'. He took us to see Walt Disney's Pinocchio, explaining that my brother and I were his puppets still in the carving stage….My brother… remains psychologically locked into those traumatic childhood years and is obsessed with Disney themes and productions to this day. His house is decorated in Disney memorabilia; he wears Disney clothes, listens to my father's instructions on his Disney telephone, and maintains 'When You Wish Upon a Star" as his favorite song, which has locked his children into the same theme."*[3]

Cathy's formal induction to the Monarch Program gives a clear connection to the Catholic Church. At her first Holy Communion she was given the "Rite to Remain Silent." This is a ritual where the victim supposedly enters into a covenant with God, which they are told is a promise to keep the secrets that the Catholic Church has always known and which the Pope keeps locked away in the Vatican. Victims are dressed appropriately for the ceremony in red, white and blue; and are then bathed in the blood of a sacrificed lamb. The basis for this programming was anchored in the Vow of Silence which the Jesuit monks take "not only to keep secrets, but so they can still their mind and hear their inner guidance." In some cases the victim is told that "The walls have ears and the plants have eyes so your silence is tantamount to success." It is explained to the victim that the sea shells and the plants have the ability to hear, and that a sensitive occultist (programmer) can psychically pick up what the plants and sea shells hear. In the Britney Spears video, *I Wanna Go*, Britney is interrupted during a press conference by a man with a sea shell, who turns around to reveal himself as her robotic demon handler.

During her ritual experience, Cathy received a Rosy Cross necklace which would lead her through the rest of her mind controlled existence. Her abuser told her that he worked for the Vatican and now, so did she. *"After the Rite to Remain Silent was installed, the voices of my multiple personalities that I had previously heard in my head ceased. In the silence of my deliberately created memory compartments, I could only hear the voices of my abusers who created them...commanding my silence."*[4]

***

"On the altar of the Devil, up is down, pleasure is pain, darkness is light, slavery is freedom, and madness is sanity."
—The Satanic Rituals

Programming

Programming centers around the concept of inverted reality and illusion, where nothing is as it appears to be, up is down, yes is no, pain is pleasure, and the line between reality and dreams is blurred. Not being able to determine what is real and what is illusion/dream/fake is used in mind control to get targets to give up on reality and succumb to the alter-ego programming. One way to describe the split, is to say that the child's mind is thinking "This isn't happening to me, it's happening to someone else" and a split in the personality occurs. The mind of the victim is not only divided from itself, but the very process of torture makes the victim distrustful of humans in general.

This victimization of body and soul transforms the person into a complex computer program. A file (alter) is created through trauma/torture, repetition and reinforcement. In order to activate (trigger) the file, a specific access code, password, cue or command is required. About seventy five percent of victims are female, since they possess higher tolerances for pain and tend to dissociate easier than males. The victim is called a "slave" by the programmer, who in turn is perceived as master or god. Monarch programming is also referred to as the "Marionette Syndrome." A marionette is a puppet that is attached to strings and is controlled by the unseen puppet master. Handlers used to carry around a black or grey three ring binder, now they use a lap top computer, which lists the Monarchs access keys and triggers. The term Uncle is often used to refer to a person's handler as in Uncle Sam. An example of this was the Mouseketeers where children were instructed to call Walt Disney "Uncle Walt."

***

Alters

The basis for the success of the programming is that different personalities called 'alters' can be created who do not know each other, but who can take over the body at different times. An alter is a dissociated part of the mind which has a separate identity and is given cue codes by the programmer, to trigger that part of the mind to come to the front of consciousness. The alter's "identity" may be anything from another person, a gem, a rock, a tape recorder, an animal or even think of itself as a demon. An Alter Fragment is an even further dissociation which is programmed for a single specific purpose. Stephen Spielberg's TV show, *United States of Tara*, features a housewife with at least five different alters who take over the body when she is triggered by some type of trauma. The initial part of a person's mind before splitting occurs, is called the core. Part of the drama that is carried out during the entire victim's life is that their mind tries to protect this innocent core essence of themselves from being touched. The PINK alters are core related alters; they maintain the true feelings of the true self apart from the cult programming. These are viewed as weak and fragile because they are emotional and often break down and weep.

***

Hypnosis & Electricity

Hypnosis or hypnotic trance is a form of dissociation and has always been an occult science. Hypnotic cues can be given to cause the body to go into various dissociative states. The cues use all the senses and are tied to everyday objects to enhance the programming and everything in life becomes a cue to reinforce this. The limit to this is simply up to the programmer's creativity. One method for inducing children into a hypnotic state is to have them stare at a spinning top as the colors whirl around. Programmers will often use a "hand spinner"; a handheld high speed hypnotic device, designed to quickly put you in a deep state of hypnosis. Jay Parker says that his father owned and used such a device. In the *South Park* episode titled *The Return of Chef*, this technique can be seen used by The Super Adventure Club, an elite group of child molesters.

Flashing lights have been used to put people into altered states for a long time. It was discovered that if a strobe is flashed into the eyes at ten hertz, the brain will retune itself to that frequency. The consciousness will downshift to an alpha or below and the entire cortex is influenced by the strobe. During the programming, the child will be strapped down, naked on a gurney with an I.V. in one hand or arm. There will be wires attached to their head to monitor brain patterns. They will see a pulsing light, most often described as red, white and blue.

Another basic component of the Monarch program involves the use of electro shock, to create dissociation and later to remove the memories of what the slave has carried out on a mission. Many survivors remember the electrified cages called Woodpecker Grids, used to give shocks to children locked inside to make them multiples. Cathy O'Brien recalls a programming center at Tinker A.F.B. in Oklahoma: *"I was escorted away from the two by a nurse, who purported to be tending to my injured arm. In fact, she was preparing me for the 'Tinker-belle cage'—an electrified metal cage with an electrified grid bottom. Locked inside, I was subjected to high, direct current voltage to compartmentalize the Peter Pan theme mind-control programming that I endured. Like Peter Pan's Tinkerbelle, I learned to 'ride the light' as a means of travel. Additionally, my instilled Tinker-belle theme mind manipulation included a sense of Never-Never-land timelessness that was rooted in my 'natural' inability to comprehend time due to my MPD/DID."[5]*

The Masonic lodges have been using a mild form of hypnosis and electroshock therapy for a long time. *"Certain forces are sent through the candidate's body during the ceremony, especially at the moment when he is created, received and constituted an Entered Apprentice Freemason. Certain parts of the Lodge have been heavily charged with magnetic force especially in order that the Candidate may absorb as much as possible of this force. The first object of this curious method of preparation is to expose to this influence those various parts of the body which are especially used in the ceremony. In ancient Egypt, there was another reason for these preparations, for a weak current of physical electricity was sent through the Candidate by means of a rod or sword with which he was touched at certain points. It is partly on this account that at this first initiation the candidate is deprived of all metals since they may very easily interfere with the flow of currents."[6]*

***

The Structuring of a System

The purpose of the mind control is to build a System within the mind that is a human robot. In the beginning, the programmer must bring order out of the chaos he has just created and must use some kind of structure to place worlds. The victim has an internal world built inside their mind in which the hundreds and thousands of alters must live in. When the programming begins, it must be simple enough that a child can understand it. During the Monarch programming, an average System will have at least 1,000 alters but not all of these will be personalities designed to hold the body. They understand that their victim of multiple personalities is, in essence, a city of people, and so they used that understanding to construct, in the victim's head, all of the structures and features of a geological land. Survivors report that the map of Oz was frequently used. Slaves in high level positions will have their System structured on the Tree of Life and these alters consider themselves gods or goddesses. The movie, *Labyrinth,* is a portrayal of what the internal world of a Monarch slave may look like. The hideous ruler of the castle played by Kabbalist, David Bowie guards the stolen baby which represents the innocent core.

The alters are organized in a system of layers, or levels. Generally speaking, the deeper the layer, the worse the trauma memories. Cult memories are usually found at the deeper levels of the internal system. In real life, the carousel is used as a device to teach dissociation and how the alters are to go up and down in trance and an internal carousel is built into a System. In a Castle System child alters are hidden and disobedient ones may be locked up inside. Other systems can be based on things such as a Chess Board, Double Helix, Flowers, Hour Glass, Potter's Wheel, Puppets, a spider's web, stairwell, a tornado, or Umbrella.

Mirrors are used a great deal in programming. Within a slaves mind countless mirror images are made and they see mirror images everywhere. Many of today's superstitions derive from ancient concepts of the supernatural. Bad luck caused by a broken mirror comes from the idea that a man's reflection represented his soul. The shattering of mirrors represents the persons mind and the creating of alters. What have witches used for millennia to see beyond time and space? Mirrors. In the 1957 Disney TV show, *All About Magic,* Walt turns the pro-

gram over to a character with a green mask in a dark mirror who was called "The Slave of the Mirror." In some cult programming, mirrors are placed into the System and the demons are layered behind the mirrors. If an alter would shatter a mirror, the demons behind it are released and all hell breaks loose in their mind. When a deep alter is needed to perform, they are sent into the looking glass world where a looking glass person carries out the command.

***

Levels of Programming

The levels of programming correlate to the frequency of brainwave activity and both are symbolized by the Greek letters of the alphabet. Alpha represents general programming characterized by extremely pronounced memory retention along with substantially increased physical strength and visual ability. Alpha programming is accomplished through deliberately subdividing the victim's personality which, in essence, causes a left brain-right brain division, allowing for a programmed union of L and R through neuron pathway stimulation. People with Multiple Personality Disorder will sometimes develop super-human

skills such as a photographic memory, visual acuity forty-four times greater than average, and a high pain threshold.

Beta represents the sexual alters and early sexual abuse will be used to anchor this programming. Beta alters generally see themselves as cats or kittens and are programmed to have charm, seductive skills, charisma, and creativity. Beta alters' primary function is to provide sex for the people who run our visible and invisible government as "Presidential Models"; in other words, sex slaves for the President or whomever else he chooses to share with. Betas are taught how to perform sex in rituals, or programming related to prostitution, including producing and directing pornography. This programming eliminates all learned moral convictions and stimulates the primitive sexual instinct, devoid of inhibitions. This accounts for the pervasiveness of feline imagery surrounding models, actors, actresses and musicians.

In Gamma programming, alters are possessed by demons layered in to their system. Blood rituals are used to attach demons to alters in a particular way. However you want to

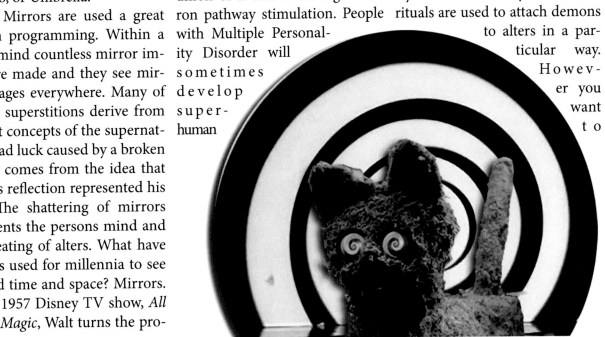

define "demon" is up to your own beliefs, but these entities are a reality to the victim and something they must grapple with every day. The ceremonies to demonize a victim occur before they are born and generational spirits are very important to them. Great effort is taken to make the victim certain that God has rejected them. The slaves are repeatedly warned that God is cruel, judgmental, and full of wrath and wants to destroy them for all the wicked things they have done. The Gamma programming also has to do with System protection and the art of deceit is a part of that. These alters will provide misinformation to their therapist, try to misdirect, tell half-truths, and protect the system by making sure certain secrets are kept.

Delta models are slaves whose purpose is assassination. Also known as "killer programming", it was originally developed for training special agents or elite soldiers of the Delta Force, CIA, Mossad, MI6, and KGB in covert operations. With the optimal adrenal output, subjects are devoid of fear and systematic in carrying out their assignment. No doubt, Jason Bourne from the movie trilogy has had some Delta programming. Omega is the "self-destruct programming"; because Omega is the last letter of the alphabet. The corresponding behaviors include suicidal tendencies and/or self-mutilation and cutting. This program is generally activated when victim/survivor begins therapy or interrogation and too much memory is being recovered. There are other levels not listed here that correlate with the rest of the Greek alphabet.

***

> "Sometimes in art therapy, I have observed MPD patients to enter an apparent trance state after looking at another patients art work."[7]

Triggers

The stimuli which bring about particular programmed behaviors and states of consciousness are called triggers. These can be anything from words, sounds, tones, rhythmic patterns, hand signals, colors, symbols or hand held objects. Virtually any stimulus can be used for the purpose of eliciting a pre-programmed response if that particular cue was previously used as a signal for a repetitively traumatizing procedure. Practically anything can be used as a trigger to create a trance and dissociation, and the corporate world is set up in a way that the victim is surrounded by as many triggers in everyday life as possible.

> "My television programming was then expanded to include the shows that every Project Monarch Mind–Control slave had to watch: I Dream of Jeannie, The Brady Bunch, Gumby and Pokey, and Bewitched."
> —Cathy O'Brien

One of the basic ideas of creating a mind-controlled slave is to control the entire milieu of the slave. That is to say, they can never escape because their environment is designed for what is called "story immersion." For instance, a Monarch who has been given the basic "Alice in Wonderland" and "Wizard of Oz" script will see objects connected to these

story lines almost everywhere they go. The constant bumping into programming paraphernalia or pictures helps focus the victims mind on the programming and keeps them dissociative. As a way of enhancing the effect of the programming that they can never escape, Monarch slaves are conditioned to place trigger items into their lives. According to survivor, Cisco Wheeler, the first step in neutralizing a code is to look at them with the alters, to go over it consciously, and know it is a trigger. Once the conscious mind knows something is a trigger it is harder for it to work.

***

> "The annual televising of Wizard of Oz was celebrated as a grand holiday around my house. This was to prepare my mind for future base programming on the theme that I, like Dorothy, could 'spin' into another dimension"[8]

The Wizard of OZ

This story was chosen in the late 1940's to be the basis for the Intelligence community's trauma based programming. One of the most important concepts of the programmers is having slaves "go over the rainbow" which is another term for going into a trance. The yellow brick road is the script one must follow; no matter what fearful things lay ahead, the Monarch slave must follow the Yellow Brick Road which is set out before them by their master. Tin Man programming is an all purpose program and it means that the slave is a well oiled machine. In upper level slaves, "Dorothy" represents the Mother of Darkness alters. Some alters live "over the rainbow" and some do not. For those who live over the rainbow they serve their masters in such a deep hypnotic trance that they perceive reality like it's a dream.

The Wizard of Oz contains many themes commonly used by programmers. All of Dorothy's nightmarish experiences stemmed from her desire to risk her own life to protect her threatened pet. Nearly all MPD/DID's have suffered the loss of pets during ritual torture. The close relationship between Dorothy and her dog is a very subtle connection between the satanic cults use of animal familiars. A Monarch slave child will be allowed to bond with a pet. The child will want to bond with a pet anyway because people are too terrifying at this point, then the pet is killed to traumatize the child. Oftentimes the Oz theme is used to rationalize that what the child has experienced was "just a bad dream", like Dorothy was told upon her awakening in her bed at the end of the movie.

The history behind the Wizard of Oz suggests that it has been an integral part of the occult and programming world all along. The author of the Oz books was L. Frank Baum, a member of the Theosophical Society. He was supposedly inspired by "some spirit" who gave him the "magic key" to write the story, *The Wonderful Wizard of Oz*, which came out in 1900. The books were to be a "theosophical fairy tale", incorporating the ancient wisdom of the Mystery Religions.

The word OZ is important to all Thelemic magicians as it is not derived from children's stories, but from Gematria. In Hebrew the word OZ is spelt with the letters Ayin and Zayin and adds up to 77. According to Aleister Crowley, this number represents magic acting on the world of matter. It can be expressed as eleven, the grand number of ritual magic, multiplied by seven, the number of manifestation (7-11). In addition to this, the word Oz also has sexual and satanic undertones. Its first letter, Ayin, represents the male goat of the Witches Sabbath and identified by Crowley as the 'Devil' of the Tarot deck. The short manifesto by Crowley print-

Disneyland California circa 1958

ed in 1942, *Liber Oz*, contains the basic creeds of Thelemites, "There is no god but man" and "The slaves shall serve." Thelemites believe that during Creation, monsters from Universe B were irresponsibly unleashed, and are the same as the beings referred to as the Nephilim in the Bible. Kenneth Grant says the generic name for these beings is Oza. Cathy O'Brien's abusers told her that Oz was another dimension like hell or purgatory.

***

Alice in Wonderland

The Rev. Charles Lutwidge Dodgson was a teacher of mathematics at Oxford and a deacon of the Anglican Church, who wrote under the pen name Lewis Carroll. Alice Liddell, the young girl upon whom the fictional Alice was based, had a relationship with Carroll that started when she was just four years old. He created the Alice character during a row boat ride with her and her two sisters. Dodgson had many underage companions and didn't care much for adults in general. He far preferred the company of young girls with whom he would dine alone in his quarters. Although no one has ever come forward to accuse him, with only diaries to go by, the suspicion that he was a pedophile continues to this day. Dodgson's affection for what he called his "child friends" was always mingled with a vague, lustful yearning. He once wrote to one 10-year-old girl, *"Extra thanks and kisses for the lock of hair. I have kissed it several times - for want of having you to kiss, you know, even hair is better than nothing."*[9]

Dodgson's major hobby was photography—very candid photography. Over half of his subjects include nude and semi-nude girls. *"I confess I do not admire naked boys in pictures. They always seem... to need clothes, whereas one hardly sees why the lovely forms of girls should ever be covered up."*[10] It's clear that Dodgson had a submerged erotic fascination with the nubile female form. If those pictures had been found today on his computer, Carroll might be registering with the Sheriff downtown. Whether or not Dodgson ever acted on his impulse to molest children, his stories continue to supply programmers with one of the most classic mind control motifs. Due to its inversion of reality, "Alice in Wonderland" provides the perfect themes for Monarch programming. The white rabbit is an important figure who allows the victim to go to otherwise inaccessible places for "adventure." He represents the master, programmer or handler.

Since its publication, *Alice's Adventures in Wonderland* has never been out of print. In 1998, Lewis Carroll's own copy was sold at auction for $1.54 million to an anonymous American buyer, making it the most expensive children's book ever sold at the time. It was originally titled "Alice's Adventures Under

Ground" and Tim Burton's characters in his adaptation of the story make reference to this when they call the Wonderland, "Under Land." Walt Disney's desire to turn the story into an animated film stretched all the way back to 1923 when he was a 21-year-old filmmaker. Between 1924 and 1927, Disney made a series of fifty-six silent Alice Comedies where she romps around in a combined live action and animation make-belief world. A few of the 1920's Alice silent cartoon titles include: *Alice's Wonderland, Alice's Spooky Adventure, Alice Plays Cupid, Alice Rattled by Rats,* and *Alice's Mysterious Mystery*. Disney used his Mouseketeers to play all the roles in an Oz movie called *Rainbow Road to Oz*, which was never shown to the public. Adults today who received Mickey Mouse programming during the 50's through 70's can still be seen with Mickey Mouse clocks, watches, lampshades, knick-knacks, and tee shirts. Just like Dodgson, children were the center of everything Walt Disney did. The occult world that backed Walt believed that

if they could bring out that part of a person called "the child" by various psychologists, then they could appeal to the curiosity and feelings of the "child" part of adults.

***

The Presidential Model

Marilyn Monroe was the first poster girl of the Monarch program. She is possibly the most iconic figure in American culture and the most recognizable sex symbol of all time. Marilyn was indeed manipulated by high level "mind doctors" who controlled every aspect of her life. At age eleven, little Norma Jeane was declared a ward of the state. She lived in a total of eleven foster homes throughout her youth and when there was no foster home available, she sometimes ended up at the Hollygrove Orphanage in Los Angeles. Norma Jeane's unstable and sometimes traumatic youth made her a perfect candidate for Monarch mind control. Norma Jeane recalled being treated harshly in several of the foster homes and, even worse, she was abused in at least three of them. Marilyn often claimed that she had multiple personalities. "Jekyll and Hyde" she would call herself, but there were more than two. *"I'm so many people. They shock me sometimes. I wish it were just me!"*[11]

Before becoming famous, Norma Jeane went by the name of Mona and worked as a stripper in Los Angeles where she came into contact with Anton LaVey at a club called The Mayan, where he played the organ. LaVey's biography also mentions an "affair" with Monroe, which was probably more than that. *"When the carnival season ended, LaVey would earn money by playing organ in Los Angeles area burlesque houses, and he relates that it was during this time period that he had a brief affair with a then-unknown Marilyn Monroe."*[12] Throughout her career, Marilyn was in and out of psychiatric hospitals where she had little to no personal freedom. As several biographies have revealed, she was not allowed contact with her extended family, and her handlers isolated her in order to further control her and to avoid real people from helping her to realize that she was being manipulated. The only people that she was in contact with were her psychologists and her handlers. In a book by Lena Pepitone, who was hired to take care of Marilyn, it states that in her house *"floor-to-ceiling mirrors were everywhere. Even the dining alcove at the rear of the living room had a table with a mirrored top."*[13]

Marilyn was the first high profile presidential model slave, a situation that required her handlers to exercise extreme control on everything she said and did in public. High level Monarch slaves are often identified with gems and stones which identify their status; presidential models are reportedly identified with diamonds. Marilyn Monroe is the ultimate symbol of Beta Programming. At the height of her career, she was involved with the highest power figure in the world, President John F. Kennedy. While some historians classify their relationship as just an affair, when she sang Happy Birthday to him publicly, wearing barely any clothes, they were acting out a demoralization play for the rest of the American public. Sadly, Monroe died not three months after that famous appearance.

The last months of Marilyn's life were characterized with erratic behavior, strange anecdotes and several "intimate" relationships with high-powered individuals. As she was increasingly showing signs of serious mental distress, she also had affairs with several men including Bobby Kennedy and Marlon Brando. Even as her life was very stressful, she had no symptoms of being suicidal. She was very happy the day that she died and was excited about the future plans she had made for her life outside of Hollywood. While her death was classified as a "probable suicide" due to acute barbiturate poisoning, it is still one of the most debated conspiracy theories of all time. A well-documented chapter about Marilyn Monroe in the book, *Dead Wrong*, by Richard Belzer and David Wayne, proves that she could not have ingested all the drugs they found in her system when she died. The only way they could have been delivered to her bloodstream without her body rejecting them was anally. After her death, new owners of Marilyn's Brentwood home hired a contractor to replace the roof and remodel the house, and discovered a sophisticated eavesdropping and telephone tapping system that covered every room in the house. The components were not commercially available in 1962, but were in the words of a retired Justice Department official, "standard FBI issue."

It is obvious that Beta slaves are programmed to emulate Marilyn. Over forty years after Monroe's death, her image continues to be used ad-nauseam to identify those who are following in her footsteps, by the same system that controlled her entire life. Fellow Monarch, Britney Spears, is reportedly "obsessed" with Marilyn. Britney demands that a collection of Marilyn Monroe DVDs be on-hand in all her hotel rooms. She also visits Marilyn's grave regularly and wants to be buried in the same cemetery. Actress Megan Fox had Marilyn's likeness tattooed on her arm, but had to get it removed because of its "bad vibes."

***

The Freedom Train

What would happen if a slave tried to physically escape his master or handler? This has happened countless times and the mind control is so solid that they really don't have anything to worry about. Programmers will create alters to watch over and report back to the handler everything that the slave is doing. These alters are fiercely loyal to their masters and will undermine any outside help that the victim seeks. Some alters are programmed for suicide whenever they feel that the security of the System is breeched. Any alter who betrays the abusers is labeled a Judas and is programmed to act like the Judas of the Bible by hanging themselves.

When slaves outlive their usefulness or their programming begins to break down they are murdered and this is known as being "thrown from the Freedom Train" because Freedom Train is a code for the entire trauma based mind control program. What is the first thing you come upon when entering the Disneyland theme park? The train station. The first defense of the programmers is that the victim has no idea that he is MPD/DID or that they

When the handler loses control of a System, "Sleeping Beauty" is kept sleeping by spiders who bite her in a coffin while "Daddy demon" and "the black princess" rule from the castle dungeon. The alters who were on the "light side", so to speak, are under attack, bound and isolated by walls and put into a cocoon which leads to death.

***

Disney's Role

Hollywood movies and children's books provide an infinite pool of resources for programmers. One of the most effective and easiest ways to put children into a hypnotic trance is to say "Imagine you are watching your favorite TV show or movie." This is why Disney movies are so important as they are the perfect hypnotic tool to get the mind to dissociate. According to victims' testimony, MOST of Walt Disney's films are used for programming while some of them are specifically designed for mind control.

During the 1950's, 60's and 70's at least ninety percent of Monarch victims were subjected to watching *Fantasia* in order for them to build the foundational imagery. The score of Stravinsky's Rite of Spring, featured in *Fantasia*, was originally conceived as a pagan ritual meant to evoke a sacrificial virgin dancing herself to death. Child victims had their eyes taped open and sat one on one with their primary programmers so that they could give the scripts as the child watched the film over and over while the child was under a guided LSD trip. This trip makes the colors and effects increased about a thousand times.

Fantasia premiered in 1940 and was a financial disaster, but was re-released to theaters in '46, '56, '63, '69, '77, '82, '85, and '90, in order to catch every generation of children. The scene with Mickey Mouse as the sorcerer's apprentice is very telling. When Mickey attempts to subdue the bewitched broom he has created, he takes an axe and kills the broom by splitting it and armies of brooms are formed from the dead broom. The broom dies and then multiplies when it comes back to life. This is a clear picture of what the programmers want the child's mind to do. They will traumatize almost to the point of death and then have the tortured alter multiply itself into many more duplicate alters. The trauma death of the broom is evidence that this film was meant to be used for training children in multiplicity.

***

The Tragic Kingdom

Disney used some misdirection magic and created subsidiaries which has allowed them to keep their good image while secretly becoming the world's largest distributor of pay-per-view pornography. Disney studios got involved in the cable television in the early eighties and they became a full-fledged partner with the pioneer of the pay-per-view

are being used as a slave. Essentially, the System is in a trance pretty much all of the time. If the person suspects he is being controlled and finds out that he is MPD, the more they dig, the more the occultist nature of the programming becomes apparent. This will discredit their testimony because most people think that magic is hocus pocus and who would believe anyone who said they were raped by Satan, Mickey Mouse and George Bush?

It is almost impossible for a victim to be isolated from being accessed by a handler. Person to person access is as easy as an eye wink, blink, hand signal, body gesture or the arrival of a particular person. Access codes through the media include flashing colors, story schemes, and pictures in the newspaper, television, ads, radio, and news events that are broadcast in all fashions. It is very difficult to protect a victim from everything that might be a code or trigger. The princess programming is a back up program that kicks in if serious deprogramming, tampering and integration is occurring.

company called Viewer's Choice. In 1993 they took a sharp turn into the soft-core porn industry by launching a service called Hot Choice. They bought the rights to a Playboy television series called *Soft Bodies,* which became the most widely watched program of its kind in the world. They also hired the porn industry veteran, Marilyn Chambers, to produce films and she has appeared on the network more than any other performer.

The name Disney is practically synonymous with sainthood. Many people all over the world regard visiting these parks as the highlight of their life and in turn share this with the next generation. Not many people know that they are also fundamentally important programming centers for mind control slaves. Disneyland's subterranean underworld provides a perfect place for rituals, porn and other secret activities. According to de-programmed ex-slaves, during the 1960's, the Brotherhood needed to shift their programming centers away from the military bases to a place that people from all over the world could come without raising suspicion because too much publicity was shined on the military bases. According to witnesses, the programmers got a big laugh out of using Disneyland as a major base for criminal activity. Under the disguise of entertaining the world, they carried out money laundering, child slavery laundering, and mind-control. They nick-named Disneyland "the little syndicate of mind-control." The theme park

creates the perfect atmosphere for programming as it meets all the criteria. They are a fantasy land full of characters, with plenty of opportunity for hypnotism and trance coming from rides and flashing lights. A Ferris wheel or carousel could be used to create dissociation while also going along with some fairy tale programming script.

Some Disneyland rides can be absolutely terrifying to small children. Presentations such as Alien Encounter, Snow White's Adventures and The Haunted Mansion send children away in tears daily. Still, schools and churches from all over the country work closely with Disneyland theme parks making field trips to The Magic Kingdom part of regular curriculum. High schools use the parks for proms, senior nights and international choir performances. You can even have your fairy tale wedding with Cinderella's castle as a backdrop and a reception theme based on your favorite Disney tale. *Modern Bride* even ranked Orlando as the number one honeymoon destination in the world.

Of all Disney's secrets, none is as dark or troubling as the growing number of active pedophiles in and around the Magic Kingdom. Criminology experts rank Disney World as the great-

est attraction in the world for both children and pedophiles. The law enforcement receives the least amount of cooperation from Disney for crimes of this nature. They are even willing to cover up crimes and destroy crime scenes to protect their image. Disney has a "zero tolerance" policy when it comes to employee and guest petty theft, but when it comes to sex crimes, the Mouse looks the other way. Within the company there is a subculture of voyeurs so large and open that even new employees can get involved fast, if they choose to.

***

The Military Occult Connection

Lt. Col. Michael Aquino, leader of a satanic organization called the Temple of Set, was a High Priest, while simultaneously serving in the armed forces as a military intelligence operative and psychological/propaganda warfare expert. Throughout much of the 1980s, Aquino was at the center of a controversy involving the Pentagon's acquiescence to outright Satanic practices inside the military. He was also a prime suspect in a series of pedophile scandals involving the sexual abuse of hundreds of children of military personnel serving at the Presidio U.S. Army, stationed in the San Francisco Bay Area. According to an article in the *San Francisco Examiner*[14], one of the victims had identified Aquino and his wife as participants in child rape. According to the victim, the Aquinos had filmed scenes of the child being fondled in a bathtub. The child's description of

> "On top of that I really want to scare kids. I want to go to Disneyland and see a 10 year old kid crying. 'Oh mommy the clock tower's going to come to life and eat me!' That's my fondest dream. Disney scared the pants off me when I was a little kid. Disney needs to scare kids!"
> —Warren Spector, video game developer for Epic Mickey

the house, which was also the headquarters of Aquino's Satanic Temple of Set, was so detailed, that police were able to obtain a search warrant. During the raid, they confiscated thirty-eight video tapes, photo negatives, and other evidence that the home had been the hub of a pedophile ring, operating in and around U.S. military bases. Even as Aquino was being investigated by Army Criminal Investigation Division officers for his involvement in the pedophile cases, he retained highest-level security clearances, and was involved in pioneering work in military psychological operations or "psy-ops".

Michael Aquino was one of Cathy O'Brien's handlers. *"Aquino and I were called to Washington D.C. to revise my base core programming to override Senator Byrd's control for security reasons…Much to Aquino's dismay and embarrassment, Reagan admired the occult role that this Army Lt. Colonel played for mind-control traumatization purposes, as it fit in with the public promotion of religion that Reagan had launched. Reagan claimed to believe that the masses were easiest to manipulate through their religion, as were mind-control slaves like myself…While Reagan had Aquino in D.C., he demanded that he wear his black ritual robes to a White House party to reinforce the controlling superstitions of a few South/Central American diplomats. Aquino appeared foolish in the eyes of his peers….Aquino got even with Reagan. Minutes before I was prostituted to Reagan that evening, Aquino ordered me into a closed side room where he very quickly had intercourse with me. When he finished ejaculating, he slapped me on the behind and disrespectfully said, "Take that to the Chief".*[15] One of the programming nicknames of Aquino happens to be Mickey Mouse. Mickey works well as a programming device because it plays on humans' subconscious genetically transmitted fear of mice. Anyone who has had ever had an issue with mice in their house can tell you that they can be vile creatures. Mickey's image can help create a love-hate relationship which is so valued during the traumatization process.

***

Demonology

From the programmers point of view, they first try to create alters and then demonize them. Within the Brotherhood, demonology is not taken lightly but is considered to be the real science of the Sciences of Mind Control, and they believe that the mind control will not work without the assistance of the Lord of the Abyss, named Choronzon or Typhon. Some alters consider themselves to be on "the dark side" and have names like Satan, Lucifer, Beelzebub, Asteroth, etc. The birthright of a child born to elite brotherhood parents is to be allowed into satanic coven activity. Within the ranks of the bloodline slaves, many of their codes and structures come from Satanic Witchcraft. This is because their programmers are witches themselves and Satanism is their world-view. Satan himself is known within a Monarch system often by the name Belial, Bilair or Bilar which are his cabalistic names. It kind of makes you wonder about The Fresh Prince of Belair. The everyday demons, whom the alters have to contend with if they step out of line, are called the Jokers who can jump out of the mirrors and drag an alter into the looking glass world. Alters wandering into the System away from their assigned living quarters end up in mazes of mirrors. The mazes of mirrors can't be broken because demons are placed behind the mirrors.

The power that exists in Satanic and Luciferian cults is reflected in an organizational hierarchy with incremental ranks. The most common positions include page, knight, priest/ess, prince/ess, high priests/ess, king, queen, savior, god and goddess. As one increases in rank, one is taught more about the programming cues, or triggers, used in ceremonies with the other followers of the cult. The pursuit of power begins with victimization. Those who have been forced into situations of extreme powerlessness will seek more and more power as both a defense and offensive mechanism. All members of Satanic cults play the victim role in rituals until one's rank increases in the cult and the extent of the victimization decreases. Throughout the cult members' rise to power, they are placed increasingly into the role of the perpetrator of painful ceremonies and procedures. Getting power decreases the harm experienced by the individual and the power of "the dark side" may be sought because they have lost all hope of protection from a "good" deity.

***

"When you find the same highly esoteric information in different states from Florida to California and from different countries, you start to get an idea that there's something going on that is very large and very well coordinated, something that is systematic and requires a great deal of communication. So I have gone from someone kind of neutral and not knowing what to think about it all to someone who clearly believes ritual abuse is real, and that the people who say it isn't are either naive—like people who didn't want to believe the Holocaust—or they're dirty"
—Prof. D. Corydon Hammond in lecture: Hypnosis in MPD: Ritual Abuse

The Pedos Stack Up
While Sigmund Freud was practicing psychoanalysis in the 19th century, he found himself coming across the phenomenon of ritual abuse victims, however, their stories were so fantastical that he did not believe them. His theory was that people commonly fantasize about such abuse, particularly during early childhood. This is the prevailing attitude among psychologists today. At the heart of the Monarch program is pedophilia and today it is almost impossible to keep track of all the high profile cases of child abuse. Among the multiple charges against individuals in the Catholic Church, the pedophiles keep stacking up. There are literally hundreds of cases of pedophile sex rings among the elite that even the mainstream press reports. Operation Cathedral was a police operation that broke up an international child pornography ring in 1998 called "The Wonderland Club." It was led by the British National Crime Squad in cooperation with other police forces around the globe, who arrested 107 suspects across 12 countries *"In September 1998, another ring was raided – what the BBC described as "a larger and more sinister pedophile network called Wonderland." The network was so named in honor of Lewis Carroll's revered children's book, Alice's Adventures in Wonderland. Carroll was widely known to have a predilection for underage girls and boys, and is now something of a patron saint of pedophiles around the globe."*[16] One reason for the high profile of the operation was the unusually high number of images possessed, produced and distributed by the Wonderland Club which was about 750,000 images with 1,200 unique identifiable faces.

In 2002, Operation Ore investigated hundreds of child welfare professionals, police officers, care workers and teachers, who have been identified as 'extremely high-risk' pedophiles by an investigation into internet porn. The discovery came after U.S. Operation Avalanche passed on more than 7,000 names of UK subscribers to an American-based child porn website. When police examined a sample of the most dedicated users, they discovered that many worked with children.

In 2006 an Immigrations and Customs child pornography sting operation called Project Flicker eventually helped authorities identify 30,000 people from around the world who bought child pornography from 230 websites run by a ring of criminals. This operation produced payment records proving that at least 5,200 of them were U.S. military personnel. At first, the Pentagon failed to examine 1,700 of the cases as they claimed it "wasn't a priority." In 2010 the Pentagon released investigative reports that were part of a broader effort initiated by Operation Flicker, which implicated individuals working with agencies including the National Security Agency and the National Reconnaissance Office, which operates U.S. spy satellites. *The Boston Globe* disclosed the results of the investigations after obtaining the documents through the Freedom of Information Act. Cases included contractors for the Security and Intelligence Directorate of the Defense Advanced Research Projects Agency, or DARPA, in Arlington, Va. One case in California involved more than a dozen individuals with ties to the Defense Department several of whom had top secret clearances.

In 2012, almost a year after his death, claims were widely publicized that the English DJ and BBC television presenter, Jimmy Savile, had committed sexual abuse with his victims ranging from prepubescent girls and boys to adults. The Metropolitan Police Service launched a formal criminal investigation, called Operation Yewtree, into historic allegations of sexual abuse by Savile and other people, over four decades. It stated that it was pursuing over 400 separate lines of inquiry, based on the claims of 200 witnesses, via 14 police forces across the UK. It described the alleged abuse as being "on an unprecedented scale" and the number of potential victims as "staggering."

Hollywood also seems to have a hideous epidemic on its hands. One of the most famous child actors from the 1980's, Corey Feldman, has opened up about the sexual abuse he suffered at the hands of older men in Hollywood and details the events in his book, *Coreyography*. He claims that "pedophilia is Hollywood's biggest problem." In 2011, Martin Weiss, a forty seven year old Hollywood manager who represented child actors, was charged in Los Angeles with sexually abusing a former client. His accuser, who was under twelve years old during the time of the alleged abuse, reported to authorities that Weiss told him what they were doing was "common practice in the entertainment industry." That same year, Fernando Rivas, an award-winning composer for *Sesame Street*, was arraigned on charges of coercing a child "to engage in sexually explicit conduct" in South Carolina. He was also charged with production and distribution of child pornography. Registered sex offender, Jason James Murphy, worked as a casting agent in Hollywood for years before his past kidnapping and sexual abuse of a boy was revealed by the *Los Angeles Times*. Murphy's credits include placing young actors in kid-friendly fare like *Bad News Bears, The School of Rock, Cheaper by the Dozen 2* and *The Three Stooges*.

"Since 1983, the country has been shocked by the epidemic of allegations, coming from parent groups and law enforcement spokesmen, that American children in day-care centers and pre-schools are being sexually molested and forced to take part in barbaric rites. The villains are identified as the adult followers of a nationwide secret Satanic cult who have worked themselves in to teaching and administrative positions to gain access to the children. The testimony of kids in these cases is astonishingly similar in content—to similar to have been fabricated, some experts say. They tell of being forced to commit sexual acts with robed, chanting adults, of being made to drink blood, eat feces, witness animal and human sacrifice, and taste the flesh of roasted babies. Special task forces have been set up within police departments to investigate Satanic and occult-related crimes, parent groups have formed to combat the 'conspiracy' and Phil Donahue, Oprah Winfrey, 20/20, and Nightwatch, among others, have devoted segments to this phenomenon."
—Satan Wants You, Arthur Lyons

On March 22nd, 2014, the International Common Law Court of Justice and the International Tribunal into Crimes of Church and State in Brussels announced that they had compiled shocking evidence against the Catholic Church and the Royal Family of England, linking the defendants with the operation and protection of a global child trafficking network involving the routine and systematic kidnapping, rape, torture and sacrificial murder of newborn infants and children up to age fourteen. The documented ring, known as the "Ninth Circle", including former Popes John Paul II and Benedict, is one manifestation of this network. The Circle supposedly operates according to a canon law statute designated as "THE MAGISTERIAL PRIVILEGE", which is filed within the sealed archives of the Vatican library. Mass graves of trafficked children were identified in Canada, Holland and the United States, and are linked to the Ninth Circle sacrificial cult. Children's remains and records were ordered destroyed by Archbishop of Canterbury, Justin Welby, acting for Queen Elizabeth. Jorge Bergoglio (aka "Pope Francis"), Adolfo Pachon (Jesuit Superior General) and Justin Welby (Archbishop of Canterbury) will stand trial in absentia on April 7, 2014, after refusing to challenge or deny the criminal charges made against them in the Trial Division of the Common Law Court of Justice in Brussels.

According to witnesses, the Ninth Circle Satanic Cult is globally based and centuries old, operating at Roman Catholic cathedrals in Montreal, New York, Rome, London and dozens of other locations, including protected forest groves in America, Canada,

France and Holland. It routinely utilizes children taken from Catholic orphanages, adoption agencies, hospitals and schools. There have been thirty-two mass child grave sites identified at native residential schools across Canada, Holland and the United States. The schools were mainly run by Catholic Jesuit priests. Excavations commenced by Mohawk elders on the grounds of the Jesuit-run Mohawk Indian Residential School in Brantford, Ontario, Canada, revealed bones that had been cut up in sections. Two of these bone fragments were positively identified as being those of a small child by senior forensic pathologist, Dr. Donald Ortner, of the Smithsonian Institute in Washington, D.C. who died of undisclosed causes shortly afterwards.

The exposure of pedophile rings should increase in the future as this in only the tip of the iceberg. Right now, measures are being taken in the medical and psychiatric community to make pedophilia legal or at least decriminalized. Using the same tactics used by militant gay rights activists, pedophiles have begun to seek similar status arguing their desire for children is an "alternative lifestyle" and a sexual orientation no different than heterosexual or homosexuals. Researchers with Canada's Centre for Addiction and Mental Health have stated that pedophilia is a deep-rooted, unchangeable predisposition.

"Pedophilia has been widely viewed as a psychological disorder triggered by early childhood trauma. Now, many experts see it as a biologically rooted condition that does not change — like a sexual orientation — thanks largely to a decade of research by Dr. James Cantor at the Centre for Addiction and Mental Health. Cantor's team has found that pedophiles share a number of physical characteristics, including differences in brain wiring. It's now thought that about 1 to 5 per cent of men are pedophiles, meaning they are primarily attracted to children."[17]

"Nothing that happens in the circle can be told outside of the circle. There is no way out because there is no end to it.

"Your parents have given you to us. They know what is happening."

A page from a child's book about satanic ritual abuse called *Don't Make Me Go Back, Mommy*, by Doris Sanford

In the McMartin Preschool case, about 800 children were witnesses whose stories collaborated that Satanic Ritual Abuse and programming was done, but the media and the judicial system were able to cover it up and make it look like the abusers were the victims. It wasn't until after the case was over and the property sold, that the tangible proof of secret tunnels with ritual paraphernalia were found. The news media covered that up as well. Allegations of sexual and Satanic abuse go back a long time. So long so that a counter group has been set up called the False Memory Syndrome Foundation founded in 1992 by a couple who were accused by their own daughter of sexual abuse when she was a child. Its original board member was Dr. Martin T. Orne, hypnosis expert and a senior CIA Navy Researcher at the University of Pennsylvania experimental psychiatry laboratory. It was created to deny the existence of ritual abuse and is staffed with psychiatrists connected to the CIA. Whether you believe one side or the other, the bottom line is: either preschool children are conspiring together in lies, or government officials are.

***

Hospital Birth Protocols

There is something seriously wrong with the way babies are coming into this world and that is because modern day hospital birth protocols mirror Monarch mind control techniques. Not so long ago, babies used to be born at home, guided by a midwife or a family member. Only in the past seventy years has the trend shifted when it became fashionable to give birth with a doctor at a hospital. This is also the time frame of the systematic immersion of the entire population into trauma based mind control.

Studies are showing that 95% of American hospital births are considered "traumatic" and 45% of those are considered severely traumatic. One in ten women experience post-partum depression. Extreme bonding and breast-feeding problems almost always occur with caesarian births. In the United States, one out of every nine babies ends up in the intensive care unit. Child birth experts are deeming humanity a species in crisis in terms of how children are brought into the world and this trauma is having an impact on civilization. Humanity is being altered.

Over eighty percent of hospital births are induced by a drug called Pitocin, undermining the ability of humans to experience authentic love. Pitocin is the artificial form of Oxytocin which is the hormone of well-being and bonding. For this reason, it is sometimes referred to as the love hormone and you literally inherit it from your mother. During the natural birth process, the mother's body is flooded with Oxytocin, facilitating easier delivery, breastfeeding and bonding. When Pitocin is received during labor the mother's brain will not send the Oxytocin. This causes longer and stronger contractions which puts enormous amount of pressure on the baby and also deprives him of oxygen and the Oxytocin rush in the birth canal. If the contractions become too strong, an epidural is administered or C-section is performed. It is also for this reason you will see the C-section as the preferred method of birth for Hollywood stars. After a delivery through C-section, the mother's chemical biology is closer to that of grief, as if the baby had died.

The inability to secrete Oxytocin is interfered with at the moment of birth it will stay that way for life, deliberately interfering with the capacity to experience genuine love. Recent studies have begun to investigate Oxytocin's role in various behaviors, including social recognition, pair bonding, anxiety, and maternal behaviors. Data shows low levels of Oxytocin are linked to decreased empathy, sociopaths, psychopathy, narcissism and general manipulative behavior. Most other birth protocols are just ways of inflicting unnecessary trauma. The amniotomies, ultra sounds, immediate clamping and cutting of the umbilical cord, vaccines, and circumcision are just the beginning of a life of trauma in the new Monarch-eugenics program.

***

1. *Cult and Ritual Abuse*, James R. Noblitt & Pamela Sue Perskin
2. *Trance-Formation of America*, Cathy O'Brien w/ Mark Phillips
3. Ibid pg. 92
4. Ibid pg. 88
5. Ibid pg. 106
6. *Freemasonry Universal* Vol. 5, (1929)
7. *Cult & Ritual Abuse*, James R. Noblitt & Pamela Sue Perskin
8. *Trance-formation of America*, Cathy O'Brien w/ Mark Phillips
9. *Still She Haunts Me*, Katie Roiphe
10. Ibid
11. *Goddess*, Anthony Summers.
12. *Anton Szandor LaVey: A Biographical Sketch*, Magus Peter H. Gilmore,

13. *Marilyn Monroe Confidential: An Intimate Personal Account*, Lena Pepitone

14. *San Francisco Examiner*, October 30, 1987

15. *Trance-Formation of America*, Cathy O'Brien w/Mark Phillips

16. *The Pedophocracy*, David McGowan

17. *The Toronto Star*, Dec 22, 2013

Books:

The Illuminati Formula Used To Create An Undetectable Total Mind Controlled Slave, Fritz Springmeier

The Control of Candy Jones, Donald Bain and Long John Nebel

Thanks for the Memories, Brice Taylor

Disney: The Mouse Betrayed, Peter & Rochelle Schweizer

Mind Control, World Control, Jim Keith

The Manchurian Candidate, Richard Condon

The Search for the Manchurian Candidate, John D. Marks

Physical Control of the Mind, Jose Delgado

The Brain Changers: Scientists and the New Mind Control, Maya Pines

Operation Mind Control, Walter Bowart

The Mind Stealers: Psychosurgery and Mind Control, Samuel Chavkin

The Mind Manipulators, Alan Scheflin and Edward Opton

I Swear by Apollo: Dr. Ewen Cameron, the CIA and the Canadian Mind-Control Experiments, Don Gillmor

Journey Into Madness: The True Story of Secret CIA Mind Control and Medical Abuse, Gordon Thomas

U.S. Mind Control Experiments on Children, Jon Rappoport

Psychic Dictatorship in the USA, Alex Constantine

Satan's Underground, Lauren Stratford

Stripped Naked, Lauren Stratford

The Only-Good Heart, Beth Goobie

Unshackled: A Survivors Story of Mind Control, Kathleen Sullivan

Uncovering the Mystery of MPD, James Friesen

More Than Survivors, James Friesen

The Franklin Cover-Up, John W. DeCamp

Conspiracy of Silence, Sandra Butler

The Biggest Secret, David Icke

Children of the Matrix, David Icke

Angelic Defenders & Demonic Abusers: The Memoirs of a Satanic Ritual Abuse, Kerth Barker aka "Kathy"

Twenty-Two Faces, Jenny Hill, Judy Byingon

Other Resources:
Red Ice Radio: Guest, Janice Barcello
www.vigilantcitizen.com

WeirdStuff! Pedobear

Pedophilia has an icon and it is the Teddy Bear. In mind control it represents the slave in their helpless condition and the fact that they are nothing but a toy to the programmer. A teddy bear or other toy may be given to a child after a trauma session to serve as a trigger in the future. The internet's favorite pervert is named Pedobear, the mascot of molestation. The brilliance of the Pedobear mythos is that none of it is apparent in this innocent picture of a teddy. That's why he has sometimes ended up in ads for children's clothing. In the many photo shopped images of Pedobear, he chases little girls he calls "loli." His favorite target is Stephanie, the teen star of the kids' show, Lazytown. He also shows up with a lot of anime characters and Dora the Explorer. Generally anyone over fifteen gets Pedobear's stamp of disapproval as "too old." Pedobear is the internet's meme for saying, "You're being creepy about a kid." Many times, Pedobear is added to a picture to point out real-world sexualization of kids, but it's alternately shown as an acknowledgment of being inappropriately attracted to a child. In the art of trauma based mind control victim, Kim Noble, can be found a piece called "What Ted Saw."

MONARCHS, ZOMBIES, & ROCK 'N' ROLL

WILL BLOW YOUR MIND AND ROCK YOUR BODY-THETANS

"Here is the very essence of the cultural revolution taking place in America: the rejection of America's religious heritage and its replacement with something contrary. It is not the devil behind rock and roll—it's another god."
—Robert Pielke**

Remember when Nanna told you that Rock & Roll was Satan's music? You should listen to her more because, although she might not have all the facts, she knows what she is talking about. Even David Bowie agrees: *"Rock has always been the Devil's music. You can't convince me that it isn't."*[1] Artists who openly admit they sold their soul to the dark lord for fame in the industry include Bob Dylan, Dr. Dre, Katy Perry, Kanye West, Eminem, Snoop Dog and many, many more.

The modern history of rock and roll begins with a pact with the Devil. Robert Johnson was called the King of the Delta Blues. He was the most mysterious musician who had a profound and frightening influence on Muddy Waters, B.B. King, Eric Clapton, Keith Richards and numerous others. Born and raised in the Mississippi delta, Johnson started playing guitar in the late 1920s. His wife and child died in childbirth around 1930 and he then devoted himself fully to the

guitar. Blues master and Johnson's mentor, Son House, said that before his "transformation" he was a talentless and irritating player whose technique was so bad he made audiences angry. *"He'd sit at our feet and play during the break and such another racket you never heard."*[2]

Soon after, Johnson left Son House and Willie Brown in Robinsonville, Mississippi for the area around Martinsville, possibly searching for his natural father. Here he learned other guitar styles from Isaiah "Ike" Zimmerman, who was rumored to have learned to play guitar supernaturally by visiting the graveyard at midnight. The Beauregard Cemetery is still there today. Robert and Ike would take a small dirt road through the woods, cross over a crossroads, and walk into the then white-owned cemetery to play music. When Johnson next appeared in Robinsonville, he seemed to have acquired a miraculous guitar technique. It was during this journey that he supposedly made the age old deal.

The legend went that if an aspiring bluesman waited by the side of a deserted crossroads on a dark and moonless night, the Devil himself would come and tune his guitar, sealing a pact for the bluesman's soul and guaranteeing a lifetime of easy money, women, and fame. Though no one was there to witness it, many claim that Johnson had done just that. At the stroke of midnight, he walked down to the windswept crossroads at the junction of Highways 61 and 49 in Clarksdale, Mississippi. Reciting an ancient incantation, he called upon the Devil to make his bargain. In exchange for Johnson's immortal soul, the devil tuned his guitar, thereby giving him the abilities which he so desired. When he returned to Son House and the band, he asked if he could play a lick or two. At first they denied him but agreed to let Johnson show them what he had learned. The young man played his instrument with an unearthly style, his fingers dancing over the strings. When he finished their mouths were standing wide open. His voice moaned and wailed, expressing the deepest sorrows of

a condemned sinner. His song, *Crossroad Blues*, is a type of hymn, each verse invokes imagery used in voodoo ceremonies. Other songs like *Hell Hound on My Trail*, and *Me and the Devil Blues* tell of black magic and damnation. Johnson wasn't the only one who attributed his success to the devil, early blues singer Peetie Wheatstraw called himself the Devil's Son-in-Law and the High Sheriff of Hell. Robert Johnson recorded just twenty-nine songs between 1936 and 1937 and then died at age twenty-seven, the first member of the infamous "27 Club" made up of musicians who died tragically at that young age.

***

Voodoo Ancestors

Robert Johnson's songs are the foundation of modern blues and rock and roll. It has long been recognized that rock music derives from the American South, from spiritual and gospel music, from jazz, rhythm and blues. Less widely recognized is the fact that these forms of music derive, in turn, from a system of religious beliefs known as voodoo. If black music is the father of rock, voodoo is its grandfather. The words may be new, but the beats are ancient. They originated in Africa with the banging of drums made out of skins of sacrificed animals. These drum beats were used to call out spirits as the African tribes practiced their rituals.

Voodoo is a mixture of the distinct religion of West Africans called Vodun. For tribes who speak the Fon language, a *vodu* is simply a god, spirit or a sacred object. In the ancient capital city of Abomey, Africa, the spirits that speak through humans are called vodun and the word means

"mysteries." From vodun comes voodoo, and it is to this belief system that we must look for the roots of popular music. Voodoo's spread to the new world is due to the adaptability of its paradigms to mix with the host cultures and religions. It began with the arrival of the first batches of slaves in Haiti in the 17th century who had no trouble combining their traditions to build up a new syncretic religion. Voodoo is not so much Africa *in* the new world as it is Africa meeting the New World, absorbing it and being absorbed by it. In some areas it was the old religion of Dahomey mixed with Roman Catholicism. In Cuba it is known as Santeria, in Jamaica it is called Obeah, in Brazil, Macumba and in Haiti, Voudou. For captured slaves, it was the only way they could rebel or enact some sort of cosmic justice on their slave handlers.

There are thousands upon thousands of Voodoun Gods; it would be nearly impossible to list them all. Every voodoo rich culture brings more into the list, as Houn'gan (priest) or Mambos (priestess) die, they too, are added into the fold. Nana Buluku is the Supreme Deity of the Fon people. He made the universe and everything in it, however, they do not worship him because he is so far above them, all they can do is acknowledge his existence. At the head of the Haitian Voudon pantheon is the similar, Bon'Dye, a creator god who was so dissatisfied with his product that he abandoned it. He put into play emissaries called *loa* who were given the power over earth. Because Bon'Dye is unreachable, Vodouisants say their prayers to the lesser entities. Unfortunately these spirits don't like people very much and must be appeased with offerings and sacrifice. According to one gnostic voudon text[3], there was once a school of powerful magicians in Atlantis, who did not die in the cataclysm, but became spirits with amphibious bodies so they could continue their work under the ocean. They can be called upon, and through them anyone can become a "big lucky Hoodoo."

The loa are called down through ritual and can possess objects, people, animals or even an entire area can be blanketed by a consciousness. Multiple people in the area of possession can easily be taken by the same spirit. The loa are the same forces recognized in other African-based religions throughout the world and are sometimes called "orishas." The names may differ, but the force or power remains the same, with practitioners recognizing the same attributes of these forces.

The indigenous religion of West Africa is called *juju*, and is the practice of the Yoruba speaking people of Nigeria from which vodoun evolved. The Voodoo that originated with the Fon speaking people has similar gods and goddesses from juju, and shares many similar practices and beliefs as well. The gods and goddesses of juju are called orishas, just as they are in Santeria. These religions are ever changing in subtle ways by a process called Syncretism, which is the merging of different, seemingly contradictory belief systems. Far from what the Western world thinks as hocus pocus, juju is as formal and structured as any other religion. It is the worship of primal

forces, and a quest for total power and control. Juju fundamentally differs from other religions, for instance Christianity, where the doctrine is based on love and redemption, juju is based on fear and domination. Protestantism and Voodoo are always at odds and as an old Haitian saying goes, "If you want the loa to leave you alone—become a Protestant."

Jujumen seek only to appease the gods of evil, whom they fear. They believe that every misfortune in life is due to the evil orishas and so they must be placated with offerings to leave them alone. They are essentially slaves to these spirits. They see no point in appealing to a god of love who would care for you no matter what you do. In the secret symbolic language of juju, they refer to themselves as goats and everyone else as sheep. Many Africans who are nominally Christians or Muslims continue to practice juju in private. Author, Isiah Oke, recounts his upbringing as the grandson and successor of an important *babalorisha*, or juju high priest, in West Africa. Oke describes the traumatizing ceremonies he underwent in his training and also the ritual torture and murder that he was required to inflict on others. These practices all have the common themes of trauma based mind control, including demoralization, food deprivation, dissociation, and memory loss and spirit possession.

Juju is practiced openly in West Africa, but there is a secret and hidden side, one might say, a religion inside a religion that is believed to give power through blood. *"Our rituals are designed to appease the most horrid of our gods. And because our gods are so

fearsome-so must be the rituals: We believe that nothing better appeases the fierce spirits of juju than blood."[4] The relatively benign juju ceremony takes place in the public temple, but there is another sacrificial place hidden in the forest that they call the Shrine, where the gruesome and bloody rituals are performed. This secret dark side reflects many of the ancient mystery religions who functioned in the same manner as modern secret societies, with members sworn by oath not to reveal what goes on at meetings. *"Each of the pagan gods had, besides the public and open, a secret worship paid to him, to which none were admitted but those who had been selected by preparatory ceremonies called Initiation. This secret worship was termed the Mysteries."*[5]

***

The Crossroads

One of the most significant images in voodoo is that of the crossroads, which symbolizes the gate of access to the invisible of gods and spirits. The crossroads features prominently in Robert Johnson's music, and in today's popular culture. Musician, Eric Clapton, holds a special affinity with the crossroads. When Britney Spears had her breakdown in 2007, she had just checked out of his Crossroads clinic in Aruba. Most voodoo rituals and ceremonies commence with a salutation to the god who guards the crossroads and to pass the crossroads is to enter into voodoo initiation. A crossroads is never merely the visible intersection of two highways; it is also the representation of the meeting point between men and gods. The action of staking a vampire corresponds with the widespread tendency in the past to bury suicides, executed criminals, or witches with stakes in their hearts, at the crossroads. So, crossroads are even today feared by some people as highly haunted places, crowded with ghosts that have been unable to leave their gravesides.

A god both juju and voodoo have in common is Legba the Gate Keeper. Papa Legba is the synthesizing god of voodoo. He stands at the crossroads between the loa and the humans and is their intermediary. To the Yoruba people, Legba is the god of gates and is not a friend to man, but the enemy of an enemy. Legba battles Fate who is the bringer of bad fortune, so they pray to Legba in order that he will trick his enemy into leaving them alone. In voodoo ceremonies, Legba gives or denies permission to speak with the spirits. He is the chief, or king, of the loas, and is symbolized by the sun, and gold; and he is called the Master of the Highway. They say that any crossroads is a very spiritually dangerous place and every direction but one is wrong. Legba can help or hinder you; if he feels like it he will send you the wrong way and perhaps you will never return.

Kalfu is Legba's dark twin, and his name literally means crossroads. Kalfu is part of the Petwo family of Loa and the word *petwo* can also mean drum. The Petro rite in voudon is considered the darker self-serving ritual where the practitioner attempts to gain some godlike powers for himself. It is dedicated to the loa, Kalfou of un-tempered power, and usually involves an animal or human sacrifice, ecstatic dancing, mass possession, demonstration of powers, possible orgy, exor-

cism and sleeping in the ritual area. In Haitian Voodou, Kalfu is often envisioned as a young man or as a demon; his color is red and he favors rum infused with gunpowder. He is often associated with Satan and is the god of black magic. When Kalfu mounts a person, everyone at the service stops speaking because he allows evil loa to come to the ceremony. As the evil god of the crossroads, he controls all who venture within it, creating confusion and disorder wherever he goes. He often plays the trickster, impersonating his brother or following behind him, nullifying his deeds. He is the uncontrollable force of bad luck, grinning as he throws everything around him into disarray.

At the crossroads of life and death stands Baron Samedhi, a member of the Gue'de family who are the spirits of the dead. As keeper of the cemetery, Baron Samedhi is both the lord of eroticism and god of the grave. He represents the currents of death and sex and his symbol is a skull and cross, graves and shovels. He loves children but is very lustful. Baron Samedi holds a high status as a Freemason. Skeletal designs used in 32nd Degree initiation ceremonies, all-seeing eyes, skull and crossbones, funeral tools—these all belong to Baron Samedi as Grand Master of the celestial Lodge of Vodou Heaven.

In witchcraft, the crossroads are sacred to Diana/Hecate. One of the ancient trinities was that of Diana, Luna and Hecate, who are three aspects of the same female energy. She was called Diana on earth, Luna in Heaven and Hecate in Hell. Hecate is a premier deity in Satanism and she is their version of Aphrodite and Venus. Hecate is portrayed as both a virgin and a whore, and crossroads are her sacred places. It is at crossroads that witches, Grand Masters and Freemasons perform their rituals, because the crossroads are symbolic of the vortex points created where ley lines cross. In ritual sex magic, the wearing of clothes of the opposite

sex and the performance of bi-sexual acts are called "Crossroad Rites" and the women involved were called dikes. Crossroads are also places of human and animal sacrifice and Hecate is known as a 'sex and death goddess' as well as a goddess of witchcraft and sorcery. The significances of the crossroads make it a suitable place for holding Sabbaths and making pacts with the Devil.

A list of common hiero-glyphs compiled by Sir Alan Gar-diner is considered a standard reference in the study of Ancient Egyptian. The glyph O.49 is an O with and X inside and this he identifies with the Crossroads. It is used in Egyptian hieroglyphs as a determinative for the names of towns or city place names and is also an ideogram in the Egyptian word "city". When Aleister Crow-ley died, his successor Kenneth Grant, took over the O.T.O. Grant identifies the Mark of the Beast as the fusion of O and X. (the Phallus and the Kteis) *"The Heart of the Sigil of Nodens is identical with the Mark of the Beast... the fusion of O and X which produces the lightning flash."*⁶

***

*"The search for the use of music in devil posses-sion resulted in finding two main avenues. One is the use of beats in music to call the spirits or gods. The other is the altered state of consciousness."*⁶

Possession

Practically every religion that came before Judaism, Christiani-ty and Islam, practiced some form of spirit possession as a staple. The ancients knew exactly how to use music to elicit a mystical experience. Dance and music are so closely woven into the practice of ancient cults that one could al-most call them "dance religions." The dance itself is linked with di-vine possession, the mechanism by which the gods communicate with the faithful. Voodoo and its variants retain a number of key elements including music, chant-ing, dance, the sacrifice of hu-mans and animals, the eating of flesh and drinking of blood. Most

important of all, however, was the induced state of trance, or pos-session. Voudon is a possession cult with a formal liturgy and to be possessed by a god or spirit is the ultimate objective of the en-tire ceremony. When possession occurs they are literally mounted by the spirit as a man mounts a horse and is able to take control of its body.

Those cultures that choose to access the spirit world by possession have often used some form of rhythmically con-trolled noise to facilitate the com-munion. The shamans say they "ride their drum" to the World Tree. The classic possession cul-tures teach that the orisha ride the rhythm of the drum down into the dancing bodies and it is called the trance drum. Specific rhythms correspond to specific gods and it is the rhythm identi-fied with each god that is a pri-mary instrument in summoning him. No worship of the orisha is possible without the rhythms that call and speak for the god. By coming to the "drum trance" area, the natives were entering into a pact with the spirits that would permit them to take control of their minds and bodies and it can happen to anyone.

The people have learned that when the spirits enter their bodies, they feel no pain, they are gloriously excited and exhilarated, wave their arms, dance around wildly, and fall on the floor in apparent ecstasy. Amid the excitement of these rituals, the natives are overcome with an intense urge to want to have sex. Men wearing masks take young women into the bushes and have their way with them. They feel no remorse and are never confronted because their excuse it that they were quite literally possessed. Children conceived as a result of these rituals are considered illegitimate and are abandoned in the wilderness or sold to witch doctors. The spirits inhabiting their bodies can also give them feelings of depression, anger, and violence. The tradition of possession led from Africa to the shores of America. It began with ragtime, led to blues, and then jazz and later became rock 'n' roll. It was the intensity of the drums which came as a great shock attack on the physiology of men and women. The incessant, monotonous beats were the key to reviving the possession cults of the East and Africa in America. From America, through rock, it has been carried around the world.

It is easy to see how much a rock concert resembles a spirit possession ceremony. All of the elements are present. The rock star as priest, trance inducing rhythms and lights, faithful worshippers and willing vessels for possession. Like the Rolling Stones, and other rock figures, blues singers regularly performed a type of shamanistic ritual to induce a state of ecstatic hysteria in the audience. Blues singer, Bessie Smith for example would elicit from her listeners what was described as "religious frenzy." This would later come to characterize the rock concert, only adding increasingly explicit sexuality.

The Beatles were once barred from performing in Israel following an investigation that prompted the education ministry to conclude their performances caused mass hysteria. John Lennon talked openly about possession and his music. *"It's like being possessed, like a psychic or a medium"*[7] *"I felt like a hollow temple filled with many spirits, each one passing through me, each inhabiting me for a little time and then leaving to be replaced by another."*[8] *"Song writing is about getting the demon out of me. It's like being possessed. You try to go to sleep, but the song won't let you. So you have to get up and make it into something, and then you're allowed to sleep."*[9]

John Lennon is among those that can be quoted as having sold their soul for rock and roll. His wife Yoko Ono recounts the event: *"Finally it was a time to consummate all these spells by making a living sacrifice and signing a pact with the devil. For Lena was not a "white" witch. She was the real thing – a practitioner of black magic. There was no knowing what she planned to do to seal the bond of Lucifer. All she would say was that a witch's moon was nigh, and they had to make ready for the sacrifice. 'What sacrifice?' Yoko kept demanding. To which the old witch would reply, 'Don't be silly, girl. We've got to make a sacrifice with the blood of an innocent to the one who has the power.'"*[10]

***

"One could argue that multiple personality disorder is merely a modern, Western, term for what has been known for centuries as possession."[11]

Monarch Zombies?

In voodoo, a *zombi* is a person who has died and was buried, but who is later found in the possession of a *bokor*, or sorcerer, as his imbecilic slave. For them, the zombi are the living dead—corpses which have been extracted from their tombs and raised by a process which no one really knows. Recently it has been reported that a zombie like state can be brought on by the drug, scopolamine, which is called "Devil's Breath" and can block free will, wipe memory and even kill. It is said that the bokor breathes his soul into a bottle then passes it beneath the corpse's nose. The spark of life which the sorcerer gives the corpse is not enough to fully restore him. He has no memory or knowledge of his condition. The zombi is a beast of burden which his master exploits without mercy. Their docility is total, provided you never give them salt. If they are given even one grain, the fog in their mind will lift, they will act revenge on their master, and then go in search of their tombs.

The zombie phenomenon in popular culture is a perfect allegory to Monarch programming. If rock music belongs to the Devil, then Pop music is most certainly the product of the CIA Monarch Mind Control Program. Could it be that most of our entertainers are prototype mind controlled zombies? Many of the mind-controlled slaves report having had voodoo rituals as part of their trauma, and many have "voodoo dolls" placed into their Systems. When vows and oaths are made, a personal object is given to the satanic cult for the Keeper of the Seals to guard. If the vow is broken, voodoo magic can be used against the offender by using the object given in the sealing.

In the late eighteenth century, German physician, Franz Mesmer, was exploring the healing possibilities of hypnosis, when he discovered an entirely different person could emerge when a patient was in a hypnotic state, another "self." Shortly after, psychologists coined the phrase "alter ego" to describe patients struggling with Dissociative Identity Disorder or multiple personalities. The Monarch programming phenomenon would explain why so many rock stars have alter egos. David Bowie is Ziggy Stardust, his "Martian messiah who twanged a guitar." Rapper Eminem is also Slim Shady, his "evil" side who able to say what Marshall couldn't and specialized in rape, murder, drugs and gore. Lady Gaga is alternately Jo Calderone, a swearing, chain smoking, and crotch grabbing male persona. Garth Brooks had an episode as Chris Gaines, a proto-emo figure created by Brooks to explore pop music. Rapper Nicki Minaj reportedly has three famous alter egos called Barbie, Roman Zolanski—her gay male twin, and Martha, Roman's mother.

Therapist James Noblitt, gives a detailed account of his work with MPD patients in the book *Cult and Ritual Abuse*. During his practice, he began to notice a common thread among his patients that were from var-ious different lives and backgrounds. In one group therapy session he used the phrase "deeper and deeper" and accidentally put his entire group into a trance. He found that most people who suffer with multiple personality disorder were also victims of some form of satanic ritual abuse. Noblitt gives fourteen commonalities between MPD and demonic possession. Both phenomenon are more frequently identified in females; occur sometime after traumatic experiences; are associated with ancient and modern cults; and have a sense of secrecy. In both cases victims experience co-conscious awareness; exhibit uncharacteristic behavior that defies physical limitation; and demonstrate paranormal psychic abilities.

Darker than just an alter ego, some stars seem to be suffering from a literal demonic possession called Disturbia, the name used for Rhianna's video, where she is seemingly possessed by the devil. Eminem states in one song *"My soul is possessed by this devil, my new name is Rain Man."* In 2008, Beyonce unveiled her dark alter, Sasha Fierce, a devilish seductress who battles with Beyonce's light side. Shasha was born during the music video *Crazy in Love* with Jay-Z, where the old Beyonce is locked in a car and burns to death. Pictures displayed on beyonce.com reveal Sasha posing behind a motorcycle with a goat of Baphomet on it. The theme of the album, *I Am... Sasha Fierce*, revolves around the duality between the godly Beyonce and the evil Sasha. *"I created my stage persona to protect myself, so that when I go home, I don't have to think about what it* is I do. Sasha isn't me."[12] *"It's like a blackout. When I'm onstage I don't know what the crap happens. I am gone."*[13] Apparently, that alter of hers is dead now as Beyonce told *Allure* magazine that she killed Sasha in 2010, although she may have made an appearance at the 2013 Super Bowl where here facial expressions were so "fierce", demonic and unflattering that her publicist's tried to have them removed from the internet.

The word monarch is not only defined within the context of royal nobility or the government project, but also refers to the feeling a person gets when they are undergoing trauma induced by electroshock. A feeling of being light headed is reported; as if one is floating or fluttering above their body like a butterfly. There is also the symbolic representation of the transformation or metamorphosis from one creature to another. Pay attention to the infinite number of times a young celebrity is pictured in the Monarch butterfly motif. They are proving to you who is owned by them and they go through a tremendous amount of effort to inject as many references to Monarch programming into popular culture as possible.

The idea that a butterfly's wings might create tiny changes in the atmosphere that ultimately cause a tornado is called the "Butterfly Effect." The flapping wing represents a small change in the initial condition of the system, which causes a chain reaction of events leading to large-scale phenomena. In a book called, *The Tipping Point: How Little Things Can Make a Big Difference*, author Malcom Gladwell, cites examples of the small percentages of a total population required to act, "at

Lady Gaga told *Rolling Stone Magazine** "I do have morbid dreams. But I put them in the show. A lot of the work I do is an exorcism for the fans but also for myself...The [video] piece in the show where I'm eating the heart, its a real bovine heart....I have this recurring dream sometimes where there's a phantom in my home. And he takes me into a room, and there's a blonde girl with ropes tied to all four of her limbs. And she's got my shoes on from the Grammys. Go figure —pyscho. And the ropes are pulling her apart. I never see her get pulled apart, but I just watch her whimper, and then the phantom says to me, 'If you want me to stop hurting her and if you want your family to be OK, you will cut your wrist.' And I think that he has his own, like, crazy wrist-cutting device. And he has this honey in, like, Tupperware, and it looks like sweet-and-sour sauce with a lot of MSG from New York. Just bizarre. And he wants me to pour the honey into the wound, and then put cream over it and a gauze." GaGa was confused by her dream and turned to other sources to find out its meaning."So I looked up the dream, and I couldn't find anything about it anywhere. And my mother goes, 'Isn't that an illuminati ritual?' And I was like, 'Oh, my God!'"

which the momentum for change becomes unstoppable" for the entire society. "*Ideas and products and messages and behaviors spread like viruses do...The success of any kind of social epidemic is heavily dependent on the involvement of people with a particular and rare set of social gifts.*" Entertainers make perfect puppets for social control. Musician and founder of ethnomusicology, Béla Bartók, spent his entire life studying the folk music of various cultures. He deduced that the music produced by a culture is inseparable from the nature of that culture. Singing and dancing serve to draw groups together, direct the emotions of the people, and prepare them for joint action, and more often throughout history, the action for which the crowd was being pre-

pared for was warfare. The modern day zombie characters do not need a sorcerer to resurrect them, their ailment is viral. They have the ability to self-replicate by feeding off of healthy brains. By placing Monarch slaves in key positions of influence and leadership, could they be creating a "butterfly effect" of mass demonic possession?

***

"I like to think of the history of rock and roll like the origin of Greek drama. That started out on the threshing floors during the crucial seasons, and was originally a band of acolytes dancing and singing. Then, one day, a possessed person jumped out of the crowd and started imitating a god."

—Jim Morrison

Cult Leaders

All control of the population remains on the level of the emotions and the nervous system. Whoever controls the dance floor holds influence over generations. Thanks to the media we can witness the effect of music on the masses. Singers and musicians exercise tremendous power over crowds of adoring fans. They can very easily be likened to cult leaders with both demonic and godlike influence. Bob Dylan called Elvis "the deity supreme of rock 'n' roll religion as it exists today." Elvis Presley was the King of Rock and Roll and would often state that when he was on stage he was possessed by a surge of electricity. Elvis' father, Vernon Presley, states that when Elvis was born, the entire house was surrounded

by a strange blue light. They also witnessed a UFO, many years later, over Graceland, which triggered Vernon's memory about Elvis' birth. Unknown to most fans, Elvis testified that he encountered cosmic beings as a child who allowed him to peer deep into the future and invested him with supernatural powers, including the ability to move clouds, levitate objects, and heal the sick. Whenever the King did healing prayers, he would invoke the words "First we must think of the blue light." The beings also told him of his origins from a blue planet far away in the Orion constellation. Elvis told close personal friend, Wanda June Hill, that the beings were "light forms" who often came to him when he was in the closet being punished and played music for him, and spoke to him about his home planet. Eyewitness accounts of Elvis report that he absolutely had the ability to perform miracles. On one occasion during a long bout of rain, someone complained that they wished it would stop. Elvis threw open the curtain, stepped out onto the patio and commanded the clouds to part, which they immediately did.

In Larry Geller's biography of Elvis Presley, *If I Can Dream: Elvis' Own Story*, Elvis admits to receiving help from the spirits and was obsessed with UFO's of which he encountered many. According to Geller who was Elvis' hairstylist and spiritual advisor, he always traveled with a portable bookcase containing over three hundred volumes of esoteric books. Among his favorites were, *Isis Unveiled* by Madame Blavatsky, *Secret Teaching of All the Ages* and *The Mystical Christ* by Manly P. Hall, *Esoteric Healing* by Alice Bailey, *The Inner Life* by Charles Leadbeater, *Aquarian Gospel of Jesus the Christ* by Levi H. Dowling, *The Prophet* by Kahilil Gibran, *The First and Last Freedom* by Krishnamurti, *The Urantia Book*, *The Rosicrucian Cosmo-Conception*, *The Book of Numbers* by Cheiro, *Chariots of the Gods* by Erich Von Däniken, and the six-volume set *Life and Teaching of the Masters of the Far East* by Baird T. Spalding. Elvis was an enormous fan of Theosophist leader Madame Blavatsky who published the journal called *Lucifer*. He was so enamored with Blavatsky's book, *The Voice of Silence*, which contains Tibetan incantations, he sometimes read from it onstage and was inspired by it to name his own gospel group, "Voice." Madame Blavatsky and the Theosophical Society heavily influenced Hitler and taught about the existence of ascended masters called the Great White Brotherhood. Elvis believed that he was working under the aegis of these masters.

Who can forget Elvis' first performance of *Hound Dog* on the Ed Sullivan show in 1956? With every thrust of his pelvis the audience screamed hysterically. America had never seen anything like it. Elvis Presley was the first high profile product of African music in America which the official culture could not ignore. When whites started playing rock 'n' roll, the whole aesthetic of Western performance changed. In voodoo ceremonies, the devotee is spurred by a god within him and throws himself into a series of improvisational bodily movements. The only difference between a rock concert and a voodoo ritual is that in voodoo, the audience knows that it is the loa, and not the performer, to which their admiration goes. The rite of possession by the spirits became the standard of American performance in rock 'n' roll. Jim Morrison credited unseen forces he nicknamed "The Lords" for helping him write and perform music, and claimed when he was onstage the spirits of dead Indians took over him. Little Richard, Jerry Lee Lewis, James Brown, Janis Joplin, Joni Mitchell, Jerry Garcia, Santana, Prince;—they all let themselves be possessed by a god they sometimes could not name, but more often than not it turned out to be some form of Satan.

At one Elvis concert, on August 31, 1957, hysterical crowds trampled people, including Canadian reporter, John Kirkwood, who wrote: "*It was* like watching a demented army swarm down the hillside to do battle in the plain when those frenzied teenagers stormed the field. Elvis and his music played a small part in the dizzy circus. The big show was provided by Vancouver teenagers, transformed into writhing, frenzied idiots of delight by the savage jungle beat music. A hard, bitter core of teenage troublemakers turned Elvis Presley's one-night stand at the Empire Stadium into the most disgusting exhibition of mass hysteria and lunacy this city has ever witnessed."

Pop Star Ke$ha considers herself a cult leader and openly admits it. She began her career in the business by co-writing the Britney Spears song, *Until the End of the World,* and appeared in Katy Perry's music video, *I Kissed a Girl.* The lyrics of her song, *Dancing with the Devil,* state openly that she has sold her soul for fame and now she can never escape. The art on the cover of the single is classic Monarch symbolism—her head has been cracked open and stitched back together. The video for her song, *Die Young,* features Ke$ha in a black veil, posing as if she was some sort of religious statue. She is then carried on the shoulders of four men, as in cultures where people carry statues of the Virgin Mary in the streets. They break into a chapel and trash the place. Upside down crosses, pentagrams, and VV symbolism hypnotically flash across the screen. Ke$ha pulls the "Devil" card from the Tarot. Flashes of mating wolves reinforce the 7th Satanic Statement that man is just an animal. Since the song is called *Die Young,* we are lead to think that Ke$ha is shot and killed by the police in the end. This song was topping the charts at the time of the Sandy Hook school massacre, and was dropped from the airwaves for its eerily prophetic message. Her song, *Supernatural,* is about an incubus that comes to her in the night and she has confessed to actually having "sexy times" with ghosts, and told Jimmy Kimmel in 2013 that her vagina is haunted and needs to be exorcised by her "hypnotherapist." During her tour called "Sleazy" she can be seen drinking blood from a heart and dancing with her mother who is wearing a giant penis costume.

It would be no surprise if we start seeing cults develop around the loss of the King of Pop, Michael Jackson, whose career is also heavily laden with Monarch symbolism. We all know that these people have power, but ultimately they are someone else's slave, whether they answer to their handler or directly to Satan, only they can say. Either way, that sounds pretty stressful. Elvis Presley's involvement in the military makes him a prime candidate for the Monarch mind control program and Ke$ha's symbolism suggests the same thing. They are just front men to hypnotize and zombify the masses; and if you think you've heard that annoying song on the radio one too many times, according to the techniques of famous cult leaders, Charles Manson and Adolf Hitler, they both agree that repetition is the key.

***

"If I told you what our music is really about, we'd probably all get arrested,"
—Bob Dylan, 1965

Slavery Old and New

In ancient times, the idea that some human beings should be under the absolute subjection of others was taken for granted and went virtually unquestioned. The actual practice was so widely accepted that it has been claimed that there was no action, belief or institution in Graeco-Roman antiquity that was not one way or other affected by the possibility that someone involved might be a slave.

Voodoo comes from a very specific area of Africa which was once called Dahomey, modern day Benin, and was known as the Slave Coast. At its height in the 17th and 18th centuries, slavery was a booming business. Transactions were mainly negotiated with tribal princelings who had long standing trade relations with the whites and were thirsting for European products. In the kingdom of Dahomey, the slave trade was a national industry and the economy of the whole country was based on annual raids against neighboring tribes. The African king kept a monopoly of the many thousand prisoners and sold them to the whites, keeping some back for sacrifice or slave labor. So, we see that slavery is not a matter of race, but of economics. Natives worshipped their king like good little slaves, and in turn he sold them out for European money. This continues today on a mass scale where they have turned the plantation global.

If you think about it, just about everything on earth is produced by some form of slavery. Most of your video game technology comes from factories where they would rather die than continue to make iphones. Most of the world's toys are made in China, by children. Coffee and chocolate come from plantations in South America, blood diamonds come from Africa, and so on. Even your fruit and vegetables are picked by migrant farm workers from Mexico. On the other hand, to obtain any of these things you must submit yourself to a form of slavery under contract known as a job, and it only ends at the top. What parts of our lives are not controlled? When we go to our jobs, our sovereignty is compromised and we submit ourselves to a boss. After work we are too tired so the only entertainment we can muster for ourselves is television. The situation has gotten so bad that black slaves in 1860 were freer than all Americans and all humans are today—at least they knew that they were slaves. When we consume corporate products that were made in sweat shops and mega factories, we are paying to keep humankind enslaved, even if you can't see the prisoners. If you complain about "the white man" and the atrocities of colonial slavery; but still buy Air Jordan's and listen to Jay-Z, you are the worst kind of hypocrite.

"I have experimented with some of the newest, and still the oldest, methods for control of slaves. Ancient Rome would envy us if my program is implemented."
—Willie Lynch

In the new colony of Virginia, in 1712, there was a speech delivered on the bank of the James River by a British slave owner from the West Indies named Willie Lynch. He was invited to teach his methods of mind control to slave owners there and the term "lynching" is derived from his name. His methods were as simply brilliant as they were sadistic. He used the same techniques for breaking his slaves as he did with breaking horses as he saw no difference between them, even down to the practice of breeding "mules" out of people. *"What we do with horses is that we break them from one form of life to another; that is, we reduce them from their natural state in nature. Whereas nature provides them with the natural capacity to take care of their offspring, we break that natural string of independence from them and thereby create a dependency status, so that we may be able to get from them useful production for our business and pleasure."* The goal that he hoped would propagate slavery indefinitely was to create such a psychological terror in a woman's mind that she would raise her young to never rebel against authority. *"The Black slaves after receiving this indoctrination shall carry on and will become self-refueling and self-generating for HUNDREDS of years, maybe THOUSANDS."* We can see where his methods of psychological warfare still apply across the board in popular culture today.

His first method was division into an infinite number of groups: *"I have outlined a number of differences among the slaves; and I take these differences and make them bigger. I use fear, distrust and envy for control purposes…On top of my list is age…The second is color or shade. There is intelligence, size, sex, sizes of plantations, status on plantations…whether the slaves live in the valley, on a hill, East, West, North, South, have fine hair, course hair, or is tall or short. Now that you have a list of differences…I shall assure you that distrust is stronger than trust and envy stronger than adulation, respect, or admiration…Don't forget, you must pitch the OLD black male vs. the YOUNG black male…You must use the DARK skin slaves vs. the LIGHT skin slaves…You must use the FEMALE vs. the MALE, and the MALE vs. the FEMALE…You must also have white servants and overseers [who] distrust all Blacks. But it is necessary that your slaves trust and depend on us. They must love, respect and trust only us…If used intensely for one year, the slaves themselves will remain perpetually distrustful."*

His next method was controlling the language of the slave. He knew that if you could teach the population that you wish to keep subjugated a perverted form of dialect, you could make them look perpetually foolish and they would never pose any competition in the world of business, finance and politics. Today, rap and hip hop music is the largest progenitor of slang and Ebonics. *"For further severance from their original beginning, we must completely annihilate the mother tongue…and institute a new language that involves the new life's work of both. You know language is a peculiar institution. It leads to the heart of a people. The more a foreigner knows about the language of another country the more he is able to move through all levels of that society….For example, if you take a slave, if you teach him all about your language, he will know all your secrets, and he is then no more a slave, for you can't fool him any longer.…So you have to be careful in setting up the new language; for the slaves would soon be in your house, talking to you as 'man to man' and that is death to our economic system."*

There are more black people under correctional control today than were enslaved in 1850. According to The Sentencing Project, an advocacy group dedicated to changing how we think about crime and punishment, *"More than 60 percent of the people in prison are now racial and ethnic minorities. For black males in their thirties, one in every ten is in prison or jail on any given day."* The United States has a higher rate of incarceration than any other nation and spends billions every year to keep people behind bars. Privatized prisons are individually owned prison companies which enter into contractual agreements with the government to house prisoners and receive a per diem or monthly rate for each prisoner confined in the facility. Because of this, there is a major incentive for pushing violence, crime, drugs and easy money in music that young men listen to. Inmates are used for slave labor and produce for the world's biggest corporations for pennies on the dollar. Each month, California inmates process more than 680,000 pounds of beef, 400,000 pounds of chicken products, 450,000 gallons of milk, 280,000 loaves of bread, and 2.9 million eggs from 160,000 inmate-raised hens. Starbucks subcontractor, Signature Packaging Solutions, has hired Washington prisoners to package coffees as well as Nintendo Game Boys. Subcontractor, Third Generation, uses South Carolina inmates to sew lingerie and leisure wear for Victoria's Secret and JCPenney. Federal Prison Industries, a.k.a. Unicor, says that in addition to soldiers' uniforms, bedding, shoes, helmets, and flak vests, inmates have produced missile cables and wiring harnesses for jets and tanks. Inmates are also used in call centers for political campaigns.

***

"There is nothing more efficacious to drive away evil spirits than Musical Harmony"
—Agrippa, *Three Books of Occult Philosophy*

The Magical Power of Music
Music can directly affect those centers of the brain which govern emotion and in turn this can govern and transform a personality. It neutralizes rational judgment and can elicit all manner of emotion from worship to arousal, sorrow to joy, love to hate or even terror. Song and dance is employed in all classical Mystery Schools to induce altered states of consciousness. Music's power has been used since the first shaman and was mathematically formalized in Ancient Greece. The very word "music" can be traced back to Greek mythology when humans often prayed to the Muses for good voices. They were

Big Jay McNeely at the Los Angeles Olympic Auditorium in 1953 was immortalized in photos by Bob Willoughby

the goddesses of singing, art, and science and were believed to inspire excellence in these pursuits. The Sirens were similar to the muses, born from the muse Terpsichore, and competed with them in singing contests. The sirens were tricksters and known to sing beautiful songs on the rocky shorelines to lure sailors to their deaths.

"Both the universe and man, the macrocosm and the microcosm, are constructed on the same harmonic proportions."—Pythagoras

For the Pythagoreans and Hermeticists, "harmonic attunement" was the governing principle of the universe, along with the microcosm/macrocosm. To them, harmony was equal to beauty which was equal to goodness. This applied not just to music but the whole of creation which was perceived as a single, all-embracing musical instrument where harmony was the binding agent. Through the conduit of music, cosmic energy could infuse with the individual. The powers of the cosmos could be invoked not by beseeching them, as in conventional prayer, but by placing oneself "in tune" with them. *"The Hermetic magicians of the Renaissance believed that the sounds of specific words, intoned by a human voice, conjoined with mathematically perfect calculated precision could shatter the barriers between dimensions of reality, just as a note struck on a tuning fork can shatter glass. When such perfection was achieved, the resulting invocation became activated. Thus, the invisible and elemental forces of the cosmos could move freely and intermingle with the human world.*

Music, in short, was akin to prayer, imbued with a dynamic and active potency."[14]

The Greek legend tells how the god, Apollo, gave Orpheus a lyre which produced harmonies that joined all of Nature together in peace and joy. Inspired by this Orphic tradition of music and science, Pythagoras conducted perhaps the world's first physics experiment. By plucking strings of different lengths, he discovered that sound vibrations naturally occurred in a sequence of whole tones that repeat in a pattern of seven. Like the seven naturally occurring colors of the rainbow, the seven tones and all of Creation is a singing matrix of frequencies. In music theory, the circle of fifths is a visual representation of the pentagram, the Phi ratio and the Fibonacci sequence. The fifth is the interval found in most sacred music, and has a powerful harmonizing effect on the human energy system. It is the first harmonic sounded by a plucked string, and is what gives the note its depth and beauty. Its sacred sound is the hallmark of the Gregorian chant. In fact, most divinely inspired music, including some New Age music and that of indigenous cultures, is built around the musical interval of the fifth. Pythagoras recognized the fifth for its universal beauty and described it as an archetypal expression of harmony that demonstrates the "fitting together" of microcosm and macrocosm in an inseparable whole. The fifth is a beautiful sound because it demonstrates how the universe works.

"You can hypnotize people with music, and when you get them at their weakest point, you can preach into their subconscious whatever you want to say."—Jimi Hendrix

In 1665, the Dutch scientist, Christiaan Huygens, noticed that if two clocks were placed next to each other, they would soon begin ticking synchronously—and so was discovered the Law of Entrainment. Because of entrainment, music is often used beneficially to control heart rate and other rhythms in the body and also to facilitate altered states of consciousness. It is also possible to use the rhythm of sound to control the rhythm of brain waves. Twentieth-century scientists discovered an ancient usage of different tones and entrainment and successfully used them to produce an altered state of consciousness. A drum beat synchronized with the beat of the human heart will, if gradually accelerated, cause the heart to accelerate to match tempo. In its pulsating appeal to heart and blood, certain kinds of rock music can stimulate something basic, elemental and unquestionably sexual. In mythology, the fertility god, Pan, played sensual pipes that were credited with the power to drive an individual insane with lust. In 1922, Trixie Smith released a record titled, "My Man Rocks Me with One Steady Roll." The term "rocking and rolling" was used back then as slang for dancing or sex. The word "roll" is used to describe the rolling in bed with the sexual partner as they both "rock" together. The phrase was later coined by Ohio disk jockey, Alan Freed, in 1951.

Rock & Roll is the focal

point of youth culture and in order to understand it you must go all the way back to the earliest days of human civilization. The concert is a direct descendant of the ancient Mysteries; the drugs, crashing drums, wild costumes, screaming flutes, pyrotechnics, sex, and a feeling of transcendence, all of the elements are present. Mystery cult centers were the ancient equivalent of today's concert halls which is why so many have names like the "Orpheum", "Apollo" and "Palladium." One of the earliest mysteries were practiced in ancient Egypt. They were known by many names in Greece, *mysteria*, *bakchoi*, and *orgia*, where the modern word "orgy" comes from. The initiates mostly worshipped "suffering gods" and experienced their dramas and deaths through ritual theater and music. The cults practiced secret initiations which were never to be shared with outsiders on pain of imprisonment or death. Each mystery cult was usually centered on a single god among many others they recognized. The cults weren't so much about dogma as they were about the experience of *being* the god, and sex was often a crucial part of the process. The Egyptian mystery cults had their very own version of pop stars in the form of sultry temple singers who were known as the "harem of the gods." There are many similarities between the voodoo traditions of the Yoruba people and the Egyptian Mysteries. Many historians believe that the West African traditions were imported from ancient Egypt when the ancestors of the Yoruba migrated west as a result of political upheavals.

***

"Writing for a penny a word is ridiculous. If a man really wants to make a million dollars, the best way would be to start his own religion."—L.R.H.

Scientology & Babalon Working

We've all seen the mammoth buildings in the heart of every metropolis, adjacent to some of the world's busiest tourist attractions and nestled away in the most luxurious private locations. Most days there are attractive, normal-looking people out front offering a free personality test to curious passersby. If you have two hours to kill, you can take a quiz that will illustrate supposed strengths and weaknesses in your psyche, and if you have enough money, they'll be happy to tell you more. If not, you're welcome to come back when you do have thousands of dollars to spend. If you can't afford it, you will never know the secrets o f true bliss and just what the heck Dianetics is. Are the Scientologists merely a foundation to supply gold medals for Tom Cruise and John Travolta, or is it something more sinister? The founder of Scientology is L. Ron Hubbard, who

throughout the 1930's wrote a large variety of mystery, action, and sci-fi pulp fiction stories. Hubbard joined the U.S. Navy in 1941 and allegedly acquired knowledge of subliminal mind control through his military service with Navy Intelligence.

In 1945 Hubbard was recovering from various ailments that led to his discharge from the military. It was during that time that he became good friends with famous Thelemite, Jack Parsons who took a great liking to him. Parsons, sometimes called Crowley's most promising pupil, was an unorthodox genius whose solid rocket fuel helped NASA send spacecraft to the moon and a lunar crater on its dark side is named for him. Parsons was also another self-proclaimed Antichrist who performed magick rituals to create a new sort of human being that would finally destroy Christianity. Parsons owned a great mansion in the Pasadena hills where he invited anyone who had an "atheist and bohemian nature" to live with him. His residence also served as an O.T.O. lodge and meeting place for science fiction writers such as Robert Heinlein and Ray

Bradbury.

Hubbard's incredible war stories made him popular in the group. Parsons saw much potential in L. Ron and allowed him to move into his compound. He provided Hubbard with the formal training that he lacked, revealing to Hubbard the secrets of the highest grades of the O.T.O. In a 1946 communication to Aleister Crowley, Parsons wrote about Hubbard: *"Although Ron has no formal training in Magick, he has an extraordinary amount of experience and understanding in the field. From some of his experiences I deduced that he is in direct touch with some higher intelligence…He describes his Angel as a beautiful winged woman with red hair whom he calls the Empress and who has guided him through his life and saved him many times. He is the most Thelemic person I have ever met and is in complete accord with our own principles. He is also interested in establishing the New Aeon."*[15]

When Hubbard moved in, he immediately put the moves on Parson's girlfriend, Sarah "Betty" Northrup, and stole her from him. This was a huge blow to Parson's ego, not only because of the transfer of affection but also because Parson thought of himself as a god-man and above petty human emotions. In order to deal with his jealousy, Parsons dedicated himself to conjuring a new "magical partner" in his workings of sex magic. It seemed a necessity to Parsons that the Aeon of Horus be fulfilled by a passive complement to Horus, and he saw this as being the force of the goddess Babalon. Spelled

with an "a" instead of a "y" for its numerological significance, this goddess is very prominent in the Thelema pantheon of deities. They collaborated on a magickal endeavor to evoke her, called the "Babalon Working." Its purpose was the elemental manifestation of the force of Babalon to produce an avatar or incarnation that would bring to fruition the Aeon of Horus. The Scarlet Woman of the O.T.O. has an interesting connection to juju and the mysteries of the Yoruba people. Odudua or Iya Agba is the Supreme Genetrix worshipped by the people of Dahomey, Benin and neighboring kingdoms. Her name means "the black one." Odudua was the presiding deity of the city of Ado, which means "whoredom" where a temple of sacred prostitution was established in her name. The initiates of the O.T.O. believe that Ado is a terrestrial power zone where, according to tradition, the earth menstruates. Thus, they equate Odudua to the Scarlet Woman.

Despite Hubbard's betrayal of Parsons, he was determined to continue on with the

working and believed he needed Hubbard's assistance. In a series of rituals, undertaken in January 1946, they attempted to summon an "elemental" who would participate in further rituals. Hubbard acted as a scribe noting the results of the ritual. During one ceremony where Hubbard was "scrying in the Aethyr" while Parsons took notes, he described a vision he had of a savage and beautiful woman riding naked on a great cat-like beast. This, they thought, must be Sophia incarnate. The rituals performed drew largely upon the Enochian magical system devised by John Dee, magician and consultant to Queen Elizabeth I, and Sir Edward Kelley. They were also heavily based on rituals and sex magic outlined by Crowley, who borrowed many aspects of his Babalon from combining the goddess Ishtar, with the figure of Mystery Babylon, the Great Whore in the Book of Revelation.

Their elemental arrived a short while later in the form of a red haired woman named Marjorie Cameron, who remained in the dark about the working until long after it was completed, even though they used her for the next phase. According to Cameron the next part of the Babalon working consisted of her and Parsons spending two weeks in bed together. The ultimate purpose of the working seems to have been the birth of a child, a Moonchild, into whom Babalon would incarnate. The "magical child" Parsons was pursuing was one outlined by Crowley as conceived by "a certain perversion of the Office" meaning unorthodox ritual sex. This female child would be a product of her magically influenced environment rather than her heredity and according to Crowley, would be "mightier than all kings of the earth." No such child ever manifested, and although Parsons and Cameron both referred to Cameron as Babalon, the working was clearly aimed at bringing the goddess down to earth from somewhere else.

The relationship between Jack Parsons, L. Ron Hubbard and Aleister Crowley was crucial to reinforcing government scientists and the military into black magic rites. Parsons, Hubbard, and the O.T.O. knew that during the first atomic bomb blast at the trinity site in New Mexico, a large steel cylinder had been placed near ground zero. They were obsessed with the idea that this cylinder had been a means of radioactively animating a tiny person, known in alchemy as a homunculus. In the inner lore of the O.T.O., nuclear power is regarded as a form of diabolic consciousness, a literal demonic energy. O.T.O. doctrine, reflecting ancient occult tradition, holds that only by first animating the homunculus and keeping it incarnate on earth could tampering with nature advance to the state of genetic engineering, cloning and crossbreeding.

Soon after the Working, Hubbard ran off with Parsons' girlfriend and a great deal of his money. Reduced to living in abject poverty, it still took a while for Parsons to accept that he had been defrauded by his magickal partner. Hubbard later claimed that his actions had been under the orders of Naval Intelligence

the entire time. During one of his transmissions from the other side, Parsons had been told that he would become "living flame" before Babalon incarnated; and this prophesy proved to be chillingly correct. On the afternoon of June 17, 1952 he dropped a highly unstable explosive, a fulminate of mercury, and died of horrific injuries an hour later.

***

Dianetic Success

The year 1950 was an unexpected success for Hubbard, who was then broke and living in New Jersey. He published the book, *Dianetics*, what he called "the modern science of mental health" and went from being unheard of to a guru almost instantly. Mailman would deliver sacks of letters daily from the unhappy and desperate who had read the book and wanted Hubbard to take them to psychological paradise. That same year he opened a Dianetics clinic, where the hopeful and newly converted could come for a fee, and their ills, from loneliness to cancer, would be cured. Dianetics was the new scientific revolution and L. Ron Hubbard was its prophet.

Essentially a confessional, auditing is one of the main services of Scientology and is also called counseling or processing where one Scientologist, the "preclear" is questioned by someone called the auditor who charges up to hundreds of dollars a session. The auditor's basic aid is the "E-meter", a skin galvanometer that is said to help him diagnose the problems of his client. Advertised as a self-help therapy, it is based on the premise that by recalling negative experiences or "engrams", a person can free him-

self from repressed feelings that cripple his life. The process was a sort of regression hypnotherapy whereby the clusters of body thetans that inhabit all of us are removed allowing us to regain our divine potential.

What is a body theatan you might ask? This is the secret, Kirstey Alley, Beck, Lisa Marie Presley and many more have paid upwards of $350,000 to learn. The Xenu story is part of the Church of Scientology's secret OT III "Advanced Technology." These events are known within Scientology as "Incident II" and considered a sacred and esoteric teaching. According to Hubbard, it all began 75 million years ago with an intergalactic alien ruler named Xenu who was in charge of seventy six planets in this part of the galaxy, including Earth, which was known as "Teegeeack." Xenu had quite the problem, all of his planets were overpopulated, so he formulated a plan. With the help of his renegades and evil psychiatrists, he called in trillions of people for "income tax inspections" but when they showed up for their audit they were swiftly injected with a paralyzing mixture of alcohol and glycol.

The unconscious people were loaded onto space planes that looked like DC-8s, except that they had rocket motors and could fly three hundred light years in nine weeks. These space planes flew to earth and the unconscious people were stacked around the bases of the volcanoes and hydrogen bombs were lowered into the volcanoes and detonated. All of the souls of the dead people, the thetans, were blown about by the nuclear winds. Xenu and the renegades captured the thetans and placed them into boxes and shipped them to huge cinemas where they spent days watching special 3D motion pictures. These films implanted ideas of Christianity, Judaism, Islam and other lies into the thetans, confusing them. As they left the cinema they began to cluster together, believing they were one entity. The theatan clusters inhabited the few living bodies that were left—our ancestors. Meanwhile, Xenu was finally overthrown by the Loyal Officers and locked away in a mountain

sealed by a force field that is powered by an eternal battery where he remains to this very day. All religions as we know them are merely the remnants of thoughts that were implanted into the thetans. These body thetans inhibit us all, warping our perception of reality. The souls of these immolated aliens, now cling to us like body lice, through reincarnation after reincarnation, and can only be removed through hours of auditing at a cost of hundreds of thousands of dollars.[16]

During the 1960s, Scientology was run from a ship called the *Apollo* that carried Hubbard and his followers. His trusted aides were teenage girls who wore a uniform of platforms and hot pants and referred to Hubbard as "Commodore." He would eventually add other ships to his fleet he called Sea Org and ran his operation in typical trauma based mind control protocol. Cadets went through severe demoralization, sleep deprivation, forced abortions, and torturous punishments, such as being bound and thrown overboard and later rescued, when they made a mistake. Everyone who joins the Sea Org signs a contract for a billion years making a commitment to return and serve the church for endless life times to come.

Starting in 1973, the church was responsible for "Operation Snow White", which planted operatives inside the IRS, FBI, Justice Department, and the American Medical Association. These operatives stole and copied thousands of documents that could be used in silencing Scientology opponents. The group began calling itself a church at conveniently the same time the Internal Revenue Service started demanding tax payments from them. For decades Scientology fought the IRS, until an odd thing happened in 1993—the IRS capitulated and granted Scientology tax exempt status after one of the groups high ranking officials had an unscheduled, closed door meeting with the then head of the IRS. Along with their tax exempt status, Scientology can boast that they have more visible celebrities than any other denomination in the United States. In 1955, Hubbard made an interesting proposal to his followers, they should pick a celebrity and try to get him or her to join Scientology. He ordered his followers to recruit celebrities by any means necessary and not take no for an answer when trying to bring your celebrity in for formal auditing sessions.

One aspect of the Church of Scientology is an example of a controlled opposition, revealing a portion of the ugly truth to sell you a solution. They claim that what the doctors tell you about mental illness is a myth and that modern day psychiatry is infested with evil and in league with the pharmaceutical industry to keep people enslaved. This is true. Priscilla Presley is a devoted member and speaks publicly for the religion's anti-psychiatry front group, the CCHR. In 2013, Jayden Smith created a scandal on Twitter urging kids to drop out of school claiming "School Is The Tool To Brainwash The Youth" Also true. According to Radar Online, Jayden attended the New Village Leadership Academy in Los Angeles, which his parents founded in 2008 on a curriculum influenced by Scientology, but is now home schooled.

***

104

"So the idea of Scientology 'auditing' or 'counseling' or 'processing' is to free yourself from your body and to return you to the original godlike state or, in Scientology jargon, an operating Thetan—O.T. We are all fallen gods, according to Scientology, and the goal is to be returned to that state."
—L. Ron Hubbard Jr.

Science or Satanism?

L. Ron Hubbard Jr. was born in 1934, weighing 2.2 pounds, after only six and a half months in the womb. He was the result of failed abortion attempt by his father. Ron Jr. claims to recall, at six years old, another vivid scene of his father performing an abortion ritual on his mother with a coat hanger. This, he says, stems from his father's secret life in which he was deeply involved in the occult and black magic. When Hubbard Sr. was sixteen and living in Washington. D.C., he read *The Book of Law* by Aleister Crowley and was fascinated by the creation of a Moon Child, *"When Crowley died in 1947, my father then decided that he should wear the cloak of the beast and become the most powerful being in the universe."*[17]

Ron Jr. claims that his father was a staunch Satanist before anything else and this was the foundation of everything that he did. *"I believed in Satanism. There was no other religion in the house! Scientology and black magic. What a lot of people don't realize is that Scientology is black magic that is just spread out over a long time period. To perform black magic generally takes a few hours or, at most, a few weeks. But in Scientology it's* stretched out over a lifetime, and so you don't see it. Black magic is the inner core of Scientology—and it is probably the only part of Scientology that really works. Also, you've got to realize that my father did not worship Satan. He thought he was Satan. He was one with Satan. He had a direct pipeline of communication and power with him. My father wouldn't have worshiped anything. I mean, when you think you're the most powerful being in the universe, you have no respect for anything, let alone worship."*[18]

He recalls LRH Sr. as an angry drunk and a drug fiend. Just like Walt Disney, Hitler and others with a guilty conscience, LRH Sr. had to have his clothes washed and washed and washed and would take showers half a dozen times a day. Ron Jr. was just sixteen when *Dianetics* was published and witnessed the watershed transition of his father from broke science fiction writer to religious icon. Ron Jr. was not only a disciple but a willing organizer in the new movement and was to be so throughout the 1950's. He calls Scientology a power-and-money-and-intelligence-gathering game. Ron Jr. was involved in all manner of processing of the church which included pioneering experiments in hypnosis, lobotomy, electroshock, sensory deprivation, ESP and drugs all rolled into a method he called "Soul Cracking."

"The explanation is sort of long and complicated. The basic rationale is that there are some powers in this universe that are pretty strong. As an example, Hitler was involved in the same black magic and the same occult practices that my father was. The identical ones. Which, as I have said, stem clear back to before Egyptian times. It's a very secret thing. Very powerful and very workable and very dangerous. Brainwashing is nothing compared to it. The proper term would be 'soul cracking.' It's like cracking open the soul, which then opens various doors to the power that exists, the satanic and demonic powers. Simply put, it's like a tunnel or an avenue or a doorway. Pulling that power into yourself through another person—and using women, especially—is incredibly insidious....It is the ultimate vampirism, the ultimate mindfuck, instead of going for blood, you're going for their soul. And you take drugs in order to reach that state where you can, quite literally, like a psychic hammer, break their soul, and pull the power through. He designed his Scientology Oper-*

ating Thetan techniques to do the same thing. But, of course, it takes a couple of hundred hours of auditing and mega-thousands of dollars for the privilege of having your head turned into a glass Humpty Dumpty—shattered into a million pieces. It may sound like incredible gibberish, but it made my father a fortune."[19]

***

More Crowley Inspired Counterculture

The British invasion did not come as four long haired young boys, but a little old bald head on the cover of *St. Pepper's Lonely Hearts Club Band*. This curious figure in the top left, looking like Uncle Fester, is none other than Aleister Crowley, the unsung hero of the 1960's rock movement and the O.G. of sex, drugs and rock and roll. The Scarlett Woman also makes an appearance in the artwork as a little four armed lady in red on the bottom center. Most people are quite aware of Crowley's appearance on the album among the Beatles' other heroes, but few ask why he made the cut. John Lennon made the connection clear in an interview with *Playboy* when he said that *"The whole Beatle idea was to do what you want, right? To take your own responsibility."* Lennon was paraphrasing "Do what thou

wilt," which is one of the central doctrines of Thelema. The Beatles were only the first of many counter culture rock musicians in the 1960s to openly cite Crowley as a major influence. Other famous devotees include the Rolling Stones, Iron Maiden, Hall & Oats, and Ozzy Osbourne who wrote a song about him, titled *Mr. Crowley*. Led Zeppelin's guitarist Jimmy Page was so invested in Thelema that he bought Crowley's mansion on the Loch Ness in Scotland.

Apart from the rock stars who helped to popularize the New Aeon, we can see the others who revolutionized western culture in deep and lasting ways. Harry Smith, was a Thelemite whose influence on folk and rock music cannot be overstated. Aldous Huxley once dined with Aleister Crowley in Berlin, and the rumor goes that Crowley introduced him to peyote. Timothy Leary said on national television that he saw himself as continuing Crowley's work. These are only a few of the major streams of influence that Crowley had in shaping the movement of the 1960s. Crowley's efforts to make Eastern philosophy more accessible to the West, helped to inspire the whole New Age movement. Gerald Gardner, the man who brought contemporary Wicca to public, was heavily inspired by *The Book of the Law* and his involvement in the O.T.O. *The Book of the Law* appears to

accurately predict the Nazi era, the psychedelic sixties, and the growing return to pagan practices and ancient Egyptian black magic. However, it's not much of a prophecy if what you're claiming to channel you were later on instrumental in creating anyway. No wonder the Beatles included Crowley on that album cover as one of the most influential people of the 20th century. He was the orchestrator, the stage manager and the director of the show.

***

Release the Stars

As I travelled around the country in 2012, I would often hear the same phrase repeated over and over, from coast to coast, from 11 to 60 year olds. The phrase was, "I *love* Lady Gaga!" The inflection and cadence was the same every time, as if it were instantly downloaded to everyone at once. Today's popular culture creates an interesting relationship between us and our entertainers. They help us escape boredom and make us use our imagination, they show us new worlds and characters, and they are there at every major milestone in our lives. Their movies are watched on our first dates and their music is played at our weddings, birthdays, funerals and anniversaries. Nothing can bring back nostalgia like your old song on the radio or your favorite movie or TV show. Who wouldn't want to spend time with their favorite musician to thank them for touching your heart, and in that way they sort of become like extended friends and family.

On the other hand, we scrutinize and judge them, build them up and tear them down, take their art and throw it in their face. With help from the CIA tabloids they are traumatized and stalked by the paparazzi in the name of fame. Their slavery and demoralization should upset us, but the audience is part of the problem. If you really loved your idols you wouldn't just take from them. You wouldn't pay to watch them debase themselves, and then spit it back in their face. You wouldn't use their trauma based mind controlled spectacle to further your career in the media. You wouldn't secretly enjoy their performance and then call them a slut afterwards. If you really loved your celebs then you would want to see them free of their mind control prison.

If you had lived through the American Civil War would you have been pro or against slavery? Would you have had the courage to be part of the Underground Railroad, helping other humans to freedom under punishment of hanging if you were caught? If you lived in Europe during WWII would you have sheltered Jews and other targeted individuals in your home, even if it meant you and your family potentially dying in a firing squad? It is too easy to say yes, of course I would. Today we have an unprecedented and precious opportunity to begin freeing all mankind from all forms of slavery and it all begins with spreading awareness. We realize that this is a cult of secrecy and disbelief so we will attempt to spread the word.

In our culture, celebrities have the largest following and social influence. We encourage high profile, and all other, whistle blowers and recovering victims to come forward with their stories. We offer a knowledgeable and safe community where the information will be shared for the largest impact. We believe that by helping to "release the stars" of their mind control that it will be easier for other low profile victims to follow. By highlighting the evidence of mind control in the media face to face, and through independent media, we may be able to provide the public with the keys of knowledge to decode the agenda for themselves.

WeirdStuff! Insane Clown Posse's *Miracles*

If the Satanists can secretly incorporate the devil into the pop music, can angels hide God in rap music? The tale of ICP's video Miracles is super weird stuff. In April, 2010, the rap duo shocked the world when they announced that they were secretly evangelical Christians in the lyrics of their song, *Thy Unveiling*. Then came their mind-blowing video, *Miracles*, which was about 180o away from anything they had ever done before. Violent J and Shaggy 2 Dope claim that have spent the last twenty years faking their thuggish persona in order to trick fans into accepting Jesus with hidden messages in their songs. Of course, one might argue that twenty years was an incredibly long time for them to have pretended to be insane murderous clowns. The news shook the Juggalo community to its core. While some fans claimed they'd actually had an inkling, having deciphered some of the hidden messages in several songs, others said they felt deeply betrayed and outraged—they'd been innocently enjoying all those songs about chopping people up and shooting women, and it was Christian music all along??

*Rolling Stone Magazine, Issue, July, 2010

1. Rolling Stone Magazine, February, 1976
2. The Blues: The Experts Guide to the Best Blues Recordings, Michael Erlewine
3. Voudon Gnostic Workbook, Michael Bertiaux
4. Blood Secrets, Isaiah Oke
5. Revised Encyclopedia of Freemasonry, Albert Mackey
6. Demon Possession and Music, Dr. Juanita McElwain
7. The Playboy Interviews with John Lennon and Yoko Ono, Berkeley, 1982
8. People Magazine, August, 1988
9. The Playboy Interviews
10. The Lives of John Lennon, Albert Goldman
11. Cult & Ritual Abuse, James Noblitt & Pamela Sue Perskin
12. Parade Magazine, December 2006
13. GQ Magazine, Feb, 2013
14. The Elixir and the Stone, Michael Baigent & Richard Leigh
15. The Great Beast: The Life and Magick of Aleister Crowley, John Symonds
16. An Illustrated History of Scientology, L. Rick Vodicka
17. Penthouse Magazine, June, 1983
18. Ibid
19. Ibid

Books:
Voodoo in Haiti, Alfred Metraux
The Supernatural, Douglas Hill & Pat Williams
Planet Drum, Hart, Lieberman, and Sonneborn
A Treasury of Afro-American Folklore, Harold Courlander
Music and the Mind, Anthony Storr

Perdurabo: The Life of Aleister Crowley, Richard Kaczynski
Aleister Crowley: The Biography, Tobias Churton
Sex and Rockets, John Carter
The Secret History of Rock & Roll, Christopher Knowles
Cults of the Shadow, Kenneth Grant
Alien Rock, The Rock 'n' Roll Extra Terrestrial Connection, Michael C. Luckman

**You Say You Want a Revolution, Robert Pielke

Other Resources:
Essay: A New and Greater Pagan Cult: Gerald Gardner & Ordo Templi Orientis, Rodney Orpheus

"In a society in which nearly everybody is dominated by somebody else's mind or by a disembodied mind, it becomes increasingly difficult to learn the truth about the activities of governments and corporations, about the quality or value of products, or about the health of one's own place and economy.

In such a society, also, our private economies will depend less and less upon the private ownership of real, usable property, and more and more upon property that is institutional and abstract, beyond individual control, such as money, insurance policies, certificates of deposit, stocks, and shares. And as our private economies become more abstract, the mutual, free helps and pleasures of family and community life will be supplanted by a kind of displaced or placeless citizenship and by commerce with impersonal and self-interested suppliers...

Thus, although we are not slaves in name, and cannot be carried to market and sold as somebody else's legal chattels, we are free only within narrow limits. For all our talk about liberation and personal autonomy, there are few choices that we are free to make. What would be the point, for example, if a majority of our people decided to be self-employed?

The great enemy of freedom is the alignment of political power with wealth. This alignment destroys the commonwealth - that is, the natural wealth of localities and the local economies of household, neighborhood, and community - and so destroys democracy, of which the commonwealth is the foundation and practical means."
—Wendell Berry,
The Art of the Commonplace: The Agrarian Essays

Do what thou wilt

Radioactive Seawater Impact Map (update: 10.08.11)

shall be the whole

of the Law.

PROGRAMMED FOR WAR

"In the early months of WWI, on Christmas Eve, men on both sides laid down their arms and joined in a spontaneous celebration. Despite orders to continue shooting, the unofficial truce spread across the front lines. Even the participants found what they were doing incredible: Germans placed candlelit Christmas trees on trench parapets, warring soldiers sang carols, and men on opposing sides shared food parcels from home. They climbed from the trenches to meet in 'No Man's Land' where they buried the dead, exchanged gifts, ate and drank together, and even played soccer."
—Stanley Weintraub, Silent Night

There is one secret so powerful that, were it revealed, it would cause such an upheaval to the matrix, that the spell of the sorcerers might instantly be broken. This occult knowledge is so shocking that the reader might, at first, find hard to comprehend, but try to suspend your disbelief for the following statement: **Humans are good.** Contrary to an abundance of evidence that suggests otherwise, it is a fact that people are not really that great

at killing each other. We know you're thinking this outrageous statement couldn't possibly be true, since you're constantly running from people trying to murder you on a daily basis, right? Or, could it be that billions of us all over the planet move about their entire existence without harming any one? Human beings instinctively going out of their way to try not to hurt each other? Crazy, we know...

***

"There is a substantial body of evidence demonstrating humans' seemingly natural aversion to killing. Much of the research in this area has been conducted by the military; analysts have found that soldiers tend to intentionally fire over the enemy's head, or not to fire at all... What these studies have taught the military is that in order to get soldiers to shoot to kill, to actively participate in violence, the soldiers must be sufficiently desensitized to the act of

killing. In other words, they have to learn not to feel—and not to feel responsible—for their actions. They must be taught to override their own conscience. Yet, these studies also demonstrate that even in the face of immediate danger, in situations of extreme violence, most people are averse to killing."
—Melanie Joy, *Why We Love Dogs, Eat Pigs and Wear Cows*

Natural Born Killers?

In the midst of the fierce fighting during the Second World War, as the battles intensified, the US Army was faced with an extraordinary number of cases involving mental breakdowns among their troops. More than 800,000 men were classified unfit for duty due to psychiatric reasons. An additional 504,000 soldiers were lost from the fighting effort due to psychological collapse. Almost half of all men evacuated from combat were sent home suffering from what we now call post-traumatic stress disorder. In desperation, the Army turned to psychoanalysis to try and deal with the steadily rising influx of combat fatigue related injuries in soldiers returning home from combat. *"Shocked by the appalling percentage of the emotionally unstable revealed by the WWII draft figures, congress, in 1946, passed the national mental health act which recognized for the first time that mental illness was a national problem."*[1] Using techniques developed by Freud, doctors tried to convince soldiers that breakdowns were not the direct result of combat, but were merely pre-existent childhood memories of violent feelings and subconscious desires which they had repressed because they were too frightening. The

military concluded that an averse attitude toward killing was driven by irrational, primitive and violent forces. What's that soldier? You don't like killing people? Report to the nearest psycho analysis center for your hypno-regression therapy, on the double! In 1946, President Truman signed the National Mental Health Act, born out of these war time "discoveries" by psychoanalysts that millions of draftees were suffering from "hidden anxieties and fears." The aim of the act was to deal with an invisible threat to society called Mental Health, insinuating that people who were opposed to killing others and being shot at should please visit their nearest psychological guidance center to learn how to control their emotions. Among the psychiatric literature on war, repugnance toward killing is referred to as "acute combat reaction." Psychological trauma resulting from slaughter is called "stress." Psychologist, Peter Marin, has argued that military history is largely "a massive unconscious cover-up" in which we hide the true nature of combat. Even among the psychological and psychiatric literature on war, there is, according to Marin, "a kind of madness at work." He notes that psychological trauma resulting from "slaughter and atrocity is called 'stress,' as if the clinicians…are talking about an executive's overwork."

In 1755, a French engineer named Du Perron presented the young Louis XVI with a "military organ", which discharged twenty-four bullets at the same time. It was the forerunner of the modern machine gun. The weapon was considered to be so deadly that the offer was refused and the

inventor was admonished by the king, who deemed Du Perron an enemy to humanity for creating such a deadly weapon. Despite an unbroken tradition of violence and war, man is not by nature a killer. The vast majority of combatants throughout history, who, at the moment when they had the opportunity to kill the enemy, have found themselves hesitant and unable to do so. Lt. George Roupell, a commander in WWI, stated that the only way to stop his men from firing into the air was to draw his sword and walk down the trench, beating the men on the backside and telling them to fire low. As an infantry platoon leader and company commander in WWII, Colonel Albert J. Brown observed that *"Squad leaders and platoon sergeants had to move up and down the firing line kicking men to get them to fire. We felt like we were doing good to get two or three men out of a squad to fire."*[2] In the Vietnam War, more than fifty-thousand bullets were fired for every one enemy soldier killed. Of the 27,574 muskets recovered from the Civil War's famous Battle of Gettysburg, nearly ninety percent of them were still loaded.

Prior to WWII it was assumed that the average soldier would kill in combat simply because his country and his leaders told him it was essential to defend his nation. What they found was that only about 15 to 20 percent of soldiers would take any part in their weapons or fire at the enemy. Even highly trained soldiers, in the heat of battle, will choose to run supplies, relay messages, load, pass weapons, tend to the wounded—anything but actually fire the killing shot. All of this and more is evidence that there exists a powerful, innate human resistance to killing one's own species, and many times humans will die before they can overcome it.

The application of the fight or flight response model, one that traditional psychology holds as a law of nature, is the appropriate set of choices for creatures faced with danger *other* than that which comes from its own species. For responses of creatures confronted with aggression from their own kind, the set of options is expanded to include posturing and submission. Posturing is intimidating but is mostly harmless. Deadly animals rarely use their full force against each other, instead they go through a series of posturing, mock battle and submission that is vital to the survival of the species. Among tribesmen and primitive warriors in almost every culture, there are patterns of aggression and very highly orchestrated and ritualized displays of physical prowess and competitiveness; but only a tiny level of actual bloodshed. Tribes in New Guinea who are excellent marksmen, will take the feathers off of their arrows rendering them useless before they go to war. The American Indian form of battle called "counting coup" or simply tagging their opponent, was considered to be far more important and humiliating than wounding or killing.

So, if we are such a peaceful species, then why does there always seem to be so much conflict? Most, if not all of the wars throughout history, were orchestrated by invisible governments, who use agent provocateurs to manipulate the masses and capitulate the violence. Modern mili-

tary training techniques can partially overcome the inclination to posture. The history of warfare is the search for more effective means to condition men to overcome their natural resistance toward killing their fellow man. Military conditioning employs methods of trauma based mind control, such as thousands of hours of repetitive drilling, paired with the ever present incentive of physical violence as the penalty for failure to perform correctly.

Lt. Col. Dave Grossman is a military expert on how to condition people so that they will kill. He writes in his book, *On Killing*, that the same process the government has used to condition soldiers to kill, is being utilized by the entertainment industry. The only major difference is that in the military, men are taught to kill only on command. To be efficient and desensitized killers, who are loyal, and will act on command, while society and our children are constantly being exposed to death, and killing with the entertainment industry, which is also desensitizing, and is ultimately conditioning all of us, subliminally, to relate our real life experiences with things we have witnessed though the media. Our children are being taught to kill whenever they want to, via TV's "entertainment." It begins innocently with cartoons and then goes on to the countless acts of violence depicted as the child grows up. Then the parents, through neglect or conscious decision, begin to permit the child to watch R rated movies featuring vivid depictions of knives penetrating and protruding from skin, long shots of blood spurting from severed limbs, and bullets ripping into bodies and

exploding out the back in showers of blood and brains. *"In a kind of reverse Clockwork Orange classical conditioning process, adolescents in movie theaters across the nation, and watching television at home, are seeing the detailed, horrible suffering and killing of human beings, and they are learning to associate this killing and suffering with entertainment, pleasure, their favorite soft drink, their favorite candy bar, and the close, intimate contact of their date."*[3] Rifts in society combined with violence in the media and in interactive video games indiscriminately condition children to kill. The same process the military uses to effectively enable killing in young draftee soldiers is being applied to the civilian population of this nation. Negative interaction content in video games indiscriminately and cunningly deceives our children into thinking that killing is just a normal part of life, while desensitizing us further from innocence and shifting our perspective closer towards darkness, and familiarizing us with the thought of death. The military uses the same process to effectively justify war, and condition its soldiers into becoming virtual killing machines that see killing as the only viable option in conflict. This is the same tactic of manipulation and conditioning, which is being applied to the civilian population of this nation through subliminal and esoteric means.

Countless scholarly studies have proven that if we put media violence in a child's life, we are more likely to get violent behavior. When people become angry or frightened, they stop thinking with their forebrain, the mind of a human being, and start thinking with their midbrain which is indistinguishable from the mind of an animal. They are literally "scared out of their wits" and start behaving with survival instinct, like a cornered animal in danger. Through popular culture, children are conditioned to become desensitized to overcome their biological inhibitions toward killing and to see the world as a threatening place. George Gerbner is a pioneer researcher on the long term effects of television on society, known as Cultivation Theory. He argued that people who watched a considerable amount of television tended to think of the world as an intimidating and unforgiving place. *"The primary proposition of cultivation theory states that the more time people spend 'living' in the television world, the more likely they are to believe social reality portrayed on television."*[4] Cultivation leaves people with a misperception of what is true in our environment. He coined the term "mean world syndrome" to describe a phenomenon where the violence-related content of mass media makes viewers believe that the world is more dangerous than it truly is.

One major method of turning innocent babies into killers is they must be made to override their own conscience. In 1943, Walt Disney released a cartoon called *Education for Death: The Making of a Nazi*. The film features the story of little Hans, a boy born and raised in Nazi Germany, who is educated to become a merciless soldier. The narrator says: **"To begin with, Nazi control over a German child starts as soon as it's born."** As Hans grows, he hears a distorted version of Sleeping Beauty where the prince rescues the princess, representing Germany, from a wicked witch called Democracy. The knight in shining armor is none other than Adolf Hitler. Can you imagine the audacity of the Nazis, using fairy tales for mind control? Because of this distorted children's story, Hans becomes greatly fascinated with Hitler as he and the rest of the young members of the Hitler Youth give his portrait the "Sieg Heil" salute.

When Hans is sick and bedridden, his mother prays for him and we see he learns what it means to be compassionate. A Nazi officer bangs on the door to take Hans away, but his mother says he is too sick and needs more care. The Nazi officer orders her to heal her son quickly, implying if the child does not get well soon, he will be euthanized. He commands her not to do anything more to him that will cause him to be weak, explaining that a soldier must show no emotion, mercy or feelings whatsoever. Hans recovers and resumes his indoctrination in a school classroom where he and the rest of his classmates watch as the teacher draws a cartoon on the blackboard of a rabbit being eaten by a fox. In virtue of his mother's tender care, Hans feels sorry for the rabbit. The teacher is outraged and orders him to sit in the corner wearing a dunce cap. As Hans serves his punishment, he hears the rest of the classmates "correctly" interpret the cartoon as *"the world belongs to the strong...and to the brutal!"* This sparks Hans to recant his remark, and declare that the weak must be destroyed.

Nazi ideology emphasizes that man is a savage beast and that human nature should reflect the law of the jungle. There is just one tiny flaw in this logic: you are not a fox. You are not a lion or a sheep or a reptile. You are man-kind. You were born with free will and the knowledge of good and evil. This should be recognized as our conscience. This means that every person, in their heart, knows that all life is sacred and an extension of himself. We have a natural affinity, within all of us, that acts like a moral compass, and gives us a sense of what is right and wrong. When we live in constant violation to this, when we secretly

know we are wrong, this creates a schism in the brain. A great deal of neurosis plagues the individual who recognizes that he is breaking the common rules of his own kind. He is ashamed of himself and his species, but he does not have the strength of conviction to live in the higher level of his own consciousness. The word Nazi is synonymous with mindless killing machine. Pay attention to how many times the soldier is portrayed in the media with his face darkened or obscured or in photo advertising with the top of his head cropped off. Is this a subliminal reference that his brain is missing, or symbolic of mind alteration?

***

"When the human soul suffers a greater strain than it can bear, it would thus become separated from the body, leaving the animal soul, or sidereal body in its place, and these human remains would be less alive in a sense than a mere animal. Dead persons of this kind are said to be identified by the complete extinction of the moral and affectionate sense: they are neither bad nor good; they are dead. Such beings, who are

the poisonous fungi of the human race, absorb the life of living beings to their fullest possible extent, and this is why their proximity depletes the soul and chills the heart…These are dead people whom we mistake for living beings; these are vampires whom we regard as friends!"—Eliphas Levi, Transcendental Magic

Honor & Glory

Everyone who has ever been to boot camp has experienced trauma based mind control. The military induced training methods that increased firing rates after WWII are referred to as "programming" or "re-programming." The psychological techniques used to split a personality are the same used for initiation into any type of cult. First, you must breakdown, demoralize and degrade a human. You must tell him he is nothing on his own, but by joining the military, fraternity, sorority, religion, or whatever; he could be great or become a chosen one. Groups who have all powerful leaders, who control their environment, control all information and eventually control the way their

followers think, have one basic thing in common, they have found people who are willing to take that first step of surrendering to an authority figure they hope has all the answers.

The horrors that these people encounter trying to be all they can be, doesn't just come at the hands of their "enemies." In 2013, the Senate Armed Services Committee held hearings on the epidemic of sexual assault in the armed forces. Reported rapes in the military are at an obscene level, with male on male violence on the rise. While the military has been arguing that it can clean up its act, the numbers prove otherwise. According to the Department of Defense's Sexual Assault Prevention and Response Office, there were 26,000 reported cases of sexual assault in the U.S. armed forces in 2012. Rape in the military is a lot like rape in civilian life. They rape because they can, and because the stigma is placed on the victim not the rapist. There is a huge difference between the actual numbers of soldiers who have experienced Military Sexual Trauma (MST), compared to those who fully report it. This is due to victims' fears of retaliation, including possible discharge from service or being overlooked for a promotion. Sexual predators in the military operate the same as they do in the church. The more hierarchical an institution is, the more the victim is stigmatized and the abuser gets away with it. In 2013, the Pentagon released a report that shows sexual assaults in the military have increased sharply, to the rate of seventy per day. This shocking report came just after the officer in charge of the Air Force's Sexual Assault Prevention and Response Office, Lt. Col. Jeffrey Krusinski, was charged with sexual battery.

A soldier can leave the battlefield, but that doesn't mean the war is over. When they return home they are never the same person as when they left. Men and women in the military are returning only to face a new set of struggles, as they carry physical and psychological wounds into a society that doesn't fully understand their experience or their sacrifice. Self-medicating with alcohol is common and often starts with a desperate need to get to sleep and stay asleep, but studies* show that heavy alcohol consumption exacerbates PTSD symptoms over time. The way that U.S. Government and Veteran's Administration treats its military veterans, is absolutely disgusting, proving, that they don't treat, or care for our veterans as individuals, but more like they are a number. Some of these men and women gave up everything to serve their country, protect their citizens' rights, and the freedoms of this nation. Sadly, they are often mistreated, as if they were a burden on society once deemed injured or disabled. Men and women who have literally sacrificed everything, including their lives, to serve their country are being medicated, labeled as crazy, tossed aside, and treated like human garbage by the military that sent them to combat, and the Veteran's Administration, who vowed to offer competent after care for those who need it.

You would think that wounded soldiers returning from war should easily be able to apply for the benefits that they were promised. Unfortunately, the complete opposite is the case. Applying for veteran benefits is extremely complicated, and there is a staggering amount of medical records, which are constantly being lost, or just seemingly happen to disappear within the D.O.D. VA employees are actually paid bonuses for denying claims. This explains why approximately 70% of the claims submitted to the Veterans Administration are refused or sent back to be redone. Vets have to fill out an absurdly complicated twenty-three page application and if they make even one small mistake their applications can be stonewalled for years.

The U.S. government does not prepare soldiers to come back and reintegrate into society. They kick them to the curb and hope that they can find jobs. The unemployment rate for veterans is much higher than the overall rate of unemployment in the U.S., and military veterans are becoming homeless at a much faster rate than the general population as well. A high percentage of military families have been losing their homes since 2008 and at last count there were 200,000 veterans sleeping on the streets of America. The U.S. Department of Veterans Affairs reveals that, *"The number of homeless Vietnam era veterans is greater than the number of service persons who died during the war."*

On top of everything else, the Department of Homeland Security has labeled military veterans as potential terrorists. This is not just philosophy on paper. Now, we are actually starting to see veterans rounded up and shipped off to mental institutions for evaluation if they express views that the government does not like. Once a military vet is determined to be "mentally ill", they can be arrested by the authorities at any time. After witnessing how vets are treated, it is absolutely baffling to see that anyone is still willingly registering for the armed services.

More evidence that demonstrates the humans' appetite for killing is not what they would have you to believe is the rate of suicide among military personnel. The conflict in Vietnam was the first war in recorded history whose combat deaths were later to be exceeded by the suicides of its veterans. When the boys came home from serving their country they found that, due to the horrific things they had witnessed, they could no longer function in society. The World Socialist Website reports that U.S. military suicide rates are at a record high. *"American troops are taking their own lives in the largest numbers since records began to be kept in 1980. It is indisputable that it is linked to the stresses on soldiers caused by the wars in Afghanistan and Iraq. The 'significant stresses' would include killing; repeated exposure to scenes of death and injury; the constant threat of death or injury; and the dehumanizing policing operations that American soldiers have been ordered to conduct against civilian populations."*

In 2011 the U.S. military lost 165 soldiers to suicide, a record that narrowly beat the 2009 level of 160. By the end of 2012 things had gotten much worse, and by the end of November the suicide deaths were up to 303. Putting this in perspective, that's actually more fatalities than the total number of U.S. troops slain in combat in all of 2012. In 2013, CNN announced that every day, 22 veterans take their own lives. As shocking as the number is, they estimate that it may actually be higher. The military has been desperate to get a handle on the rising suicide rate, making several very public efforts, none of which seems to have accomplished any positive results or even scratched the surface of this growing epidemic. Congress is pushing for a new law, allowing the military to ask "unstable" troops whether they own any personal guns. As with most of the legislative solutions to this problem it seems focused more on adding to the stigma of being considered "at risk" than actually encouraging people to seek help.

***

Heroes & Satyrs

Just as Princess Programming uses perverted ideology to shape the feminine psyche, so does its counterpart, the programming of the warrior. Since most people are good and want to avoid conflict at all cost, how do you make them willing to fight? What turns a perfectly good human being into a monster? You must call him a Hero and make him believe he is fighting for truth, freedom and justice. With a warped sense of morality, a Hero can be made to do almost anything. We are by nature a passive species but there can be no heroism without an enemy and without combat. The hero must be desensitized toward death. The Brotherhood knows that in order to take over the world by open force, they would have to organize a mind controlled army who would not be affected by what they do to their fellow countrymen, or even their own families. One of the ways to control a person is to create an enemy, get them angry and then channel that hate at a predestined target.

Before there was written language there were various stories about brave, superhuman heroes. These legends were created, and recounted, as a way to teach you how to behave. Mythologist, Joseph Campbell writes about the concept of the monomyth in his book, *The Hero with a Thousand Faces*. Campbell outlines that a common pattern exists beneath the narrative elements of most iconic myths, regardless of their origin or time of creation. His comparison of classical mythology, which focused on the archetypal hero and his journey, proved the same pattern has been used throughout history from Osiris to *Star Wars*. The basic stories of the hero overcoming the villain, or the great man who sacrifices himself for the greater good of the whole, are what drive civilization. In this culture creation, the people are the hardware and the mythology is the software. Stories were the basis of education in tribal culture. Once humans began to go through the process of citification, leaders no longer needed to teach people how to hunt, farm and fish for themselves. They needed "citizens" who would fall in line, without question, and fight for the empire. The youth were taught why preservation of their city was so important and why they should hate the neighboring tribe. To do this, they used thrilling tales of past heroes who fought and died valiantly for the freedoms they now enjoy.

Hercules was the greatest of the Greek heroes, a paragon of masculinity and divine ancestry. He was the son of Zeus and mortal Alcmene and was the hero who found Prometheus, killed the vulture, broke the chains, and liberated the long-suffering god. In Rome and the modern West, he is known as Hercules of extraordinary strength, courage, ingenuity, and sexual prowess with both males and females. His iconographic attributes are the lion skin and the club. By conquering dangerous archaic forces he is said to have "made the world safe for mankind" and to be its benefactor.

Hercules is the Greek version of Horus the vengeful hero. Horus is described as a god of war, revenge and bloodshed. Horus or Ares (Mars) and Hercules are identical in name and nature; the

Greek version of the war-god is based upon the Egyptian original, from which our word "hero" derives. Horus or Heru, was the Hero, the solar vanquisher of the demon of darkness and of the dragon of the deep. Aleister Crowley interpreted the onset of WWI and WWII as proof of *The Book of the Law's* power made manifest. He considered it to be the "baptism of blood", traditionally associated with the birth of a new Aeon. *"There is a Magical Operation of maximum importance: the Initiation of a New Aeon. When it becomes necessary to utter a Word, the whole Planet must be bathed in blood. Before man is ready to accept the Law of Thelema, the Great War must be fought. This Bloody Sacrifice is the critical point of the World-Ceremony of the Proclamation of Horus, the Crowned and Conquering Child, as Lord of the Aeon."* [5] This paragraph was written in the summer of 1911, just three years before its fulfillment.

Walt Disney's version of *Hercules* is born with the gods on Mt. Olympus but he is cursed by his uncle, Hades, the god of the underworld, who turned him into a mortal, but he is still able to retain his superhuman strength. When Hercules feels he doesn't fit in with society he goes searching for his true parents. He travels to the temple of Zeus, with only a symbol of the gods to guide him. Zeus explains that Hercules can become a god again and return to Olympus if he can become a true hero. On his quest he finds the satyr Philoctetes—"Phil" for short—a trainer of heroes and archetype of Pan. When I saw Phil hold up a card that said "1" and then a digit fell off to reveal the number "11", I knew this was an esoteric clue. Crowley adopted the old English spelling of the word Magick with a "k" to indicate the peculiar nature of his teachings, which had a special affinity with the number 11 which he called the One beyond Ten. Because Cabbalists regarded the number 10 as the stable number of the system of Divine Emanations, or sephiroth, the number eleven was considered accursed, because it was outside the system. Therefore, Crowley adopted this as his formula.

> "Crowley's Magick is valuable to the student, but only the advanced student could use it with profit. The formulae, too, on which he works, would be considered averse and evil by occultists accustomed to the Qabalistic tradition, for he uses 11 instead of 10 as the basis of his battery of knocks, in the magical ceremonies, and 11 is the number of the Qliphoth. No hint of this is given in the text, and it is an ugly trap for the unwary student."
> —*Applied Magic*, Dion Fortune

The god Pan, whose cult spread across the Greek world, was a leader of the faun or satyrs and the world's most infamous sex predator. Half man and half goat, he was a lustful and energetic god and a giver of fertility. Playful, but lecherous, Pan is the personification of nature, sexuality, and the masculine generative power. He played on a reed-pipe and was known for his music, capable of arousing inspiration, sexuality, or panic, depending on his intentions. The music industry is infamous for worshipping Pan who is the very embodiment of Rock and Roll. Pan's goatish image recalls conventional faun-like depictions of Satan. Egyptologist, Margaret Murray, published the book, *The God of the Witches*, in which she theorized that Pan was merely one form of a horned god, Cernunos, who was worshipped across Europe by witch-cults. As an archetype of male virility and sexuality, the Horned God is one of the two primary deities found in the religion of Wicca. He is often given various names and epithets, and rep-

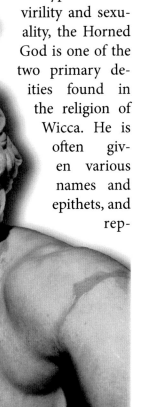

resents the male part of the religion's duo-theistic theological system, the other part being the female Triple Moon Goddess. The Greek word Pan also translates as All, and so he is "a symbol of the Universal", a personification of Nature.

Aleister Crowley coined the term, 'The Night of Pan' to represent spiritual darkness wherein the ego-self dies. NOX means 'Night' in Latin and this night is the darkness of the "Great Mother's" womb, before the initiate can be reborn and "grow up to be Himself wholly and truly as He previously was not". In mythological terms, this is the journey into the Underworld, where difficult trials must be completed and monsters vanquished, before the hero can return back to this world. The N. is identified with the Tarot symbol for Death, the O. refers to the KTEIS, PHALLOS and SPERMA, and the X. is another sign of the phallus. To initiates of the O.T.O., Pan is the Hidden God of the forest, the Abyss, the deep, the underworld; and any region withdrawn and without the range of waking consciousness. In his book, *Liber Oz*, Crowley states that "there is no god but man". The underlying doctrine of Thelma is that the initiate will be-

come god, Pan, and one with all through acts of magick and will.

"K" is the 11th letter of the alphabet and according to Crowley it is the symbol of that gigantic Power whose color is scarlet, and who has affinity with the goat of Capricorn or Babylon. The special importance of the goat is revealed by its attribution in the Indian Tradition to the goddess Kali, whose vehicle is blood. The god-form of the chimera Baphomet was said to have been worshipped by the Order of the Templars in the form of a goat which would make them the original men who stare at goats. The adorers of this sign did not consider it a representation of the Devil; on the contrary, for them it is the god, Pan, of the primitive Gnostic schools and the Christ of the dissident priesthood. For Thelemites, Baphomet is the glyph of the androgyne which conceals their secret formula of change through sexual polarity in human form. Crowley's magical title in the O.T.O. was Baphomet and he symbolizes the true will of every person as the satyr. He considered it a symbol of spermatozoa while also being symbolic of the "magical child" produced as a result of sex rituals. As such, Baphomet represents the Union of Opposites. The Sigil of Baphomet is the official insignia of the Church of Satan, and is trademarked by the organization.

Claude Debussy's *Prelude to the Afternoon of a Faun*, is first on the program in Disney's *Fantasia*. A sad, dumpy satyr lopes along through a lush garden inhabited by sleek, sultry, and nude wood nymphs. The satyr, recognizing his lack of physical appeal, attempts to beautify himself, but nothing works and he gradually shrinks away. Golden Dawn member, Arthur Machen's novella, *The Great God Pan*, has a Roman pillar dedicated to the god Nodens. The dedication is made by one Flavius Senilis, "on account of the marriage which he saw beneath the shade" and there is a strong hint that Nodens is in fact Pan. In an Orphic fragment preserved by Marobius, the names of Jupiter and Pan appear to be titles of the all-creating power of the sun. According to Plutarch, the Jupiter-Ammon of the Africans was the same as the Pan of the Greeks.

***

White Knights & Dark Heroes
Is raising your son as a superhero any better than teaching your daughter to be a narcissistic princess? As with the ladies of modern folklore, the boys all seem to have one thing in common as well. They are all orphans. How many times in the superheroes' story was the trauma of the death of his parents the catalyst that ultimately caused him to split his personality into the superhero persona or to turn to the dark side? Now you know how they create a villain super soldier, but who did they invent to play the white pawn in this cosmic game of strategy? The white knight must rescue the princess but from what he doesn't know. Today's battlefield is economics and he must save her from the worst fate of all—being poor.

It is no secret that, for the most part, men's actions are directly influenced by their desire for love from women. In popular music there is no unconditional love coming from female voices. Songs like *Material Girl* by Madonna, *Bills, Bills, Bills* by Destiny's Child, *No Scrubs*, by TLC, and *Single Ladies* by Beyonce all convey the same thing. If you analyze the lyrics of today's female singers the message is clear: "You gotta pay to get with this." For the "good guy" there is no reward because in a psychopathic system, only the psychos rise to the top. For many men who see that the world is somehow broken there is no recourse but to simply try and not be broken by it.

The idea of a knight being chivalrous instead of bloodthirsty comes from the tales of King Arthur. Throughout history, more often than not, medieval knights were the key source of terror and oppression to the general population. Their law enforcement had nothing to do with the Holy Grail quest, and they had more in common with a modern day gangster. Attempts were made to get these thugs under control, one being the chivalric code that was adopted around the 13th century. Examples like Sir Lancelot and Edward the Black Prince were raised to show knights how to behave in battle and in peace. Knights were encouraged to "defend the weak", but those were commonly interpreted as noble women and children—not peasants.

The sorcerers know that women are the motivation behind almost everything a man does. Woman is the channel through which the magical current manifests, and even the most advanced

magician's powers are not fully realized without his woman. Aleister Crowley illustrated his version of this key to magical working in *The Book of Thoth*, his commentary on the Tarot. The 11th card of the major arcana, in his version, is Lust which he equates with Strength. In traditional Tarot, the 11th card is Justice. Thelemites believe that lust has particular power in the present Aeon. The illustration on the Lust card, features the Scarlet woman as the cup bearer; the Beast is in the form of a lion with seven heads, emphasizing its connection with the stellar Cult of Set.

Starship Troopers is a military science fiction novel, written by Robert A. Heinlein. It was published hardcover in 1959 and won the Hugo Award for Best Novel. Heinlein was friends with L. Ron Hubbard and Jack Parsons and they shared his occult interests in magic, as well as inspirations from Crowley and Thelema. The story is about a young soldier named Juan "Johnnie" Rico and his exploits in the Mobile Infantry, a military unit involved in an interstellar war between mankind and an arachnoid species known as the Bugs. In the distant future, people are not considered citizens unless they have served in the military. Rico goes against his parents' demands and enlists himself because he is in love with his girlfriend who has enlisted in the air force. He finds that his grades are too low to join his girl in flight

school, and is assigned to the mobile infantry as cannon fodder.

The culture creators know that where women go, men are sure to follow. Our culture has taught men to be extremely hesitant to be husbands and fathers, and instead it has taught them to be macho sex-obsessed idiots who want to "score" with as many women as possible. In the 1942 Disney propaganda film, *Donald Gets Drafted*, it shows posters of ladies adoring men in uniform and that's why Donald decides to join up with the Army. To look smart and pick up chicks. Other posters in the cartoon show troops having breakfast in bed. Just like in *Starship Troopers*, Donald tells the recruiter that he wants to join up to fly planes, but finds himself marching in the infantry instead.

The organization of standing super-armies is the backbone of communism and according to many, America is quickly headed in that direction. Neitche convinced the world that God was dead. Darwin's followers set out to prove that humans are just apex predators on the top of the food chain. Karl Mark realized that the philosophies of Neitche and Darwin would legitimize his own philosophy of communism. The goal of socialism is communism. On

one side of the freedom spectrum you have anarchy, which means "without rulers." On the other side you have fascism, communism and socialism which constitutes total control by the state with no individuality whatsoever. Marx knew their ideas would justify brutality and the slaughter of billions which is the legacy of communism. Marx died in 1883 that same year in London a group was formed called the Fabian Socialist Society and their logo is a wolf in sheep's clothing.

***

Supermen

The desire to create a superman or a superwoman can be found all the way back in the ancient records of the Hittites. So many of the legends in comic books of super heroes run parallel to the beliefs of Adolf Hitler and the Nazis. One of the occult prophets of Germany In the 19th century was the composer, Richard Wagner. Hitler once said that to understand the Nazi doctrine you must know Wagner. In his esoteric opera, *The Ride of the Valkyries*, he declared the imminent arrival of a Master Race. In his work, *The Ring*, Wagner expressed his belief in a German "Superman", bestriding the world like the ancient pagan gods Wotan and Thor. Some researchers claim that Thor was worshipped as early as the stone-age. He rode a great chariot, pulled by two giant, fearsome and powerful goats who symbolized thunder and lightning. The Nazis believed that man is not finished. He is on the brink of a formidable mutation which will give him the powers which the ancients attributed to the gods. They also believed that alliances could be formed with the "Master of the

World" or the "King of Fear", who reigns over a city which is hidden somewhere in the East.

There was no illusion of equality under Hitler. The true blood S.S. man, an "initiate", was considered to be above good and evil. They were the supermen of the Nazi movement. Applications to the S.S. had to prove their racial purity back to 1750. They had to meet stringent physical requirements and were obligated to produce more *Übermenschen* in breeding camps of the *Lebensborn* movement. They were to

Thor, the Norse god of lightning, is depicted in a battle against the giants by Marten Eskil Wingein, 1872

abandon Christianity and study a mish mash of Celtic paganism and Tibetan mysticism. These leaders, called "Death's Heads," had access to the secret doctrine of The Legend of Thule which is as old as the Germanic race. It was supposed to be an island that had disappeared somewhere in the extreme North. Like Atlantis, the *wunderland* of Thule was the magic center of a vanished civilization. According to the Thule Society, there was once a highly developed civilization in the Gobi desert. As the result of

a catastrophe, a lush Gobi was transformed into a barren desert and the survivors emigrated to northern Europe and the Caucasus mountains. The Scandinavian god, Thor, is supposed to have been one of the heroes of this migration. The initiates of the Thule group were convinced that these survivors were the Aryans, members of the original race from which all humanity had sprung. The Thule society claimed that "Beings" from beyond would enable Germany to dominate the world and be the cradle of the coming race of Supermen which would result from mutations of the human species.

The notion of the "Unknown Supermen" can be found in all the black mystical writings both in the West and in the East. Hitler shared this belief and even claimed to have been in touch with them. Hitler said *"The new man is living amongst us now. I will tell you a secret. I have seen the new man. He is intrepid and cruel. I was afraid of him."*[6] Samuel Mathers, founder of the Golden Dawn, also claimed to be in communication with these men whom he called the Secret Chiefs. In a manifesto addressed to Members of the Second Order in 1896, he stated *"My physical encounters with them have shown me how difficult it is for a mortal...to support their presence... The nervous prostration I spoke of was accompanied by cold sweats and bleeding from the nose, mouth and sometimes the ears."*[7]

***

> "The first quality of a soldier is constancy in enduring fatigue and hardship. Courage is only the second. Poverty, privation and want are the school of the good soldier."
> -Napoleon

Public Education + Sports = Warfare

In the schools of Nazi Germany children were taught to be "human machines." They received their instruction at the Burgs after passing through the Napola preparatory schools. When inaugurating one of the Napola schools, Himmler reduced their doctrine to its lowest common denominator: "Believe, Obey, Fight. That is all." These were schools where pupils learned how to kill and how to die. Children were taught to spot "terrorists", who were the Jews, Blacks, Gypsies or anyone who was suspicious or spoke out against the government. The ordinary rank-and-file soldier was a soulless machine, a working robot. He was mass produced and chosen for his negative qualities. Here, there was no question of secret occult doctrine, only of training. Hitler said: *"We do not want to do away with inequalities between men, but on the contrary, to increase them and make them into a principle protected by impenetrable barriers. What will the social order of the future be like? Comrades I will tell you: there will be a class of overlords, and after them the rank and file of Party Members in hierarchical order, and them the great mass of anonymous followers, servants and workers in perpetuity, and beneath them, again all the conquered foreign races, the modern slaves. And over and above all these there will reign a new and exalted nobility of whom I cannot speak…But of all these plans the ordinary militant members will know nothing."*[8]

Public schools are rapidly transforming into some sort of hellish prison/boot camp hybrid. The new school is a training ground for learning how to live in a Big Brother police state control grid. Our public school students are being watched, tracked, recorded, searched and controlled like never before. In 2011, at one public school in the Chicago area, children have been banned from bringing their lunches from home. Instead, it is mandatory that they eat the food that the school cafeteria serves. The U.S. Department of Agriculture is spending huge amounts of money to install surveillance cameras in the cafeterias of public schools so that government can closely monitor what our children are eating.

> "The aim of public education is not to spread enlightenment at all, it is simply to reduce as many individuals as possible to the same safe level, to breed and standardize citizenry, to put down dissent and originality."
> -H.L. Mencken

It is far more comfortable for us to think that a lone madman could make a world war happen, rather than that there were millions of people who followed that madman's orders facilitating it. Hitler would never have been more than a mediocre painter if he hadn't had literally millions of people doing what he demanded, many of whom were perfectly happy, eager conspirators. The truth is it takes a generation of programing to prepare the youth for wars that are planned decades in advance. Upon accepting the New York City Teacher of the Year Award on January 31, 1990, John Taylor Gatto upset many in attendance by stating: *"The truth is that schools don't really teach anything except how to obey orders. This is a great mystery to me because thousands of humane, caring people work in schools as teachers and aides and administrators, but the abstract logic of the institution overwhelms their individual contributions."*

> "The dominant systems of education are based on three "assumptions" that are exactly opposite to how human lives are actually lived. First, they promote standardization and a narrow view of intelligence when human talents are diverse and personal. Second, they promote compliance when cultural progress and achievement depend on the cultivation of imagination and creativity. Third, they are linear and rigid when the course of each human life, including yours, is organic and largely unpredictable."- Ken Robinson

In 2013, Chicago Mayor Rahm Emanuel closed fifty

schools in the poorest neighborhoods but spent $100 Million in public funds to build a new basketball arena at DePaul University. The city of Philadelphia closed twenty three schools while a new $400 million prison was under construction. For many children their first group endeavor is a sport, but is this team building or the beginning of the "us vs. them" mentality of competition? Adults are placing just as much pressure to excel, if not more, in athletics as they do in academics. For many kids, joining a sports team can bring more time consuming responsibilities than a part time job. Speaking of jobs, in 2013, the highest paid public employees for thirty-nine states in the U.S. were football or basketball coach. Global sports fanaticism is the perfect hypnotic tool and continuously demands peoples focused emotional attention. It provides a placebo for real life experience as fans experience the same psychological result of winning or losing...but what, they can't say.

"The quality of education given to the lower class must be of the poorest sort, so that the moat of ignorance isolating the inferior class from the superior class is and remains incomprehensible to the inferior class. With such an initial handicap, even bright lower class individuals have little if any hope of extricating themselves from their assigned lot in life. This form of slavery is essential to maintain some measure of social order, peace and tranquility for the ruling upper class." —Silent Weapons for Quiet Wars.

The structure of sports teaches patrons to never question authority such as umpires, referees or coaches, and to do as you are told. While you are watching sports, you are constantly being bombarded with advertisements for the Armed Forces. The ads assure you will be a hero if you join, just like your favorite player. Sports teaches that competition is good, and winning is the only thing that matters. It is self-denial and that the team is more important than the individual in order to coordinate the defeat of another team. Sports values are similar to military values. They are placed not in what is wrong or right, but on obeying a set of rules just as in military boot camp with a chain of command.

No one can deny that organized sports is a tremendous cause of violence. Over the years, there have been various occasions, where global sporting events have degenerated into battles for control and dominance between opposing fans or between fans and police. Scenes of screaming fanatics, broken glass, fire, dangerous mobs, stampedes and cases of spectators being crushed have also been all too common. Often the riots provide a symbol or focus for political issues or an outlet for social unrest. Even in the suburbs, parent/fan violence has been on the rise at youth sporting events and can range from yelling to physical aggression, such as parents striking coaches or violence toward children players.

Like today's athletes, gladiators did product endorsements. Particularly successful warriors would endorse goods in the arena before commencing a fight and have their names promoting products on the Roman equivalent of billboards. The art of sports and warfare really came into being in ancient Greece. When you have young men running around screaming, "THIS IS SPARTA!" what are they really talking about? Sparta was a prominent city-state during the 10th century BC. Its military pre-eminence was unique in ancient Greece for its social system and constitution, which completely focused on military training and excellence. Not all inhabitants of the Spartan state were considered to be citizens or had full rights. Only those who had undertaken the Spartan education process known as the *Agoge* were eligible. When male Spartans began military training at age seven, they would enter the agoge system, a rigorous education and training regimen mandated for all male Spartan citizens, except for the firstborn son. The agoge was designed to encourage discipline and physical toughness and to emphasize the importance of the Spartan state. The training involved learning stealth, cultivating loyalty to the Spartan group, military training, pain tolerance, hunting, and communication. The aim of the system was to produce physically and morally strong males to serve in the Spartan army. It encouraged conformity and the importance of the Spartan state over one's personal interest and generated the future elites of Sparta. Discipline was strict and the males were encouraged to fight amongst themselves to determine the strongest member of the group. Special punishments were imposed if boys failed to answer questions "laconically", meaning briefly and wittily enough.

There is some evidence that in late-Classical and Hellenistic Sparta, boys were expected to take an older male mentor, usually an unmarried young man. Sparta is thought to be the first city to practice athletic nudity, and sources[9] claim that it was also the first to formalize pederasty. According to these sources, the Spartans believed that the love of an older, more accomplished aristocrat for an adolescent was essential to his formation as a free citizen. The agoge education of the ruling class was founded on pederastic relationships required of each citizen, with the lover responsible for the boy's training. The Spartans were among the first to connect spectator sports to warfare and citizenship. Participants were most often nude which added to the pedophile factor.

Girls can participate in high school sports, but what does the culture creation matrix claim as the most coveted position? The Cheerleader. The theme of the entire show called *Heroes* was "Save the cheerleader, save the world." The origin of the Prom Queen or the Homecoming Queen has roots in medieval England. May Day was a fertility festival and to sow the earth was perceived as a sexual act. May Day was a day of sexual license to renew the fecundity of the earth and celebrate the arrival of spring. The traditional maypole has obvious phallic implications. The "Queen of May" was chosen as an avatar for the mother goddess. She and other village virgins (women without children) would scamper off into the forest where they would be received by 'Robin of the Greenwood' and his 'merry men.' The frolics that followed would spawn a winter crop of fatherless children known as 'sons of Robin' or 'Robinsons.' Today, every year in the springtime, *People* magazine names a female celebrity as "Most Beautiful Woman", the modern day May Queen.

What exactly are they teaching girls is the most important thing in life? While public schools are making darn sure they know how to put on a condom or perform oral sex safely, most girls graduate without knowing how to open a bank account or balance a checkbook. Being a professional cheerleader looks like a great job, but just how much they get paid is one of the NFL's best kept secrets. The average NFL Quarterback salary is $1,970,982.00 per year. At the low end of the spectrum, a Tight End takes home $863,414. Teams that generate hundreds of millions of dollars of revenue each year pay cheerleaders about $70 to $90 per game. Some cheerleaders are paid monthly salaries ranging from $1,000 to $1,500 with the higher end of the scale being reserved for those with extensive cheerleading experience. After two pre-season games and eight regular season home games, most cheerleaders earn about $500 to $750 per season, depending on which team they cheer for and whether that team plays any additional home games in the playoffs.

***

"Military men are just dumb, stupid animals to be used as pawns in foreign policy."
-Henry Kissinger

The Military Occult Complex
The interweaving of military and magical powers has been evident since the beginning. The Old Testament portrays one battle after another. Miraculous victories of the Israelites against impossible odds were won with the help of a mighty Yahweh, who would lend or withdraw his power to the people as they pleased or displeased

him. One method of military divination for the Israelites were the Urim and Thummim; two stones that represented darkness and light, or yes/no. With this type of binary Ouija system, the Israelites used to cast the stones to decipher the will of God in battle. In ancient Greece, no self-respecting general would dare make a major tactical move unless first consulting with the Oracle at Delphi. The Celtic Druids were the psychic soldiers of their day, often accompanying an army to give aid, via their magical powers, in the destruction of the enemy. In Egypt there were many instances on record of wizards utterly destroying their enemies by the recital of magic words and by the performance of some apparently simple ceremony.

One of the most famous of all Egyptian magicians was King Nectanebus, 358 B.C., the last native monarch, who was skilled in astrology and divination of all kinds. Legend has it that when foreign armies marched against him, he retired to his secret sanctuary, filled a great bowl with Nile water, and fashioned wax figurines of his fleet and sailors and the ships and men of the enemy. He set them a float like a watery game of chess, his army on the one side, the enemy on the other. Donning his

mystic mantle, he took his magic wand and intoning the words of power, he summoned the elemental forces to his aid. In the bowl, the magical microcosm of the battlefield, the Egyptians were triumphant and this was reflected in the material world, where the Egyptians remained free from invaders that day. King Nectanebus was not so fortunate next time, however, when a massive alliance of armies moved against Egypt. Again, the King took to his water basin of figurines, but this time he witnessed his armies defeat in wax and on the battlefield. Nectanebus fled, disguised himself as a commoner, and escaped to

Macedonia where he lived out his days as a prophet and healer. The historian, Pseudo-Callisthenes, tells us that there, Nectanebus cast the nativity of the Queen Olympias, and sent a dream to her by means of a wax image. His goal was to persuade the queen that the Egyptian god Amun, in the form of the fertility god, Min, would come to her at night. The child she subsequently gave birth to was Alexander the Great.

Before Nectanebus fled Egypt, he had fought the battle of Mendes, with Ataxerxes II, king of Persia, whom he utterly defeated. Because of this victory, he forever after remained faithful to the

local god. The town was sacred to the worship of the god Min and the ram Mendes. Nectanebus took this devotion with him when he fled to Greece where his ram Mendes was identified with Pan. When the Ptolomies ruled Egypt after Alexander, Min was accepted as the Egyptian Pan, and the worship of the goat was combined with that of the ram. This gave rise to the cult of the Goat of Mendes, infamous in the West as the incarnation of the Devil with two horns.

Symbolism is found throughout military establishments and magical endeavors, whether it is the five-pointed star on the major general's epaulet, or the five-pointed pentagram on the wizard's breast. Hierarchical organization is a major phenomenon in both the warrior and magician castes. The salute is a gesture invoked when confronting a higher ranking being—both in camp and coven—although its form may vary with the time and territory. Ritual plays an important role in both the military and in magic. A certain cadence in a march, the execution of certain movements, etiquette, are all taught to the warrior. A place for everything and everything in its place is sine qua non for effective evocation. Thus, both endeavors

were accustomed to formal methods of movement and action.

The incorporation of violence in magical ritual has had several historical rationales. It has been claimed by some such as Aleister Crowley, that the biological energy released at the moment of death of an animal or of a human, combined with the emotional frenzy induced in the magician by the sight of blood, can be focused through the working of the ritual and sent psychically to do its work. Second, in conjurations, the blood of a sacrificed animal can allegedly be used by the demon being summoned to form a physical manifestation in this plane.[10] The adrenaline produced in combat is linked with all kinds of neo cortex damage. When they have gone through the demoralization and trauma based mind control of boot camp, when they come out, the dark occultist own them. "Human Pets" is how the puppet masters view the military and the police. They call the general public "the dead" or "useless eaters" and they call police and military "our dogs" and make them wear dog tags.

Hypnotism and mind control is used by magicians and military extensively. Colonel John Alexander was involved in many mystical performance enhancement studies for the Army in the early eighties. One of his projects was the Jedi Project which used visualization and suggestion methods to improve marksmanship. Alexander was instrumental in wedding the military with the magical and New Age movements. Along with motivational speaker, Anthony Robbins as the prime instructor, they created the U.S. Army's first psychic soldier.

Lt. Grady McMurty of the U.S. Army was a student of Crowley and adherent of Thelema. Jack Parsons introduced McMurty to the O.T.O. and after his military service, McMurty worked for the government and analyst and taught political science at George Washington University.

The period after the Vietnam War was a time when military morale and enrollment were at an all-time low. During this period, the U.S. Army needed to drastically shift approaches and prepare to defeat a vastly larger Soviet force in Europe. Army leaders called upon officers to develop creative approaches to dealing with this challenge. They were encouraged to fully explore the Army's "Be All That You Can Be" philosophy. The First Earth Battalion was a superman project headed by Lt. Colonel James Channon. It was spawned after Channon's exposure to over one hundred and thirty New Age groups in California. The purpose of Channon's "warrior monks" was supposedly to clear landing sites for UFO's and prepare to communicate with extraterrestrials.

In 2013, the U.S. Army Recruiting Command's top officer, Maj. Gen. David Mann, was called to testify before Congress after an investigation by the Inspector General's office determined that powerful subliminal messages were hidden within the iconic "Army Strong" song, commonly used as a background soundtrack recruiting commercials and videos. The investigation was launched after they had received numerous, unsolicited, independent complaints from soldiers who claimed they somehow

lost their capacity for rational decision-making and critical analysis when viewing Army recruiting media or meeting with recruiters, and subsequently agreed to enlistment under less than favorable circumstances, forgoing most, if not all, of the incentives for which they might otherwise have been eligible. Mann confirmed during testimony that the messages were part of a top-secret joint venture between USAREC and the U.S. Army psychological-operations community, to secure the maximum number of new recruits into the Army while keeping down the costs of recruiting incentives.[11]

***

"The pioneers of a warless world are the youth that refuse military service." -Albert Einstein

"Humanity is the spirit of the Supreme Being on earth, and humanity is standing amidst unseen ruins, hiding its nakedness behind tattered rags, shedding tears upon hollow cheeks, calling for its children in pitiful voice. But the children are busy singing the anthem; they are busy sharpening the swords and cannot hear the cries of their mothers." —Kahlil Gibran, *The Poets Voice*

I AM...LOVE

There is a vast amount of evidence to show that man was not always carnivorous or aggressive. It seems that, like most primates and many primitives of today, ancient men were vegetarian and frugivorous. They were given neither to war nor to violence, especially to sexual violence. A study published in *Nature Journal*** gives scientific support that humans are naturally good. In ten experiments using economic games, scientists observed that faster decisions resulted in more cooperation and generosity, while slower, calculated decisions show a decrease in cooperation and generosity. Their conclusion is that the humans automatic reaction is to be friendly, generous and cooperative, and only upon further consideration do they become greedy or violent. This particular study is just one of many proposals put forward by the scientific community in the past several decades stating confidently that corruption has nothing to do with human nature. Man is naturally inclined to want to be honorable. A great deal of neurosis is the individual recognizing that he is breaking the common rules of his own kind and is ashamed of himself. Left to his own devices and without unusual pressures, he is more or less a well-meaning and kindly creature. We have within us a sense of what is right, and when we live in constant violation of this, when we secretly know that we are wrong, this creates psychological stress.

In many indigenous, aboriginal cultures, the highest honors are placed on cooperation, and competition had little value. In fact, excessive competitiveness was considered a mental illness. Our culture has taught us the reverse of our ancestors. That greed is good and we should celebrate the most powerful competitors. But, how competitive is human nature? Scientists are discovering that not even animal nature is as competitive as you have been taught. By observing the patters of various animals, from reindeer trying to find a watering hole, to the graceful synchronized swimming school of fish, they find that instead of an alpha male making all the decisions, the animals all democratically vote through body language and sounds. Even Charles Darwin, the favorite of the eugenicists, admitted that our strongest evolutionary asset as a species is our ability to cooperate. If we were an ultimately greedy species we would fail to exist. Our bodies function more optimally in a state of empathy and decline as anger and other negative emotions increase.

All humans, dolphins, apes, and possibly elephants, have something called mirrored neurons. If a monkey observes a behavior that it, itself, has performed in the past, the same neuron of the brain is stimulated as if they were actually performing the action. In other words, there's something in the brain that doesn't distinguish between itself and others. We are geared at a cellular level to feel what another person feels and we are hardwired to have a compassionate response to the plight of others. At the Institute of HeartMath in California, they are discovering that the brain is not the dominant organ in the body. Ninety to ninety-five percent of the nerves that carry information go from the body to the brain, not the brain to the body. The heart sends far more information to the brain than the other way around.

The communist/socialist dictator of Romania, Nicolae Ceauşescu, was a sadistic sociopath. In an attempt to increase the population, Ceauşescu made abortion, contraception and sex education forbidden. He began his campaign in 1966 with a decree that virtually made pregnancy a state policy. He declared that "The fetus is the property of the entire society." A pregnant woman who failed to produce a baby at the proper time could expect to be summoned for questioning. Books on human sexuality and reproduction were classified as "state secrets," to be used only as medical textbooks. Under his regime, nearly 100,000 children from poverty stricken families were abandoned in orphanages and group homes which also housed the disabled and mentally ill. Together, these vulnerable groups were subjected to institutionalized neglect and abuse, including physical and sexual, and the use of drugs to control behavior. When his regime fell in the early 90's, the news of their isolation and neglect dovetailed with academic interest in studying the impact of deprivation on early human development. Behaviorists had a unique opportunity to study early development under conditions that could not be scientifically created for moral reasons. Although most orphanages were operating under nightmare conditions, they also discovered that mortality rates among newborns who were supplied with the basics of food and warmth, were also high. The ratio of orphans to staff was about 40 to 1, so even the best cared for infants were mostly ignored. They found that human babies could not and would not continue living if they were never kissed, cuddled, or rocked. Since the exposure of the Romanian orphanage crisis, psychologists are investigating whether attachment disorder might be the environmental root cause of sociopathic behavior.

"Attachment disorder
is a tragic condition
that occurs when at-
tachment in infancy
is disrupted... Chil-
dren and adults with
severe attachment dis-
order for whom attach-
ment was not possible
during the first sev-
en months of life, are
unable to bond to oth-
ers emotionally and
are thereby direct-
ed to a fate which is
arguably worse than
death. In the extreme
case...infants who are
not touched at all...
are prone to die quite
literally. Succumbing
mysteriously to a con-
dition then referred
to as marasmus, a Greek
word that means 'wast-
ing away'-a disorder
now called 'non-organ-
ic failure to thrive'."
      -The Sociopath Next
      Door, Martha Stout

We know that the dark sorcerers would do away with all mothers after they have given birth but thankfully this is not reality. Even if you had a terrible mother, if someone didn't love you as a baby, you literally would not be alive today. There is a force stronger than drills, peer pressure and even self-preservation instinct. The real truth is that you are not a soldier, a robot or a beast. The primary foundation of what you are is love. The act that brought you into this world is called "making love." There is something fundamentally differ-ent between machines and life, and our culture treats us as if we are pieces in a mechanical uni-verse. What we create from that is the notion that we are all separate, and honor the notion of contest and competition based on scarci-ty. We are taught to be significant at someone else's expense. To be number one. To succeed. To win. However, the way the world is set up, to succeed you must put ev-eryone else behind.

***

1. *Century of the Self*, film by Adam Curtis
2. *On Killing*, Lt. Colonel Dave Grossman
3. Ibid, pg 299
4. *Communication Reports*, "Cul-tivation Revisited: Some Genres Have Some Effects on Some View-ers" Cohen, J. & Weimann
5. *Liber ABA*, Part III Chapter 12, Aleister Crowley
6. Hermann Rauschning: Hitler m'a dit. Ed. Co-operation, Paris, 1939
7. http://www.mt.net/~watcher/hitleraliengoldendawn.html
8. *Hitler and the Age of Horus*, Gerald Suster
9. "The Dispersion of Pederasty and the Athletic Revolution in Sixth-Century BC Greece", Same-Sex Desire and Love in Greco-Ro-man Antiquity and in the Classi-cal Tradition of the West, Thomas F. Scanlon
10. *Satan Wants You*, Arthur Ly-ons pg 94
11. Investigation Reveals Sublim-inal Recruiting Messages Hidden in "Army Strong" Song, Bravo for Duffleblog.com (July 23, 2013)

*"Reciprocal Associations Be-tween PTSD Symptoms and Al-cohol Involvement in College: A Three-Year Trait-State-Error Analysis," published in the edi-tion of the Journal of Abnormal Psychology (Vol. 22/4)
**May, 2013

Books:
The Morning of the Magicians, Louis Pauwels and Jacques Ber-gier
Adventures in Understanding, Manly P. Hall
No More Heroes, Richard Gabriel
The Psychic Battlefield, W. Adam Mandelbaum

Other Resources:
Survival Was All That Really Mattered: War, Trauma, and the American Hero, WebArticle, by David Chisinger (Sept 4, 2013)

Documentary: *I AM*, Tom Shady-ac

Weird Stuff! Sympathy for Robots

Not only is humanities' empathy for each other grossly underrated in popular culture, it seems that empathy for robots could affect outcomes on the battlefield as well. Julie Carpenter, a Ph.D. in edu-cation at the University of Washington, interviewed twenty three explosive ordnance disposal personnel who regularly used robots on the job. She found that the soldiers often anthropomorphized their robots, assigned them human attributes such as genders and names, and even displayed a kind of empathy toward the machines, "They would say they were angry when a robot became disabled because it is an important tool, but then they would add 'poor little guy,' or they'd say they had a funeral for it."

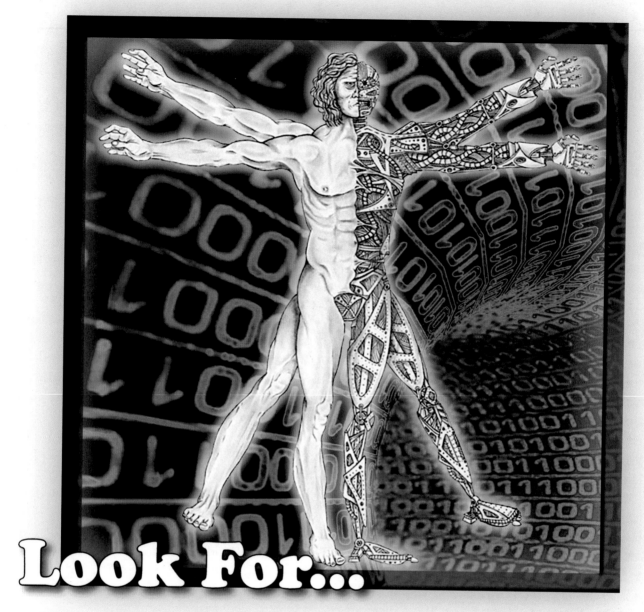

Look For...

WeirdStuff~Operation: Culture Creation Part 3!

1010101010101010101010101010101010101010101010101010101010101

Are you Man or machine? Where is the new Utopia and what does it have to do with Epcot Center and the Zeitgeist movement? Who is performing High Profile Satanic rituals in front of your face, and for what reason? Why are vampires so popular, and what do they have in common with the elite and the royal family? What is the spell of Metropolis and could it be related to Babylon? Will humanity achieve the singularity through Trans-humanism and eugenics? Find out why androgyny is so mainstream and what it has in common with the Bible Code.